# CHILTON'S
# DIESEL GUIDE

JAMES JOSEPH

# CHILTON'S DIESEL GUIDE

## Cars and Light Trucks

CHILTON BOOK COMPANY
Radnor, Pennsylvania

Library of Congress Catalog Card No. 78-22145
ISBN 0-8019-6753-8 *hardcover*
ISBN 0-8019-6754-6 *paperback*

*Designed by Anne Churchman*
Manufactured in the United States of America

Although the information in this guide is based on industry sources and is as complete as possible at the time of publication, the possibility exists that the manufacturer made later changes which could not be included here. While striving for total accuracy, Chilton Book Company cannot assume responsibility for any errors, changes, or omissions that may occur in the compilation of this data.

## SAFETY NOTICE

Proper service and repair procedures are vital to the safe, reliable operation of all motor vehicles, as well as the personal safety of those performing repairs. This book outlines procedures for servicing and repairing vehicles using safe, effective methods. The procedures contain many NOTES, CAUTIONS and WARNINGS which should be followed along with standard safety procedures to eliminate the possibility of personal injury or improper service which could damage the vehicle or compromise its safety.

It is important to note that repair procedures and techniques, tools and parts for servicing motor vehicles, as well as the skill and experience of the individual performing the work vary widely. It is not possible to anticipate all of the conceivable ways or conditions under which vehicles may be serviced, or to provide cautions as to all of the possible hazards that may result. Standard and accepted safety precautions and equipment should be used when handling toxic or flammable fluids, and safety goggles or other protection should be used during cutting, grinding, chiseling, prying, or any other process that can cause material removal or projectiles.

Some procedures require the use of tools specially designed for a specific purpose. Before substituting another tool or procedure, you must be completely satisfied that neither your personal safety, nor the performance of the vehicle will be endangered.

2 3 4 5 6 7 8 9 0     9 8 7 6 5 4 3 2 1 0

# Contents

## ACKNOWLEDGMENTS

Many persons and firms contributed information and material during the compilation of this book. The author and Chilton Book Company express their sincere appreciation to the following for their generous assistance:

Association of Diesel Specialists (A.D.S.), Kansas City, MO
American Petroleum Institute (API), Washington, D.C.
Buick Motor Division, General Motors Corp., Flint, MI
Cadillac Motor Car Division, General Motors Corp., Detroit, MI
Caterpillar Tractor Co., Peoria, IL
Chevrolet Motor Division, General Motors Corp., Detroit, MI
Cummins Engine Company, Columbus, IN
Detroit Diesel Allison, General Motors Corp., Detroit, MI
Environmental Protection Agency (EPA), Washington, D.C.
Five Star Manufacturing Co., Clarksdale, MS
Ford Industrial Engine Operations, Detroit, MI
Garret Corporation, AiResearch Turbocharger Div., Los Angeles, CA
GMC Truck & Coach Division, General Motors Corp., Pontiac, MI
Indianapolis Motor Speedway, Indianapolis, IN
International Harvester/Truck Group, Chicago, IL
Isuzu Diesel of North America, Livonia, MI
Kold-Ban International Inc., Algonquin, IL
Mercedes-Benz of North America, Inc., Montvale, NJ
Nissan Diesel Motor Co. Ltd., Japan
Oldsmobile Division, General Motors Corp., Lansing, MI
Phillips Temro Inc., Eden Prairie, MN
Porsche + Audi, Division of Volkswagen of America, Inc., Englewood Cliffs, NJ
Robert Bosch Corporation, Broadview, IL
SAAB/Scania, Scania Division, New Haven, CT
Society of Automotive Engineers (SAE), Warrendale, PA
Volkswagen of America, Englewood Cliffs, NJ
Volvo of America, Inc., Rockleigh, NJ
Wilcap Company, Torrance, CA

Cover photographs courtesy of GMC Truck and Coach Division, General Motors Corp.; Mercedes-Benz of North America, Inc.; Oldsmobile Division, General Motors Corp.; and Volkswagen of America, Inc.

# CHILTON'S
# DIESEL GUIDE

# Chapter 1

# Introduction to the Diesel

Come drive a diesel with me. You slip behind the wheel, fasten your seat belt, insert the key, and switch the ignition to RUN. On the dash an amber WAIT light flicks on. . . . Two seconds. . . . four seconds. . . . six seconds—Hardly a "wait" by other than the strictest definition. Still, if you have driven diesel before, your mind's eye perceives what's going on under the hood: energized by the battery fast-heating electrical elements, called *glow plugs,* are prewarming each of the engine's cylinders. . . . Seven seconds. The WAIT light goes out (indicating that the engine's combustion chambers have been sufficiently warmed by their glow plugs), and a green START light flicks on. You press the accelerator halfway to the floor, turn the ignition key to START (as the dashboard's green light instructed), and the engine starts with its muted throbbing, typical of the diesel.

Under this hood is no ordinary engine, but a turbocharged diesel. You push the

**Fig. 1.1** The WAIT light (the glow plug indicator at the extreme right) goes out, signaling that the engine's combustion chambers have been sufficiently warmed by their glow plugs. (Photograph by James Joseph)

automatic transmission's lever to DRIVE, and eleven seconds later you're up to cruise speed, and, if you're not careful, the speedometer's pointer is nudging past the legal 55-mph limit. The turbo-diesel's acceleration to 55 from zero is a mere 3.2 seconds slower than that of an average gasoline V-8 of the same power.

## FUEL ECONOMY AND EFFICIENCY

Times and the diesel engine have changed. Today, the emphasis is on fuel economy; and, with rare exception, the diesel's fuel economy is significantly greater than that of a comparable gasoline engine. The diesel gets better mileage than other types of engines because it is *thermally efficient,* producing greater horsepower output for fuel input, reckoned in terms of their heat equivalents. The diesel's thermal efficiency is about 36 percent, compared to 25 percent efficiency for gasoline engines, 20 percent for turbine engines, and only 12 percent for steam engines.

And this efficiency is paying off. World-wide, the production of diesel engines annually tops the three-million mark, and U.S. output alone exceeds one million. As far back as September 1975, Mercedes-Benz had turned out its 1.5-millionth diesel automobile and recently reached the two-million mark. In 1979, some 70 percent of all Mercedes-Benz cars sold in the United States were diesel (compared with 47 percent of Mercedes sales world-wide). The Volkswagen diesel Rabbit (called the Golf outside the United States) now accounts for nearly 40 percent of VW's American auto sales. Customer preference for diesel has outstripped Detroit's capacity to produce. If you have tried to buy an American-built diesel— whether an Oldsmobile, Cadillac, Buick, Chevrolet, International Scout, or any other—you probably ended up on the waiting list, and you may still be waiting. But not for long, if present trends are a reliable indication of future output. Detroit, just now seriously dieselizing, forecasts that, by the mid-eighties, 15 to 25 percent of its car production will be diesel. In Japan, Europe, and other key automotive areas, the prediction is similar, or even higher: Within the next five to ten years, at least 20 percent of all new cars will be diesel.

**Fig. 1.2** *Left:* Of 12,500 cabs on London streets, all but fifty have diesel engines. *Right:* Used London diesel cabs have found a steady market in the United States. (Photograph by James Joseph)

Virtually without exception, every one of the mammoth trucks you see on the Interstates is diesel powered. So, likely, are your city's buses and the trucks that collect your trash, clean your street, and are poised, ready to go, in your neighborhood firehouse. And England has even more widespread diesel use. For instance, of the total 12,500 London cabs, 12,450 are diesel ("Without diesel," a London cabbie tells you, "there wouldn't be a cab on London's street. We simply couldn't afford to operate gasoline engines"). Many truck diesels run 250,000 miles, even 500,000, before major engine work. Some automobile diesels do almost as well, and a few even better. When, in May 1978, Mercedes-Benz launched its "Great Diesel Search" for the highest-mileage (and oldest) Mercedes model in the United States, the company received seventy entries with 300,000

**Fig. 1.3** *Top:* The Mercedes-Benz "Great Diesel Search" turned up a 1957 180D, belonging to Robert O'Reilly, of Olympia, Washington, with 1,184,000 miles—750,000 of them on the original diesel. *Bottom:* Mileage runner-up, with 912,000 miles—902,000 on its original diesel—was a 1968 Mercedes-Benz 220D, owned by Edward Donaldson, of Eugene, Oregon.

miles or more. The high-mileage prize went to Robert O'Reilly of Olympia, Washington, whose 1957 Mercedes-Benz 180D (he was its fourth owner) had been driven 1,184,880 miles—750,000 of them on its original engine—and still delivered 37–41 mpg on the road. But another owner topped even that original engine figure: he'd driven 902,000 miles on his 1968 220D's factory diesel. Finishing behind O'Reilly's 180D in the high-mileage category was a 1968 220D with 912,943 miles in ten years—902,000 on the original engine; a 1958 180D, 847,970 miles; a 1953 170SD, 845,289 miles, and a 1961 190Db with 812,332 miles. The top twenty high-mileage vehicles located by Mercedes-Benz logged a total of 12,188,533 miles, an average of 609,000 each.

## INVENTOR RUDOLPH DIESEL

The diesel engine, of course, bears the name of its inventor, and has become so familiar that no one thinks of capitalizing it any more. Rudolph Diesel, the troubled German genius who on February 17, 1894 proved his "rational heat engine" by running the first crude, single-cylinder diesel engine for less than one minute, was in his own time to know fame, the world-wide acclaim of his peers, and fleeting fortune. And at the end, a mysterious death fraught, some believe, with international cloak-and-dagger intrigue.

Born in Paris, forced to flee with his parents to London during the 1870 Franco-Prussian War, Diesel eventually went to live with an uncle, a professor of mathematics, in Augsburg. At Augsburg's School of Industry, then a renowned technological institute, Diesel first saw one of the most intriguing devices of its time—a "pneumatic tinderbox." Resembling a glass bicycle pump, the device could ignite a piece of paper merely by compressing the air within its cylinder to the heat of ignition. Its principle was identical to that of Diesel's later rational heat engine, which similarly ignited its fuel by heat of compression.

Diesel's second significant encounter was with famed Professor Carl Linde, one of his university instructors and the man who had invented refrigeration and was first to liquefy air. Linde's refrigeration company—whose Berlin home office Diesel later headed for three years—was in the forefront of gas compression technology, the technology of Diesel's eventual engine. Backed by two of Germany's great engineering firms, one of them Krupp, Diesel began full-time work in 1893 to develop his rational heat engine, and a year later he had it running. Not for another year, however, did he prove to himself and to the scientific world what he really had: an engine four times as fuel efficient as the best steam engine of its day.

Only a handful of inventions are instantly recognized as "great" in their day, and among the historic few is the diesel engine. One evidence of this recognition was the rash of lawsuits filed against Diesel, all of them attempts to break his original patents. In 1897, only three years after the world learned of Diesel's success, Adolphus Busch, scion of the brewery empire, negotiated a million-dollar deal (big any day, but enormous in its era) with Diesel for exclusive U.S. rights to manufacture the diesel. Although poor investments and outright swindles took much of Diesel's new fortune, he was lionized everywhere in the engineering

**Fig. 1.4** Rudolph Diesel, inventor of the diesel engine.

world, particularly in America. Yet only three months after a group of American engineers, touring Germany, had invited him to be an honored guest at the 1915 San Francisco World's Fair, Diesel was to die mysteriously, at the age of 55. On September 29, 1913, he and two associates boarded the steamer *Dresden* for the overnight Channel crossing to England. When the ship arrived next morning, Diesel was missing. Eleven days later a body was found floating in the Channel, and papers taken from the body were those of Diesel's. But, as was custom, the body found at sea was consigned to the sea and allowed to float away. Suicide was one speculation. But it was also possible that the Kaiser's intelligence, as nearing conflict with England threatened world war, feared that Diesel was about to put into the hands of an eventual enemy a powerful potential instrument of war, the diesel engine.

His principle, which certainly could have been put to war use, remains unchanged, although greatly improved upon. He showed that if a gas, even air, is highly compressed by a piston within the cylinder of an engine, compression alone will increase its temperature to the "ignition point"—to a temperature at which an injected fuel will spontaneously ignite. The resulting combustion, further heating the air, causes it to expand, and the enormous pressure of the expansion itself becomes a work force, driving the piston downward and ultimately, through a crankshaft and gearing, powering the vehicle's wheels. Thus the diesel is an inter-

**Fig. 1.5** The first working diesel engine was built by Rudolph Diesel after nearly thirty months of development.

nal combustion engine, and a heat engine, and one, operating much like an air compressor, which uses air alone as the primary source of its efficiency, and an engine whose fuel ignition is spontaneous, created solely by the heat of compression.

Although the diesel engine has been around for nearly ninety years, it has been now catapulted into everyday automotives by a less-than-decade-old revolution which, world-wide, has radically changed the car owner's perception of the vehicle he or she drives. Principal promoters of this revolution are:

*the OPEC and its ever-tightening petroleum stranglehold,* almost certain to drive pump prices, whether for gasoline or diesel, to $2 a gallon and more

*inflation,* double-digited and inseparably tied to the rising cost of oil, which has doubled and may soon triple car prices, making frequent trade-ins an economic luxury of the past

*environmental laws,* whose muzzling of gas-engine emissions has reduced the gas engine's performance and its fuel efficiency

*sobering introspection,* as more people reevaluate the quality of their own lives and the economic impact of the automobile on it.

None of these factors existed a decade ago, and because they did not, the diesel's advantages were largely lost on the average car owner and buyer, although they were long recognized by those such as truck and construction machinery buyers, to whom engine economy and longevity are matters of economic survival. The diesel's strong points—fuel economy and long life—were hardly persuasive when gasoline was pump-priced at 35 cents a gallon (as it was in 1968) and when the average car owner, spurred by model changes every year, traded in and often up every couple of years. The driver trading that frequently didn't plan to keep the car long enough to reap the diesel's benefits, so was not interested in a long-lived engine. Nor, with gasoline so cheap, could buyers be persuaded to pay more for diesel (sometimes twice the price of a gasoline engine) and also pay the penalty of the diesel's then inferior road performance. Often too small, too under-powered, and too slow speeded, automotive diesels earned the reputation of being gutless slow-goers, fine once they got to cruising speed, but seemingly taking for-ever to get there. The diesel had going against it one thing most drivers would not tolerate, or buy: zilch road performance—no power on the uptake, no getaway-fast starts, no kick-in-the-pants response to a driver's foot on the accelerator, no margin of power in the squeezes, as in passing.

In 1936, when Mercedes-Benz unveiled at Berlin's Automotive Trade Show what was probably the world's first production diesel automobile, the Mercedes-Benz 260D, its maker didn't even set sights on the average car buyer, designing the 260D instead for commercial use, as a taxicab. And with considerable reason: Its 4-cylinder diesel produced a mere 45 hp. Another early production diesel car introduced at the same show, the Hanomag Rekord-Diesel, got only 35 hp from its 4-cylinder engine. In the United States, full-size cars with gas engines were al-ready going with eight cylinders and with twice to three times the power. In 1934, the 8-cylinder Hudson 8 ("with the most powerful engine in Hudson's 25-year history") developed some 113 hp, more than twice the power of the 260D and nearly three times that of the Hanomag.

## DIESEL POWER

As the seventies faded into the eighties, the diesel suddenly got what it had never had before: *power*—and, with power, *road performance* equal to that of a gas engine. Volkswagen led the power pack, unveiling in 1977 the VW Rabbit diesel, a car with the road performance of gas engine Rabbits, but with a then seemingly unbeatable fuel economy: better than 55 mpg on the highway. And the diesel version of the Rabbit cost buyers only $200 more than a gas engine Rabbit—a cost the average driver could recoup, in fuel savings, in less than 20,000 miles. Less than a year later, GM's Oldsmobile Division unveiled in 1978 its 350-cubic-inch, V-8 diesel, now the engine powering many other General Motors cars, pickup trucks, and utility vehicles. The road performance of an Olds-mobile fitted with the new diesel V-8 was the match of the gasoline engine Olds. But, typically, whereas the gas engine Olds 98 seldom managed better than 15 mpg, the dieselized Olds averaged better than 21 mpg—and promises to do even better with turbocharging. The same year, Mercedes-Benz introduced its tur-bocharged 300SD, the world's first production turbo-diesel car. The engine in the production model 300SD is a 5-cylinder diesel, the same basic engine (see com-parison, Table 1.1) that was modified for use in the C-111/3 test car that set nine speed records on a test track at Nardo, Italy, in April of 1978. The horsepower was increased to 230 through increased turbocharging, and the engine installed in a sleek C-111 test car body with an air drag coefficient of an incredible .191. The

**Table 1.1—Vehicle Comparison: 300D, 300SD, C-111/3**

|  | *300D* | *300SD* | *C-111/3* |
|---|---|---|---|
| Vehicle Type | Front engine, rear wheel drive, 5-pass. sedan | Front engine, rear wheel drive, 5-pass. sedan | Mid engine, rear wheel drive, 2-pass. coupe |
| Engine Type | 5-cyl., water-cooled fuel inj. diesel | 5-cyl., water-cooled fuel inj. diesel with turbocharger | 5-cyl., water-cooled fuel inj. diesel with turbocharger |
| Displacement | 3,005 cc | 3,005 cc | 2,999 cc |
| Power (SAE net) | 77 @ 4,000 rpm | 110 @ 4,200 rpm | 230 @ 4,400–4,600 rpm |
| Transmission | 4-speed auto with torque converter 2nd gear start | 4-speed auto with torque converter 1st gear start | 5-speed manual |
| Wheelbase | 110.0" | 112.8" | 107.1" |
| Length | 190.9" | 205.5" | 211.8" |
| Curb Weight | 3,515 lbs | 3,890 lbs | 2,742 lbs |
| Rear Axle Ratio | 3.46:1 | 3.07:1 | 1.65:1 |
| Tank Cap./Reserve | 21.1/3.0 gal. | 21.7/3.7 gal. | 37 gal. |
| Body | Steel | Steel with alum. hood & trunk lid | Fiber glass with carbon fiber |
| Fuel Consumption | 28 mpg (EPA hwy.) | 29 mpg (EPA hwy.) | 14.7 mpg @ 195.4 mph aver. over 12 hours |

**Fig. 1.6**  Mercedes-Benz's futuristic, turbocharged, 5-cylinder diesel experimental C-111 (forerunner of the Mercedes turbocharged 300SD) smashed nineteen major diesel and gas engine speed records in 1976 at Nardo, Italy.

car and engine used the engine's power so efficiently that it set the following speed and endurance records:

**New Records Set at Nardo, Italy,
April 30, 1978 by C-111/3**

| Distance Records | Old Record | C-111/3 Record |
|---|---|---|
| 1. 100 kms | 187.66 | 196.654 |
| 2. 100 miles | 190.67 | 198.736 |
| 3. 500 kms | 183.21 | 199.994 |
| 4. 500 miles | 177.23 | 199.328 |
| 5. 1,000 kms | 177.35 | 197.787 |
| 6. 1,000 miles | 172.80 | 198.274 |
| *Time Records* | | |
| 7. 1 hour | 190.68 | 199.984 |
| 8. 6 hours | 172.38 | 197.469 |
| 9. 12 hours | 170.21 | 195.398 |

Turbocharging boosted the 300SD's power by an amazing 45 percent, compared to its similarly dieseled roadmate, the 300D. By 1980 Mercedes had managed to hike the 300SD's power another 9 percent, for an overall 54-percent power increase in only three model years. With its newfound power, the 300SD immediately became a star road performer. Automotive press surveys of owners of these new diesel vehicles found them ecstatic. Accustomed to gas engine performance, most owners said their diesels road performed just as well—and with upwards of 50 percent better fuel economy.

These later developments stem from what could be called diesel's Historic Plus Year, 1977, when *plus* road performance was added to its existing advantages, through a "miracle of necessity," as it was hailed by automotive insiders. But, while the experts can list a dozen engineering and technical reasons behind the diesel's newfound power, actual motivator of the "miracle" was a simple edict issued by the U.S. Environmental Protection Agency (EPA) that by model year 1985 the fleet economy average of all cars in any maker's line must be no less than 27.5 miles per gallon (mpg). Under this EPA standard—officially dubbed CAFE, for Corporate Average Fuel Economy—the fuel mileages of all models would be added up and the total divided by the number of models offered by a manufacturer, to arrive at a "corporate average miles-per-gallon." The CAFE standard hit Detroit (and many foreign car makers, too) where it hurt most: in their big gas-guzzlers.

CAFE is not the same as mpg, which refers to the miles that any given vehicle will travel on a single gallon of fuel. The CAFE figure is a measure of fuel consumption (a subtle difference) and refers to a manufacturer's fleet average. To determine the CAFE number, the manufacturer uses the mpg for each model in its line. (Each manufacturer is assigned an EPA mileage figure based on a weighted (55/45) average of city and highway fuel economy numbers. This number will be somewhat higher than the official EPA rating because the EPA is publishing only city ratings now.) Then a fleet, or corporate average, is computed by giving proportionate weight to the number of units sold in each model line.

Consider a hypothetical case: A vehicle getting 20 mpg and one getting 40 mpg would average 30 mpg, using the mile-per-gallon formula. But the CAFE formula is different. Let's assume that each vehicle is actually driven 100 miles. The 20-mpg vehicle would actually use five gallons of fuel to travel 100 miles, and the 40-mpg vehicle would use 2.5 gallons to go the same distance. Add the five and 2.5 gallons for a total of 7.5 gallons of fuel consumed by the two vehicles to travel a total of 200 miles. Divide the 200 miles by 7.5 gallons and you arrive at a fleet average of 26.67 mpg, not 30 mpg, as you would get if you simply averaged the two cars' mpg ratings. Using this method, not only are the gas mileage figures of each car taken into account, but also the sales mix of each particular model. It is obvious that it takes more than one high mileage vehicle to offset the sale of one low mileage vehicle.

## THE ANSWER TO CAFE REQUIREMENTS

Which brings us back to the diesel. The fuel efficiency of the diesel is currently the only way most manufacturers see to meet the increasingly stiffer CAFE requirements set down by the federal government, especially if the individual manufacturer's line is heavily weighted with larger cars. The stakes in the CAFE game are not small, either. The CAFE standard gets much tougher through 1985, as seen in Table 1.2. If the manufacturer does not achieve the required CAFE figure, a fine of $5 per vehicle for each tenth-mile it falls short can be levied.

The implications of the EPA's 1977 mileage averaging were enormous. In a single stroke, it defined the kinds of cars Americans would drive after 1985—and probably before. Scratched from the probable line-up of cars that Detroit and foreign makers might sell in the United States were some of their most popular and profitable models. Doomed to extinction were virtually all large wagons (their 1980 EPA average a dismal 15 mpg). Keeping them in a maker's line after 1985 would pull down the entire line's fuel average, probably to an overall average well

### Table 1.2—Present and Future Federal Corporate Average Fuel Economy Standards

| Model Year | Average Miles per Gallon | Percent Improvement from 1973 |
|---|---|---|
| 1973 (base year) | 13.5 | — |
| Mandated | | |
| 1978 | 18.0 | 33 |
| 1979 | 19.0 | 41 |
| 1980 | 20.0 | 48 |
| 1981 | 22.0 | 62 |
| 1982 | 24.0 | 78 |
| 1983 | 26.0 | 92 |
| 1984 | 27.0 | 100 |
| 1985 | 27.5 | 104 |
| 1990 (projected) | 35.0 | 159 |

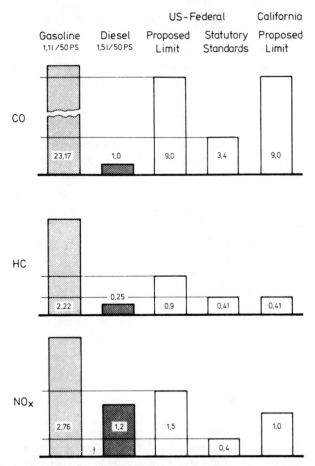

**Fig. 1.7** Proposed emission standards could be met by a subcompact car with a diesel engine, without aftertreatment. This chart shows the emissions of a VW Rabbit equipped with a gasoline and diesel engine of the same output. Compliance by gasoline engines or larger diesels with the proposed standards will necessitate expensive and efficiency-robbing exhaust emission-control systems. (*Source:* Advanced Automotive Power Systems Part I: Morphological Systems and System Analysis, SAE Paper #760591, by P. Hofbauer and B. Wiedeman, Volkswagenwerk AG)

below the required 27.5 mpg. Scratched, too, would be most large cars and many mid-size gas engine models. Not even all compacts would survive what seemed a pending wipe-out of many of America's best-known models.

A crash program to engineer better fuel efficiency into the gasoline engine wouldn't work, insiders knew. The gasoline engine, through more than eighty years of nearly year-to-year betterment, was still a fuel guzzler. Take the Cadillac, for example: Even should the engineers by some sleight of hand manage to boost its fuel efficiency 50 percent, it would still be below EPA 1985 standards.

There was, however, one obvious solution: the already fuel-efficient diesel. Boost the diesel's fuel economy even higher, engineers reasoned, and the diesel cars in any manufacturer's line would significantly raise the "fleet" mileage average above the EPA's mandated 27.5 mpg. That would permit Detroit, as well as its foreign competitors with similar CAFE problems, to sell in the U.S. market many of their less efficient gas engine models. But to do it, car makers would have to make the diesel's road performance acceptable to car buyers. In the short run, doing so would solve an automaker's immediate 1985 fuel average problem. In the long run, particularly should fuel prices grow out of hand (as they already have in Europe), it would allow the orderly transition from gasoline to diesel for all or most of a car maker's models.

Vehicle makers worked their "miracle of necessity" in a number of ways. Some turbocharged their existing, middling road performance diesels—as did Mercedes-Benz. Others—Oldsmobile and Volkswagen, for instance— "dieselized" their already powerful gasoline engines, creating a new diesel, little resembling the gasoline engine from which it had sprung, other than in road performance. Still others set about designing whole new families of automotive diesel engines (they'll be unveiled throughout the eighties) with exceptional fuel economy and road performance to match.

However they have chosen to work their "miracle," results are the same: for the once zilch road performing diesel, all the performance any buyer could want—plus fuel economy.

Thus have the 1980s become the "decade of the diesel." A new engine is in your automotive near future. It is the diesel. And today it is a star performer.

## EPA'S TOP THREE FUEL-ECONOMY CARS: EVERYONE A DIESEL

In the Environmental Protection Agency's now nearly decade-long history (the agency was established by presidential order, with the consent of the U.S. Congress, in December 1970), it has tested—generally at its Fuel Economy Group facilities at Ann Arbor, Michigan—thousands of automobiles, both domestic and foreign. While EPA test procedures have at times been criticized for too much testing on laboratory dynamometers, rather than on road runs, recent modifications by EPA in its testing methods have largely hushed its critics. And all in all, EPA test results have stood the test of time. They have become a recognized world standard for measuring, for any model of car or utility vehicle, the fuel economy and thus the fuel efficiency, of its engine and that engine's output of measured pollutants.

Makers of imported cars, like their domestic U.S. rivals, must submit their cars for EPA testing, evaluation, and certification before a model may be sold within the United States, and while it is possible that a car not yet tested—perhaps a foreign make not destined for U.S. sale—may be more economical in fuel consumption or less polluting than cars thus far tested by EPA, the existence anywhere in the world of such a "wonder car" is highly doubtful.

The contrary is more likely true. Cars that makers, notably foreign manufacturers, have reason to believe cannot stand EPA scrutiny, simply are not presented to the U.S. government testers. Says one foreign car authority, "The U.S. car market is potentially the world's most lucrative for any manufacturer. And especially for any car able to deliver maximum miles per gallon with minimum pollution, the United States being one of the few nations in the world with ever-more-strict fuel economy and pollution laws. Rare indeed is the auto maker who would intentionally deprive himself of sales in America if his car, put to EPA testing, seems assured of emerging with the 'right numbers'—with test numbers that make it competitive in fuel economy and emissions with other cars, many of them also foreign made, in the U.S. market.'' Thus the belief is generally held in the world of automotives that the cars so far tested by EPA are, in fact, the world's most fuel efficient and least polluting.

The ''so far'' looms important in at least two areas. One is the in-development of a new generation of turbocharged diesels, among them the Volkswagen Rabbit, currently on U.S. road tests, which at this writing had not been officially tested by EPA, but was scheduled for early examination. It may very well eclipse all present competitors (including its own nonturbocharged version) for fuel economy, once tested and put into production. The second qualifier acknowledges a number of cars loudly touted both by their designers and by the press as achieving all but fantastic fuel economy—the majority of them diesel engined, incidentally—but which either have never been submitted for EPA evaluation, or, if EPA tested, fell far short of their designer's claims. It is possible, of course, that one of these headlined economy cars will some day live up to the advanced billing; to date, however, none of them has.

Whatever the case, the EPA's long test history, three cars stand out in its records as, by test, achieving the highest fuel economy—and on two economy scores. The three, ranked in order, get the most miles per gallon. They lead the pack for fuel economy. And, translated to dollars annually spent for fuel, their owners (driving an average 10,000 miles a year combined city and highway mileage) can expect to spend the least for fuel. Significantly, the EPA's historic ''Top Three'' are all diesels. Two of the EPA's ''Top Three'' are Volkswagen diesels, and the other is a U.S.-designed conversion (a Ford Pinto fitted with a diesel engine).

Of the Volkswagen diesels, undisputed No. 1—the rated ''best'' economy car ever tested by EPA—is the Integrated Research Volkswagen (IRVW), still

**Fig. 1.8** The IRVW (Integrated Research Volkswagen) tops the EPA's official list of high-mileage cars with a turbocharged version of the Rabbit diesel engine.

stamped "experimental." Its diesel engine, similar to the Rabbit, is turbocharged. The IRVW is not yet in production, but it could very well be within the next few years. The other fuel-economy leading Volkswagen—ranked No. 3 by EPA—is the Volkswagen Rabbit diesel, its engine nonturbocharged. The third member of the fuel economy triumvirate—and ranked by EPA No. 2 among all cars it has so far tested—is a diesel conversion: a former gasoline engine Ford Pinto installed with a Chrysler-Nissan turbocharged diesel. This car is the handiwork of conversion specialist Tony Capanna and his California-based Wilcap Company (see Capanna interview, "Diesel Engine Conversions", in Chapter 9). The Capanna diesel Pinto made headlines and diesel fuel economy records a few years ago in a number of fuel "misering" competition runs. But it was never intended as a production car.

It seems more than likely that the Capanna diesel Pinto's EPA No. 2 place will be taken over shortly by a third Volkswagen diesel not yet officially evaluated: the turbocharged version of the Rabbit diesel, which promises to have even better fuel economy than the nonturbo Rabbit, although probably a shade less fuel misering than the Volkswagen experimental IRVW, which is a fuel-economy demonstration vehicle into which Volkswagen has put some $500,000 and the U.S. Department of Transportation $45,000. If Tony Capanna's diesel Pinto is misered from its No. 2 fuel-economy niche in EPA records, it will still likely retain a No. 3 or 4 rating, creating a new EPA "Top Four"—still all diesel.

Table 1.3, from EPA records, details findings for the three most mileage-misering cars put to the EPA test.

Concludes EPA Fuel Economy Group project manager Peter Hutchins, who had a hand in all the "Top Three" evaluations, "The Volkswagen IRVW fuel economy results were the best we've ever seen in a car . . . and the Wilcap probably falls second. As for the IRVW, it could easily, I think, become a production car."

### Diesel Increases Fuel Economy

Recent EPA fuel economy figures for so-called "standard models" with gasoline engines and for the same models installed with diesel engines dramatically

**Table 1.3—Top Three Mileage "Misering" Cars**
(According to EPA Tests)

| | *Status* | *Engine* | City *(mpg)* | Highway *(mpg)* |
|---|---|---|---|---|
| No. 1: Integrated Research Volkswagen (IRVW) | Experimental | Diesel, turbocharged | 51.9 | 63.8[1] |
| No. 2: Wilcap Ford Pinto | Nonproduction | Diesel, turbocharged | 46.1 | 60.3[2] |
| No. 3: 1980 Volkswagen Rabbit | Production[3] | Diesel, naturally aspirated; 5-speed manual transmission | 41 | 55 |

*Notes:* [1] All EPA results are the average of a number of tests. In its best city test, the IRVW scored 54.1; on its best highway test, 68.3.
[2] In its best highway test, the Wilcap achieved 63.9 fuel economy.
[3] In production car certification, only one test is run, which is the vehicle's "best" showing.

**Table 1.4—EPA mpg Fuel Consumption**

| *Make* (and transmission) | *City* | *Highway* | *Combined* |
|---|---|---|---|
| *Mercedes-Benz* (automatic) | | | |
| gasoline 2 liters | 14 | 19 | 16 |
| diesel 2.1 liters | 22 | 28 | 25 |
| diesel improvement | 57% | 47% | 56% |
| *Oldsmobile 98* (automatic) | | | |
| gasoline 5.7 liters | 14 | 20 | 16 |
| diesel 5.7 liters | 21 | 30 | 24 |
| diesel improvement | 50% | 50% | 50% |
| *Peugeot* (automatic) | | | |
| gasoline 2 liters | 17 | 22 | 19 |
| diesel 2.1 liters | 25 | 31 | 28 |
| diesel improvement | 47% | 41% | 47% |
| *VW Golf/Rabbit* (manual) | | | |
| gasoline 1.5 liters | 25 | 38 | 29 |
| diesel 1.6 liters | 40 | 53 | 45 |
| diesel improvement | 60% | 39% | 55% |

show the economy improvement possible with diesel. But these same-model gasoline-versus-diesel tests don't show the *optimum* economy possible with diesel. In most cases the principal difference between the standard gasoline engine model and the diesel was the diesel engine itself, and that reason alone makes Table 1.4 worth more than casual reading. If the fuel economy of an otherwise standard car can be so significantly improved by little more than substituting a diesel for its gasoline engine, it seems likely that further and far greater fuel economy improvement might be possible, were the dieselized model to be engineered solely around its diesel engine. Such designed-for-diesel cars are now being tested and will be available soon to the car buyer. The EPA-certified improvement with diesel over same-model gas engine cars, a fuel improvement expressed as a fuel-saving percentage *increase* over standard models, weighs heavily in favor of diesel.

## DIESEL FACTS AND MYTHS

Diesel enthusiasts say it is a far more efficient engine than the gasoline. One evidence of the diesel's greater efficiency is the 25 to 50 percent and higher mileage bonus it achieves from each gallon of fuel, compared to the gasoline engine. Another claim is that the diesel, which does not need spark plugs, a carburetor, distributor, or other gasoline engine ignition and combustion system parts, ordinarily requires less maintenance because of its fewer parts.

By the very nature of its combustion—its fuel ignited not by an electrical spark from a spark plug, but spontaneously by the heat of compression—a diesel must be more ruggedly and heavily built than its gas engine counterpart. This ruggedness gives the diesel a far longer life; whereas the average car's gas engine has a design life of little more than 100,000 miles, a diesel's life span may be two to three times longer. It is not unusual for some automotive diesels, especially the larger, more massive diesel engines that power trucks, to go 300,000 to 500,000 miles before major engine rework. Exceptional longevity has been seen also in some diesels powering cars and light pickup trucks, such as the Mercedes 220D which had been driven more than 900,000 miles before its original engine required major maintenance.

But diesel ruggedness and sheer heft carry some penalties. One is weight. Diesels weigh anywhere from a little to a lot more than comparable gasoline engines. On the little side are two 4-cylinder engines—one gasoline, the other diesel—produced by the same manufacturer. Both have identical 256 cubic inch displacements. The 256 CID gasoline engine weighs 862 pounds; the diesel, 882 pounds, only twenty pounds more. But in some other engines the weight differential is significantly greater. Even so, considering a vehicle's *total weight,* the difference may prove minimal. Oldsmobile's diesel Delta 88, not untypically, has a total (curb) weight of some 3,800 pounds, nearly two tons. Its overall weight is only 180 pounds greater than the gasoline engine version of the same model. Much of this additional weight, moreover, goes for such heavier diesel components as the injector pump and two standard-size batteries rather than one, as in a gasoline vehicle.

**Oldsmobile Delta 88**

| Engine | EPA Fuel Economy |
|---|---|
| 231 V-6 (gas) | 18 |
| 301 V-8 (gas) | 17 |
| 350 Diesel | 21 |
| 350 V-8 (gas) | 16 |
| Oldsmobile Cutlass *Engine* | |
| 231 V-6 (gas) | 19 |
| 260 V-8 (gas) | 17 |
| 260 V-8 (diesel, auto.) | 24 |
| 260 V-8 (diesel, 5-spd) | 25 |
| 305 V-8 (gas, auto.) | 15 |
| 305 V-8 (gas, 4-spd) | 17 |

Based on 1979 EPA ratings

Another diesel penalty is higher first cost. Depending on make and model, a diesel may cost anywhere from a few hundred dollars to upwards of $750 to $1,000 more. Still, longer engine life, despite higher first cost, has its ultimate reward: the diesel engine's higher resale value. With 100,000 miles showing on its odometer, a car's gas engine is ready for major overhaul, if not the scrap heap; but the 100,000-mile diesel may have yet another 100,000 miles of road life before major engine maintenance. Today, even with diesel fuel and gasoline priced neck and neck, it costs far less to fuel a diesel than a gas engine car, simply because of the diesel's often double gasoline mileage. As both gasoline and diesel fuel prices rise, as seems inevitable, the diesel's fuel cost advantage grows ever greater.

Growing greater, too, is the car-sized diesel's fuel economy. Designers of gaso-

**Fig. 1.9** The engine from the IRVW. Note the turbocharger (arrow) that enables the compact 4-cylinder engine to achieve high mileage.

line engines confess to being hard put to squeeze yet another few road miles per gallon out of what, as every engineer should know, is only a moderately efficient engine. To compensate for the gas engine's inefficiency and low fuel mileage, car makers have reduced their full-size models to intermediate, and shrunk the intermediates to compact size. Still, the diesel—in full-size models—delivers fuel mileage unmatched even by down-sized gas engine competitors. Diesel engineers have in the past few years vastly upgraded the diesel's already enviable fuel economy. By the EPA's own reckoning, the most fuel misering vehicle on the road is the Volkswagen diesel Rabbit, with a highway economy of 55 mpg. Turbocharging will soon raise the Rabbit diesel's highway average even higher, at least to 64 mpg. In one EPA highway test, the turbo-diesel Rabbit has already gotten better than 68 miles to the gallon (see Table 1.3).

Moreover, unlike gasoline engine vehicles, diesels require no pollution-squelching catalytic exhaust converter, mandated by the EPA to clean up hydrocarbons in the gas engine's exhaust. Hydrocarbons are minimal in the diesel's exhaust, primarily because the diesel burns its fuel more efficiently and completely. But the diesel faces two major pollutant problems, both potentially serious. And both are peculiar to the diesel.

One is the exhaust emission of nitrogen oxide ($NO_X$). The EPA has decreed that by the early 1980s, exhaust $NO_X$ must be reduced to a very low level—a level many, although not all, diesel makers believe they can achieve. On the other hand, many people believe that the $NO_X$ standard constitutes the greatest threat to the diesel engine. The state of California, always in the forefront of emission control legislation, has received permission from the federal government to lower the $NO_X$ standard for cars sold in that state to 0.4 gpm (**grams per mile**) in 1982. In comparison, the present and proposed standards are shown in Table 1.5.

**Table 1.5—Present and Proposed Federal and California Emission Control Standards**

| Emission | 1980 Fed. | 1980 Cal. | 1981 Fed. | 1981 Cal. | 1982 Fed. | 1982 Cal. |
|---|---|---|---|---|---|---|
| HC (Hydrocarbon) (gpm) | .41 | .41 | .41 | .41 | .41 | .41 |
| CO (Carbon monoxide) (%) | 7.0 | 9.0 | 3.4 | 9.0 | 3.4 | 9.0 |
| $NO_x$ (Oxides of nitrogen) (gpm) | 1.0 | 1.0[1] | 1.0 | 1.0 | 1.0 | .4 |
| Particulates[2] (gpm) | .6 | .6 | .6 | .6 | .6 | .6 |

[1] 1.5 if certified for 100,000 miles.
[2] Proposed legislation—not yet in effect.

The other pollutant problem is the exhaust emission of carbon particles, a by-product of diesel combustion. Exhaust particulates, specifically the diesel's, have only recently been recognized as potentially serious, perhaps even carcinogenic, air pollutants. Diesel emission of carbon particles, say researchers studying the problem, may be thirty to ninety times greater than similar emissions from gasoline engines. Now the EPA has taken aim on diesel soot.

New U.S. Environmental Protection Agency rules, designed to reduce diesel soot emissions by some 74% by 1990, have decreed that diesel cars and light trucks (weighing less than 8500 pounds) may, through model year 1984, emit no more than 0.6 gram of soot per mile. In 1985, soot reduction grows more stringent: 0.2 gram per mile for diesel cars, 0.26 gram for light trucks.

Today's diesels—at least some of them—are already within reach of both standards. The Rabbit Diesel's 0.23 gram/mile soot emission is but 0.03 gram/mile above the 1985 standard—and should easily be in compliance by that date or far sooner. Even the Oldsmobile V-8 diesel, powering most General Motors diesel vehicles seems, with its 0.84 gram/mile soot output, within reach of compliance. The major problem in meeting the soot limitation is this: in also reducing $NO_x$, soot emission is often increased.

The EPA concedes that no manufacturer knows precisely how to meet the 0.2 gram per mile standard. Yet it should not be overly difficult. Involved may be no more than fitting diesel exhausts with some kind of scrubbing device.

"The EPA's aim," says one diesel insider, "is to 'force' technology . . . to set a limit on emissions which forces the manufacturers' engineering departments to get to work on the problem and to solve it. Frankly, the idea of 'forcing' technology in any field is often a right step in technological advancement."

Thus, while a few diesel makers complain they don't know how, as yet, to meet the EPA's $NO_x$ and soot limitations, no diesel engine is actually so far off the emission mark that the doing (and engineering) should be all that difficult.

Nonetheless the diesel enters the 1980s with, on balance, undeniably the most impressive scorecard in the nearly century-old history of automotives. Weighed against an all but unbroken string of diesel pluses are, to date, one minus (exhaust nitrous oxides) and a question mark (carbon particle emission). Whether the latter is finally written into the record as a minus, or remains merely a nagging question mark, must await the final verdict of science.

One verdict is already in: nothing on the road comes close to matching diesel efficiency, fuel economy and long life.

## DIESEL PAYBACK

Is the diesel really worth buying? Some manufacturers advertise a "negative premium" to buy a diesel car, which means that a diesel model is less expensive to purchase than the gasoline engine model. Mercedes-Benz, for example, sells the 6-cylinder gasoline engine 280E, for $26,243, but virtually the same car, called the 300D, with a 5-cylinder diesel engine, is available for $24,584—a saving of $1,659. And that's not all: The 1979 (latest available with complete ratings) EPA Mileage Guide lists the following information for the two cars:

|      | Fuel Economy | Average Annual Fuel Costs |
|------|--------------|---------------------------|
| 280E | 14 mpg       | $750                      |
| 300D | 23 mpg       | $392                      |

It's not hard to see that, in this case, the savings in purchase price and fuel costs alone are considerable. Mercedes-Benz can afford to sell the diesel less expensively because the diesel has no costly emission control hardware and because they have been building diesels since 1937, so initial costs were long ago amortized.

But not every manufacturer offers a diesel model at a negative premium. In fact, most manufacturers charge a premium that ranges from $200 to $850 over the cost of a comparable model for a diesel engine version. Let's look at two popular models, the VW Rabbit Diesel and the Oldsmobile Cutlass Diesel.

Volkswagen charges a $195 premium to get the diesel model, and the Oldsmobile oil burner costs about $750 over the base V-8. Using the latest available EPA mileage ratings, does it really make sense to buy a diesel? Let's look at the numbers:

|                                  | EPA Mpg Rating | EPA Average Annual Fuel Cost |
|----------------------------------|----------------|------------------------------|
| 1980 VW Rabbit (gas)             | 24             | $563                         |
| 1980 VW Rabbit (diesel)          | 40             | $300                         |
| 1979 Olds Cutlass (gas, V-8)     | 17             | $617                         |
| 1979 Olds Cutlass (diesel, V-8)  | 25             | $360                         |

Counting fuel costs only, (at the current price of fuel) it will take less than a year to pay the diesel premium on a Rabbit, and just shy of three years to pay the diesel premium on an Olds Cutlass diesel. If you're the average driver who puts 12,000 miles per year on a car and keeps the car between five and six years, you will likely save money on either car, and could probably make similar comparisons with other diesel models.

There are other financial benefits to owning the diesel. In general, the diesel costs less to maintain. Even though some maintenance operations—for instance, oil change—MUST be done more frequently on a diesel (see the discussion of owner maintenance in later chapters), the diesel has no conventional ignition system, and does not require costly tune-ups. It is not unreasonable to assume that a diesel will run 45,000 to 50,000 miles without any major attention. In the same amount of miles, a comparably sized gasoline engine would require almost two complete tune-ups (spark plugs, ignition system servicing, and labor).

Depreciation at resale is usually less on a diesel model than on a comparable gasoline engine car. According to both the NADA Official Used Car Guide and the Kelly Blue Book, a similar publication, the 1977 Mercedes-Benz 240D and 300D models, for example, retain more value than any of the other Mercedes-Benz models of that year (see Table 1.6). The situation is the same with other manufacturers. The VW Rabbit diesel model is in such demand that the major publishers of used car trade-in values (NADA, Kelly Blue Book, and National Market Reports, Inc. Red Book) do not list a value for Rabbit diesels.

#### Table 1.6—Percentage of Value Retained—Mercedes-Benz Diesel models

|  | Kelly Blue Book | National Market Reports, Inc. Red Book |
|---|---|---|
| 1977 240D (diesel) | 83.5 | — |
| 1977 300D (diesel) | 75.9 | 77.1 |
| 1977 280E (gas) | 73 | 74.7 |

*Note:* The Mercedes-Benz 240D retains the highest percentage of value of any Mercedes-Benz model.

At Oldsmobile, you could have purchased an identically equipped Delta 88 Royale Town Sedan new in 1978 for $6,224 (V-6 gas engine) or $7,074 (diesel V-8). According to the end-of-1979 edition of the National Market Reports, Inc. Red Book, the diesel model retained 76.6 percent of its value, compared to 73.3 percent for the gas engine V-6, as shown in the following chart:

|  | New Price | 1979 Price | Percent Value Retained |
|---|---|---|---|
| 1978 Delta 88 Sedan (gas) | $6,224 | $4,500 | 72.3 |
| 1978 Delta 88 Sedan (diesel) | $7,074 | $5,425 | 76.6 |
| 1978 98 Regency Coupe (gas) | $7,841 | $5,750 | 73.3 |
| 1978 98 Regency Coupe (diesel) | $8,691 | $6,600 | 75.9 |

The cost of fuel will continue to climb; and, as the cost goes up, the savings of the diesel will be more substantial in dollars, because the diesel will deliver more miles per gallon than a comparable gasoline-powered vehicle. Obviously, the diesel is not for those who make an occasional trip to the grocery store. Its efficiency shows to greater advantage when the miles begin to pile up on the odometer. In short, the more you drive and the more fuel costs, the more you will save with a diesel. At present, the diesel stands alone in offering to those who need it the privilege of retaining use of a five- or six-passenger automobile and still getting reasonable fuel economy at the same time.

## THE DIESEL PASSENGER VEHICLE IN PICTURES

If one manufacturer's name is automatically associated with the diesel passenger car, it has to be that of Mercedes-Benz. The history of the company is one of automotive "firsts," but one of the most important has to be their early work with the diesel engine, which laid the groundwork for state-of-the-art diesel cars as they exist today. Here, in illustrations, is a brief history of the development of the diesel car.

**Fig. 1.10** The world's first (1936–1940) production diesel passenger car, the 260D Mercedes-Benz, had a 4-cylinder, 2.6-litre engine that produced 45 hp at 3,000 rpm; 1,967 of the cars were produced.

**Fig. 1.11** The two models of the 170D Mercedes-Benz (1949–1953) had a 1.7-litre engine that produced 38 hp at 3,200 rpm; 46,808 of the cars were produced.

**Fig. 1.12**   The three models of the 180D Mercedes-Benz (1954–1962) had a 1.8-litre, 4-cylinder engine that produced 43 hp at 3,500 rpm; 152,983 were produced.

**Fig. 1.13**   A total of 307,583 190D Mercedes-Benzes with 1.9-litre, 50–55-hp engine were produced (1958–1965) in three models.

**Fig. 1.14**   This 1965 Mercedes-Benz 200D used a 60-hp version of the company's 4-cylinder diesel engine.

**Fig. 1.15** The 220D Mercedes-Benz (1968–1979) had a 4-cylinder, 2.2-litre, 57-hp engine. More than 475,000 have been sold.

**Fig. 1.16** *Top:* First production of the 5-cylinder 300D Mercedes-Benz was in 1974. The 3.0-litre engine produced 77 hp. *Bottom:* In 1973 Mercedes-Benz introduced its 240D. The 4-cylinder engine produced 62 hp from 2.4 litres and got a 30-mpg city EPA fuel economy rating.

**Fig. 1.17** *Top:* The world's first turbocharged diesel production car, the Mercedes-Benz 300SD was produced in 1978. The 5-cylinder, 3.0 litre engine produced 110 hp, increased to 120 hp on 1980 models. *Bottom:* The first Mercedes station wagon, the 300 TD Mercedes-Benz, introduced in 1979, gets 28 mpg on the highway, using a 5-cylinder diesel rated 77 hp at 4,000 rpm.

## DOWN THE DECADES WITH DIESEL

### Some Diesel Milestones

*1907:* Prosper L'Orange develops the high-pressure injector and prechamber, which allows the diesel to be made in a small size practical for transportation needs.

*1923:* Probably the first preproduction diesel truck, the five-ton experimental flatbed Benz (predecessor to Mercedes-Benz), goes with a 4-cylinder, 50-hp Benz diesel engine.

*1927:* Robert Bosch Corporation produces their first diesel injection pump.

*1929:* America's first diesel automobile produced. On its inaugural 792-mile,

Indianapolis-to-New York City run in January 1930, the 1925 Packard sedan, fitted with a 4-cylinder, 50-hp Model U Cummins diesel, makes the trip on $1.38 worth of diesel fuel and averages 26.4 miles per gallon.

*1931:* One of dieseldom's most significant early endurance tests, when a truck, powered by a Cummins diesel, is driven nonstop for fourteen days and 14,600 miles, averaging 43 mph, at the Indianapolis Speedway. Same year, the first diesel race car—likewise Cummins diesel powered—enters the Indy 500. It finishes the entire race in twelfth place, without a pit stop, uses only 31 gallons of fuel, and averages 86.17 mph.

Dave Evans qualifies an 85-hp Cummins diesel-powered Duesenberg race car seventeenth in the annual Indianapolis 500-mile race. Evans finishes thirteenth at an average speed of 86.107 mph and drives the first car ever to finish the "500" without a pit stop, total costs of 31 gallons of fuel and 1 quart of oil consumed is $1.78.

**Fig. 1.18** Dave Evans drove this Cummins diesel-powdered car the full distance in the 1931 Indy 500 without a pit stop, the first time this feat was accomplished. Standing is Clessie Cummins, developer of the Cummins diesel Engine. (Photograph courtesy Indianapolis Motor Speedway)

*1934:* One of the first newsmaking diesel conversions, a Hillman sedan powered by an English Perkins 4-cylinder diesel, makes the trip from England to Moscow.

*1936:* Unveiled at the Berlin Automotive Trade Show, the world's first production diesel cars: the Mercedes-Benz 260D and the Hanomag Rekord-Diesel, both powered by 4-cylinder diesels.

*1952:* Fred Agabashian sets new one-lap and four-lap records of 139.104 and 138.010 mph, respectively, driving the Cummins Diesel Special to the pole position in the annual Indy 500. After starting No. 1, the car finishes

**Fig. 1.19** An early rec-vehicle on U.S. roads with the Hanomag combi diesel. (Photograph by James Joseph)

seventeenth, completing 71 laps before being eliminated by turbocharger failure.

*1953:*   Dana Fuller, of San Mateo, California, sets World Land Speed Record for diesel automobiles with a top speed of 169.32 miles per hour, in his diesel streamliner, powered by a 6-cylinder Detroit diesel engine. The record is to stand for eighteen years.

*1965:*   In the first of numerous speed and endurance record runs, a diesel engine Peugeot 404 coupe average more than 100 mph (161 km/hr) over a 6,200-mile (10,000-km) course.

*1965:*   Peugeot modifies a 404 diesel coupe for an assault on the diesel speed record. The resulting 161 kilometers per hour is a new record for 10,000 kilometers.

*1972:*   A turbocharged diesel Opel sets twenty speed records during a tour around a West German test track.

**Fig. 1.20** Fred Agabashian drives the Cummins Diesel Special to the pole position and sets new one- and four-lap speed records in the 1952 Indy 500 time trials.

*1974:* A 5-cylinder diesel, the first in any production passenger car, is installed in the Mercedes-Benz 300D.

*1975:* Fritz Busch, an automotive performance analyst, carries the sporty look in diesel cars to new heights with his Dieselstar. This custom-built creation covers one mile from a standing start in a record 26.4 seconds.

*1976:* New world's heavy truck speed record (D tractor class), of 144-plus mph set in a 16,000-pound Kenworth two-axle tractor powered by a turbocharged Detroit 12-cylinder diesel—by V. M. (Bill) Snyder, on the Bonneville, Utah, course.

*1976:* Nineteen major speed records are smashed in a three-day marathon at Nardo, Italy, by Daimler-Benz's futuristic, turbocharged, 5-cylinder diesel experimental C-111 (forerunner of Mercedes-Benz's turbocharged 300SD). Included in the record smash are three longstanding gas engine speed marks. Averaging better than 156 mph, the C-111 captures three world enduro-marks: for 5,000 and 10,000 miles, and for 10,000 kilometers.

*1977:* For the first time, diesel cars are rated "most fuel economical" in three of the EPA's five fuel-mileage classifications.

*1977:* A VW Rabbit finishes a 50,000-kilometer endurance run, setting 31 records during nonstop running on the Kleber Tire Corporation's test track in Miramas, France.

*1978:* New world's truck speed record (open class)—159.01 mph top speed, an average 156.796 mph over the five-mile course—set at the Bonneville, Utah, speed course by V. W. Snyder, driving a Thermo King Corp.-sponsored, 11,000-pound International truck powered by a dual-turbocharged V-8 Detroit diesel engine.

*1978:* First American manufacturer to offer production diesel automobile, as General Motors' Oldsmobile Division unveils its 350-CID V-8, first of big, economy diesel engines. Engine is initially available as diesel option in the Olds 88, 98 and Custom Cruiser (later, also in the Toronado), as

**Fig. 1.21** A new world land speed record for Class C diesel trucks, 132.502 mph, was set at Bonneville, Utah, by Pete Schmidt in his 1978 one-ton, four-wheel-drive GMC pickup, powered by a twin-turbocharged Detroit 6V-53 T diesel, developing some 450 hp with 35 pounds of turbo boost.

well as in many other GM cars and light trucks, including the Cadillac Seville and GMC/Chevrolet pickup trucks.

*1978:*  First turbocharged diesel production car, introduced by Mercedes-Benz—the Mercedes-Benz 300SD, with a top speed of 103 mph.

*1978:*  New Class C diesel truck land speed record is set by Pete Schmidt driving a twin turbocharged Detroit 6V-53T diesel powering his 1978 GMC pickup to 132.502 mph on the Bonneville salt flats.

*1979:*  EPA fuel economy tests confirm Volkswagen's own tests for its turbo-diesel Integrated Research VW (IRVW), prototype for VW's turbocharged diesel Rabbit: 63.8 mpg highway, 51.9 mpg city, best average fuel economy for any vehicle yet EPA-tested. IRVW is a joint VW/U.S. Dept. of Transportation experimental diesel vehicle.

*1979:*  First four-wheel drive utility/sports turbo-diesel vehicles, unveiled by International Harvester. Optional 6-cylinder turbo-diesel (also first for production utility vehicles) powers maker's on-road/off-road Scout sports wagons and pickup trucks.

*1980:*  First production 6-cylinder turbocharged diesel automobile introduced by Germany's BMW—accelerates 0 to 100 mph in just 35 seconds.

### Diesel Models in the United States

Following are photos of many of the currently available diesel cars and trucks that have been or are currently available in the United States. The list is by no means complete, but is representative of available cars and trucks.

**Fig. 1.22** The VW Rabbit diesel continues to be the EPA mileage champ, delivering a 1980 estimated mpg. of 42.

**Fig. 1.23** *Top:* Oldsmobile's Cutlass was among the first in GM's line to offer optional factory diesel. *Bottom:* The 1979 Oldsmobile Cutlass wagon was available with the GM 350-cubic-inch V-8 diesel. Its sedan brother was also available with the 260-cubic-inch V-8 diesel.

**Fig. 1.24**   The 240D is the only Mercedes-Benz diesel available in the United States with a manual transmission. It uses a smaller, 4-cylinder diesel that has evolved with few basic design changes from the Mercedes-Benz diesels of the early 1940s.

**Fig. 1.25**   The 300CD is the coupe version of the 300D sedan. The two cars share the same chassis and engine.

**Fig. 1.26** The 300SD can carry four adults in total comfort, has the performance and handling of a sports car, and can still achieve 27 mpg on the highway, rivaling many smaller cars.

**Fig. 1.27** The 1979 Dasher station wagon, like its sedan counterpart, is available with a diesel engine. The wagon delivered 46 mpg (highway) and 36 mpg (city) in EPA testing.

**Fig. 1.28** The Cadillac diesel Seville gets 24 miles to the gallon, compared to the gas engine Seville's 16 mpg—a 50-percent fuel economy boost. (Photograph by James Joseph)

**Fig. 1.29** Diesel power is offered in 1978 GMC light-duty trucks with Olds 5.7-litre V8 available in half-ton pickups.

**Fig. 1.30** The Olds Toronado diesel is one of the road's smoothest performers.

**Fig. 1.31** The turbo-diesel International Scout II is the first U.S. four-wheel-drive diesel.

**Fig. 1.32** GMC's Caballero sports/utility models are dieselized with the Olds V-8 diesel.

**Fig. 1.33** "Going diesel" with the Audi 5000S costs about $750 more than the gas engine version. (Photograph by James Joseph)

**Fig. 1.34**  The 1980 VW Rabbit pickup is the first mini-pickup available in the United States with a diesel engine.

**Fig. 1.35**  Volvo is the latest entry into the U.S. diesel market with a station wagon and a sedan version.

# Chapter 2

# Inside the Diesel Engine

## DIESEL AND GASOLINE: HOW THEY DIFFER

Understanding how they are alike helps to explain how gasoline and diesel engines differ. Both are *internal combustion engines* because their fuel is burnt—combusted—within the engine. Likewise, both are *reciprocating engines*—meaning the up-and-down motion of their *pistons* is translated into rotational motion through a *crankshaft*, which in turn drives the vehicle's wheels through gearing.

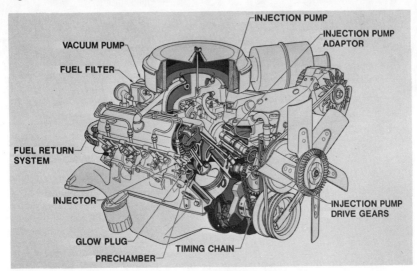

**Fig. 2.1** Cutaway view of the Oldsmobile-built GM 350-cubic-inch V-8 diesel. Note the prechamber design of the cylinder head and the gear-driven injection pump. The engine puts out 120 hp at 2,600 rpm.

35

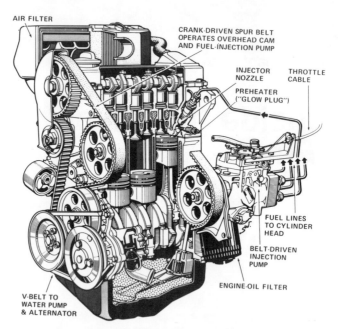

AIR FILTER

CRANK-DRIVEN SPUR BELT
OPERATES OVERHEAD CAM
AND FUEL-INJECTION PUMP

INJECTOR        THROTTLE
NOZZLE          CABLE

PREHEATER
("GLOW PLUG")

FUEL LINES
TO CYLINDER
HEAD

BELT-DRIVEN
INJECTION
PUMP

ENGINE-OIL FILTER

V-BELT TO
WATER PUMP
& ALTERNATOR

**Fig. 2.2**  Cutaway view of the VW Rabbit diesel engine. Note the swirl chamber design cylinder head and belt-driven injection pump. The unit develops 48 hp at 5,000 rpm.

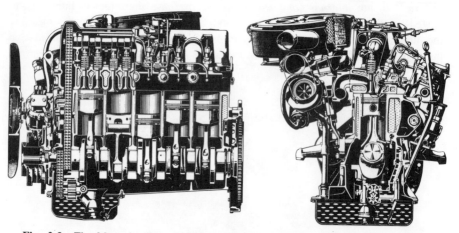

**Fig. 2.3**  The Mercedes-Benz 300SD turbocharged 5-cylinder diesel engine. Note the unusual 5-cylinder crankshaft arrangement, the prechamber design of the cylinder head, and the turbocharger underneath the air cleaner on the left side of the engine. The engine produces 120 hp at 4,200 rpm in turbocharged form, 77 hp at 4,000 rpm in the normally aspirated, unturbocharged form.

Bicycles work on the same principle. A bike's rider is a kind of reciprocating engine. His legs go up and down while the shafts (called "cranks"), on which the pedals fit, rotate much as does an engine's crankshaft, driving the bicycle's wheel through gearing. The "crank" part of an engine's crankshaft does the same thing:

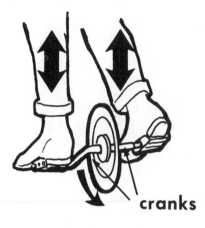

**cranks**

**Fig. 2.4** The reciprocating motion of a cyclist is similar to the motion of the pistons on the connecting rod.

converts the up-and-down motion of the pistons to rotational motion. Cranks, looking for all the world like handles, are spaced down the crankshaft—one crank for every piston, and thus each cylinder, in an engine. All of the work that an engine does has one purpose: to turn the crankshaft, thus the vehicle's wheels.

This work takes place within the engine's *cylinders,* cylindrical chambers machined into the engine's *block* (the lower part of the engine), Fig. 2.3. A single piston works within each cylinder. Even the arrangements of their cylinders are identical, whether the engine is gasoline or diesel. Cylinders may be arranged either all in line in a single row (an *in-line engine*), or in two rows or *banks* forming a kind of V (a *V engine*). The Vee arrangement of cylinders permits an engine to be built smaller and more compactly.

Similar, too, is the action of their pistons. Each heat-resistant metal piston, resembling a tin can with its bottom cut out, is connected to one of the crankshaft's cranks by a *connecting rod.* The piston end of the connecting rod turns on a *wrist pin* (also called a *piston pin*) within the piston, giving that end of the connecting rod a flexible, wrist-like motion, so it can move with and follow the piston as the piston moves upward and downward within the cylinder. Sometimes the

**Fig. 2.5** These pistons from the GM 4.3-litre gas engine (*left*) and the 4.3-litre diesel engine (*right*) show the heftier components required by a diesel engine. Note the thicker bearing caps and the beefier connecting rods. The stronger parts are one reason for the slightly increased weight of a diesel engine, compared to that of a similar gasoline engine.

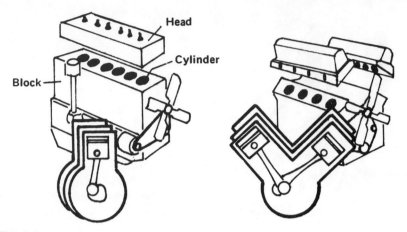

**Fig. 2.6** This simplified drawing shows the basic parts of the in-line (*left*) and V-type (*right*) engines.

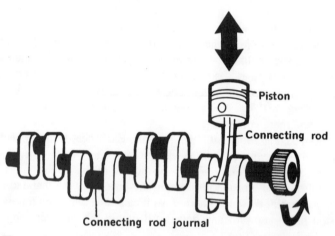

**Fig. 2.7** The rotating motion of the crankshaft forces the piston to move up and down.

cylinder is fitted with a *liner*, a replaceable cylinder within the cylinder. Whether the piston moves within the bored-in block cylinder itself or within its liner, the piston moves and behaves in the same way. Pistons, to give them freedom of movement within a cylinder, fit rather loosely. To seal the space between the piston and cylinder wall, pistons are fitted with flexible metal rings called *piston rings* that prevent combustive gases from above, under high pressure, from escaping downward past the piston. They likewise prevent lubricating oil from below, also under pressure, from escaping upward into the cylinder's combustion area.

Although the number of rings fitted around a piston and into the special grooves provided for them vary, they are generally of two types. The rings near the top of the piston are called *compression rings* because their job is to seal the piston-to-cylinder wall space against the downward escape of the highly compressed gases from the combustion chamber above. Rings at the piston's bottom are called *oil* or

**CYLINDER LINER**

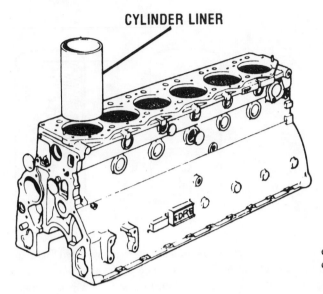

**Fig. 2.8** Some diesel engines use a replaceable cast-iron cylinder liner.

*scraper rings* because they literally scrape oil off the cylinder walls in their attempt to prevent oil from escaping upward into the combustion chamber. Between these two types of rings is a buffer ring, called an *expander*. When piston rings are worn, broken, or even missing, an engine loses power and burns oil. Power is lost because some of the highly compressed gas from the cylinder's combustion area—the *combustion chamber*—escapes downward past the piston's worn or broken rings, and its work energy is lost. Oil is burnt when, for the same reason, it escapes upward and is burned in the combustion chamber.

Tethered as a piston is to the crankshaft by its connecting rod, it can move only just so far upward within its cylinder and just so far downward. What determines the limits of a piston's up/down movement within its cylinder is the maximum up/down movement, called *throw,* of the crankshaft crank to which the piston is linked by means of its connecting rod. When a piston has moved upward within its cylinder as far as its connecting rod and the crankshaft's throw allow, the piston is said to be at *top dead center* (abbreviated TDC or T.D.C.). When it has

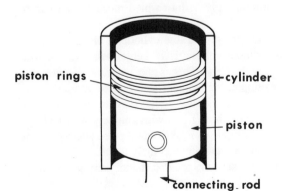

piston rings →

← cylinder

← piston

connecting rod

**Fig. 2.9** This schematic cutaway of a typical cylinder shows the parts of the piston.

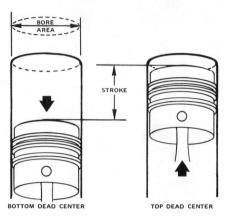

**Fig. 2.10**  The stroke of an engine is the travel of the piston from its lowest point (bottom dead center) to its highest point (top dead center).

Bore Area X Stroke = Cylinder Displacement

moved downward as far as it can, it is at *bottom dead center* (abbreviated BDC or B.D.C.). Each complete movement, up or down, is called a *piston stroke*.

The volume of air displaced within a cylinder when its piston makes one complete stroke is the cylinder's *displacement*. Displacement (in cubic inches or cubic centimeters) for any engine, diesel or gasoline, is calculated by multiplying the length of the stroke (in inches/centimeters) by the diameter of the cylinders, called the *bore,* times the number of cylinders. If an engine has six cylinders, then the engine's total CID (Cubic Inch Displacement, sometimes also expressed in liters) is equal to six times the displacement of any one of its cylinders. Generally, the more cylinders an engine has, the more power it has, and the more powerful it is in moving a vehicle, for cubic inch displacement is the measure of an engine's internal working capacity and thus the volume of air and fuel it can handle and ultimately convert to engine power through combustion.

Whereas displacement tells the "working volume" of an engine—how many cubic inches of air it can use—what indicates how efficiently it makes use of the volume of air it displaces is *compression:* into how small a space at the cylinder's top (its combustion chamber) a piston is able to squeeze, thus compress, the air it displaces. The extent to which the air displaced by the piston can be compressed is given as a ratio, called the *compression ratio*. This ratio, a measure of any engine's efficiency, is arrived at simply by dividing the maximum volume of air that the piston displaces by the minimum volume into which this same air can be compressed within the cylinder.

If, for example, the maximum cylinder volume (the cylinder's displacement) is 40 cubic inches and the minimum cylinder volume is 10 cubic inches, the ratio is 40 to 10—or, as more often expressed, 4 : 1. This is the engine's *compression ratio:* 4 : 1. It shows that, in this example, the cylinder's air can be compressed to one fourth of its original volume.

An engine's compression ratio has everything to do with engine power and fuel efficiency, for a number of reasons. Compression by itself creates energy, in the form of heat. Use of a tire pump (pumping its handle compresses the air within its cylinder) demonstrates that compressing air—or, for that matter, any gas—causes

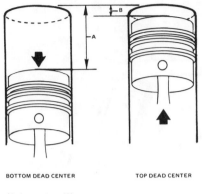

BOTTOM DEAD CENTER　　　　TOP DEAD CENTER

$$\frac{\text{Maximum volume (A)}}{\text{Minimum volume (B)}} = \text{Compression Ratio}$$

**Fig. 2.11** The compression ratio is that of the volume of air in the cylinder when the piston is at bottom dead center to the volume of air in the cylinder when the piston is at top dead center. Most automotive diesels operate at compression ratios of over 20:1.

the air to grow hotter. The harder and faster you pump, the hotter the pump grows. Using a tire pump, you have converted mechanical energy (your own pumping energy) into heat energy, through compression. Engine pistons, within their cylinders, act in much the same way. Compressing air into a smaller and smaller space creates within the compressed air mass a greater volume of oxygen, the essential ingredient of combustion. The greater an engine's compression ratio, the greater its potential efficiency in converting air and fuel to heat energy which, converted by the engine to mechanical energy, drives the vehicle's wheels.

For air to be compressed within the cylinders of an engine the pistons must move, must stroke. Most car and light truck engines, diesel or gasoline, operate on a *four-stroke cycle,* meaning that four complete strokes of a piston constitute a single combustive event. The cycle begins when the piston, at the top of its reach within the cylinder, is pulled downward by its connecting rod. As the piston starts downward, a valve in the top of the cylinder, called the *intake valve* because it permits air to enter the cylinder's combustion chamber, opens. The downward movement of the piston sucks air into the combustion chamber. Because on this piston stroke the cylinder takes in air, it is called the *intake stroke.*

As the piston, having reached bottom dead center of its stroke, starts upward, the intake air valve closes, sealing the combustion chamber. Now that the cylinder's combustion chamber is closed, as the piston moves upward, it compresses the air it has just sucked into the cylinder. This, the second of the piston's four strokes in its four-stroke cycle, is the *compression stroke.*

Now fuel, mixed with the air compressed by the piston, is ignited. The hot gases of combustion, expanding from the very small space in which they are confined (compressed) at the cylinder's top, force the piston downward on its *power stroke.* It is on this, the piston's working stroke, that the piston, through its connecting rod, delivers the cylinder's power to the crankshaft.

The piston has one final job, one final stroke. Lingering in the combustion chamber are the hot, burnt gases of combustion, and to complete the four-stroke cycle, these burnt gases must be expelled from the combustion chamber to make room for the intake (on the next cycle's first stroke) of new air. So the piston starts

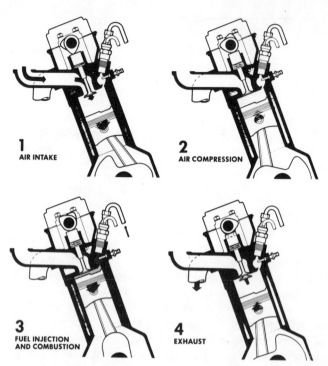

**Fig. 2.12**   How VW's diesel works: At *air intake* (1), rotation of the crankshaft drives a toothed belt that turns the camshaft, opening the intake valve. As the piston moves down, a vacuum is created, sucking fresh air into the cylinder, past the open intake valve. *Air compression* (2): As the piston moves up, both valves are closed, and the air is compressed about 23 times smaller than its original volume. The compressed air reaches a temperature of about 1,650°F., far above the temperature needed to ignite diesel fuel. *Fuel injection and compression* (3): As the piston reaches the top of the stroke, the air temperature is at its maximum. A fine mist of fuel is sprayed into the prechamber, where it ignites, and the flame front spreads rapidly into the combustion chamber. The piston is forced downward by the pressure (about 500 psi) of expanding gases. *Exhaust* (4): As the energy of combustion is spent and the piston begins to move upward again, the exhaust valve opens, and burnt gases are forced out past the open valve. As the piston starts down, the exhaust valve closes, the intake valve opens, and the air intake stroke begins again.

upward once more. As it does, the *exhaust valve* opens in the top of the combustion chamber. This *exhaust stroke,* the piston's fourth, forces the exhaust gases out of the cylinder through the open exhaust valve.

The up/down movement of the pistons, like virtually everything else concerned with the engine's internal combustion, is controlled and timed by the *crankshaft,* analogous to a watch's all-controlling mainspring. It is the crankshaft that controls the pistons' movements within the cylinders. And it is the crankshaft, through the various gears, chains, and sometimes the belts it powers, that opens and closes the cylinders' intake and exhaust valves at precisely the right moment, just as precisely introduces fuel into the cylinders, and powers a half dozen other precisely timed engine components.

Since in a four-stroke cycle engine the crankshaft receives power during only the power stroke of each piston's four strokes, it would not turn uniformly unless the thrusts of the pistons' power strokes were somehow spread out over the entire four-cycle interval. The *flywheel,* which mounts on the crankshaft's rear end, has this chore. It keeps the engine and its rotational output uniform between power strokes and thus betweeen succeeding combustions. This spread-out uniformity is especially useful at low speed and when the engine is starting. A small, relatively lightweight flywheel produces quick acceleration but uneven idling, whereas a larger, heavier flywheel smooths out idling, but provides slower acceleration. Even so, some torsional stresses, which tend to set up vibrations, do occur within the crankshaft. Helping to dampen these is the *vibration damper,* mounted on the crankshaft's front end. The vibration damper rotates at constant speed, reducing crankshaft vibration. Its all-controlling role in engine operation is unique; mechanically coupled through the connecting rods to the pistons as it is, only the crankshaft "knows" at every instant the precise position of each piston within its separate cylinder.

The *gear train* found on the front of most engines typifies crankshaft control. Here, the crankshaft powers an array of gears that in turn power and control key engine components, all of their operations timed to the rotation of the crankshaft and thus to the position of the pistons within their cylinders. Typical, too, is the crankshaft's mechanical, yet precise control over the opening and closing of the cylinders' intake and exhaust valves. A *timing gear,* driven by the crankshaft, turns a *camshaft* whose eccentrically shaped *cams* control the up/down movement of a *push rod.* The push rod in turn controls a *rocker arm,* depressing or releasing a *valve spring* that lifts (opens) or lowers (closes) the *valve.*

Although similarities between the diesel and the gasoline engine fade at the very beginning of the four-stroke cycle, it is in the diesel's combustion chamber, in the make-up of its combustive charge and the way in which fuel is introduced into the diesel's combustion chamber, that the gasoline-versus-diesel difference becomes radical. The diesel difference begins on the cycle's very first stroke, the intake. Whereas the gasoline engine's pistons suck a fuel/air mix—gasoline and air—into the cylinders, Rudolph Diesel's genius was his realization that most of the limitations of igniting a fuel mix in an engine could be overcome if what was initially sucked into a cylinder wasn't fuel **and** air, but only air. The only substance that passes through a diesel engine's intake duct is air; fuel is injected into the cylinder when the piston is near the top of the compression stroke. Compress only air within a cylinder, Diesel knew, and the air's temperature would be raised to the heat of combustion; to a temperature in which any fuel, then introduced, would self-ignite.

The fundamental economy of the diesel, as detailed elsewhere in this book, has everything to do with how it is fueled, and with the simple physics of compressive ignition—the spontaneous ignition/combustion of a fuel injected into an air mass turned torrid by compression. As the piston begins its upward *compression stroke,* it compresses into the top of the cylinder (the combustion chamber) the air which moments before it had sucked into the cylinder. Near the top of the piston's compression stroke, at top dead center, compression alone has raised the temperature of the air to 1000°F (538°C) or even higher. In the VW Rabbit diesel, heat of compression reaches some 1,650°F (900°C). But whether 1,000°F or 1,650°F, heat of compression is enough to self-ignite any fuel injected into the combustion chamber.

Now, an instant before the piston reaches top dead center, fuel is injected into the torrid air mass by an *injector,* sometimes called a *fuel nozzle*. The fuel under high pressure (necessary to break through the high pressure within the combustion chamber) is injected as a fine spray—an atomized mist of fuel, each of whose tiny molecules ignites spontaneously—and the entire fuel/air mass combusts. As it does, it expands, driving the piston downward on its power stroke. Having delivered power to the crankshaft, the piston starts upward again, on its exhaust stroke which rids the combustion chamber of the spent gases of combustion. And the cycle begins over again.

Spontaneously igniting, a diesel's air/fuel charge needs no spark (as from a gasoline engine's spark plugs) to initiate combustion. Nor does the diesel need any of the ignition-system devices for mixing fuel and air, and for igniting it. Because a diesel doesn't need them, it has no spark plugs, no carburetor, no distributor, and no other ignition-system parts required by the gasoline engine.

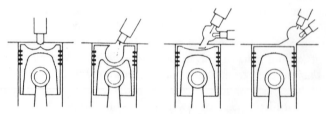

**Fig. 2.13**   Direct injection and various prechamber designs are shown here. In direct combustion (*left*) fuel is sprayed directly into the cylinder, usually onto a concave piston surface. In the Man-M system (*second from left*) fuel is sprayed into a hollowed-out piston, resulting in less noise. In the prechamber concept (*third from left*) combustion is controlled by spraying fuel into a prechamber before it reaches the cylinder. The swirl chamber concept (*right*) is similar to the prechamber, but gives better fuel consumption, more power, and less emission. (*Source:* Advanced Automotive Power Systems, Part 2: A Diesel Engine for A Subcompact Car, SAE Paper #770113 by P. Hofbauer and K. Sator, Volkswagenwerk AG)

In some diesel engines, fuel is injected directly into the top of the cylinder. This is called direct injection. More often, fuel is indirectly injected into a small chamber above the cylinder, called the *precombustion chamber*. Precombustion injection has a number of advantages. The design of the chamber aids in quick-mixing, through the swirling currents of hot air and fuel it sets up, the air/fuel mixture. Also, when the engine is cold, the small precombustion chamber is easier to preheat, thus igniting combustion and starting the diesel vehicle sooner. The preheaters that aid diesel starting, called *glow plugs,* are simple electrical elements that, when energized by the battery, turn red hot, heating the combustion (or precombustion) air around them to ignition temperature.

The precombustion chamber also produces a kind of triggering flame front which, through a passage between it and the *main combustion chamber,* helps to ignite the fuel and hot air in the main chamber more evenly. The main combustion chamber in a diesel cylinder is often only a tiny space at the very top of the cylin-

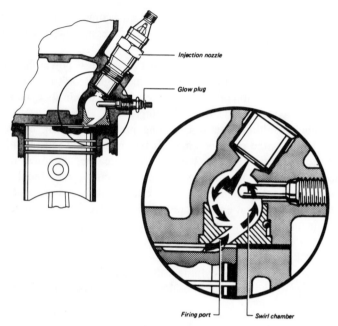

Injection nozzle

Glow plug

Firing port

Swirl chamber

**Fig. 2.14** The cylinder head of VW's Rabbit diesel is made of aluminum alloy for lightness. Combustion begins in the swirl chamber on the right when a mist of diesel fuel is injected. The burning fuel/air mix expands rapidly through the firing port into the cylinder, where combustion continues. The force of expanding burning fuel drives the piston down. The swirl chamber promotes more nearly complete combustion of the fuel, reduces the peak loads on pistons, rods, and bearing, and also permits the VW diesel to be revved to the relatively high speed of 5,000 rpm for peppy performance with low fuel consumption.

der, the space that remains when the piston has climaxed its stroke at top dead center. Sometimes this space is made effectively larger—but still tiny—by designing into the top of the piston a kind of depression, a concave configuration that becomes, once the piston reaches top dead center, part of the combustion chamber.

Whereas diesel spontaneously ignites its fuel/air charge, needs no gas engine ignition system, and compresses air within its cylinders rather than an air/fuel gasoline mix, there are fundamentally two features that make the diesel really different and they are the reasons for the diesel's being. Both have to do with diesel efficiency: the diesel's fuel miserly ways and the tremendous power it is able to extract from air, the one commodity which still remains wholly free of charge.

The gasoline engine can never provide real fuel economy for a starkly fundamental reason: Unless a very considerable amount of gasoline is used in its carefully controlled air/fuel mix, the mix simply won't spark to ignite. So, to get combustion at all, the gas engine's fuel mix must be fuel-rich, on the order of eight to eleven parts of air to every part of fuel; at very maximum, it can achieve ignition with fifteen parts air to one part of fuel.

By contrast, a diesel routinely uses far more air to fuel, usually thirty parts of air to one part fuel. And when idling, the air-to-fuel ratio may zoom to 85, even 100 parts air to one part fuel. By the very nature of its compressive combustion, the diesel is a fuel miser. Second, the diesel can compress its air-only cylinder charge to high temperatures because during compression there's nothing in the cylinders to burn, simply air.

Latent in the heat of compression is no-cost power. It is power the gasoline can never take advantage of or extract. The gasoline engine can't for yet another fundamental reason: Were it to compress the fuel/air mix within its cylinders to more than middling temperature, the heat of compression would ignite its fuel mix's volatile gasoline, resulting in power-robbing preignition. Long before its spark plugs' timed ignition, the gasoline engine's fuel mix would self-ignite, squandering most of the fuel's power before the pistons had reached the top of their upward compression stroke. From preignition combustion would come virtually no piston-usable power; the gasoline engine would be quite literally powerless. So the gasoline engine can never permit enough compression to cause heat sufficient to preignite its fuel/air mix and thus can never extract from compression its enormous latent power, as does the diesel engine.

Moreover, if the diesel is *turbocharged*—rigged with a turbine or blower that forces more air into a diesel's cylinders than normally it would take in alone—compressive power, and also the diesel's power, is raised another considerable notch.

## THE 4-CYCLE VERSUS THE 2-CYCLE DIESEL

Although the diesel powering your car, motor home, or light truck—or the diesel vehicle you plan to buy—is most likely a *4-stroke cycle* (commonly called a *4-cycle*) diesel, there is another breed of diesel engine, the *2-stroke cycle*. Because, with few exceptions, the 4-cycle is the choice of automobile and light truck designers, it's the diesel used for illustration throughout this book. The 2-cycle diesel, by contrast, but again with some exceptions, is most commonly a slower-going (meaning its piston speed is slower), heavier industrial diesel. Among the exceptions is General Motors' long and successful line of Detroit Diesels. All 2-cycle diesels, they power not only many heavy highway trucks, buses and ships, but in their 3- to 6-cylinder versions (from about 170 hp to more than 300 hp), are often the logical gasoline-to-diesel conversion choice, especially for repowering larger motor homes.

Still, the 2-cycle diesel has proved on notable occasions that it can outrun the 4-cycle, as witness the world's diesel-powered pickup truck speed record (132.502 mph), set recently by owner-driver Pete Schmidt at Utah's famed speed flats. Schmidt's GMC four-wheel drive, one-ton pickup was powered by a 2-cycle diesel—a 6-cylinder Detroit Diesel, its normal 210 hp more than doubled to 450 hp by twin turbochargers.

Afterwards, Schmidt credited his world's diesel mark to his pickup's 2-cycle engine. "The two-stroke cycle is an advantage," he declared, "because of its high horsepower-to-weight ratio." And, he added, underscoring the 2-cycle's high power despite modest rpms, "we were only turning 3,700 rpms to reach the record speed."

**POWER STROKE**

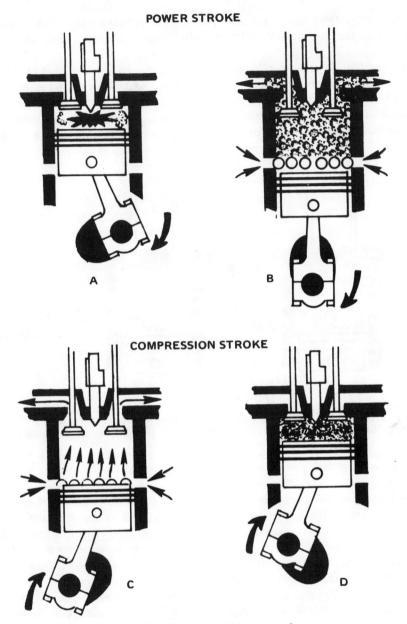

**COMPRESSION STROKE**

**Fig. 2.15**  The two-stroke power cycle.

To understand the advantages and the differences between the four-cycle and two-cycle diesels, recall for a moment the four complete piston strokes that make up, in the 4-cycle diesel, a single combustive event. Only one of the piston's four strokes (its power stroke) actually delivers power to the crankshaft, which makes *two* complete revolutions during the four-stroke cycle. Thus, only one fourth, a mere 25 percent, of the piston's work is delivered as at-the-wheel power. Put another way, three quarters of the piston's job is make-ready work, done to prepare for the one stroke out of four during which it actually powers the crankshaft.

Despite the 4-cycle diesel's efficiency that is far greater than that of the gas engine, the four-stroke diesel, quite obviously, could be even more efficient, especially if some way could be found to deliver more of the piston's power to the crankshaft, and to deliver it more frequently (say, at every crankshaft revolution, rather than at every other revolution). That done, the diesel would be a super-engine, its efficiency truly awesome.

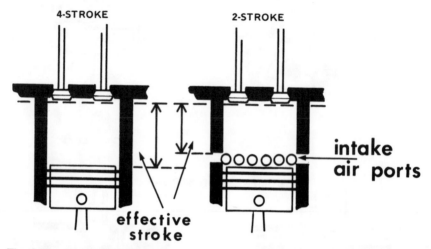

**Fig. 2.16** Comparison of the effective stroke in two- and four-stroke engines. Note that compression in the two-stroke does not begin until the piston covers the air intake ports.

That way, at first glance, would seem to be the two-stroke cycle diesel. The 2-cycle's piston makes only two strokes, a downward *power stroke* and a return upward *compression stroke*. In a sense, it makes only one round trip of its cylinder. Yet, on its two-stroke round trip it manages all of the functions of the 4-cycle's four strokes: air intake, compression, power, and exhaust. More impressive yet, every second stroke—not just every fourth stroke—delivers power to the crankshaft. Thus the crankshaft receives, in the 2-cycle diesel, power during *every* revolution, not merely during every other revolution. And now half, 50 percent rather than just 25 percent, of the piston's work is actually delivered as power at the wheels. In theory, if not in practice, a 2-cycle diesel would appear to develop *twice* the horsepower as a 4-cycle diesel of identical cubic inch displacement and speed.

At the top of its compression stroke, when the piston is at top dead center, fuel is injected into the hot, highly compressed air mass. As the fuel spontaneously ignites (by heat of compression), the combustion's fast-expanding hot gases drive the piston downward to begin the first of its two strokes, its power stroke. During compression and combustion, both valves at the cylinder's top are closed.

So far, 2-cycle and 4-cycle operation seem identical. But a split second into its downward power stroke, the 2-cycle's difference becomes apparent. That's when the piston, part of the way along its downward powering course, passes and uncovers a ring of *intake air ports* that circle the complete circumference of the cylinder. As the intake ports are uncovered, a powerful external blower—called a *scavenging blower* because its job is to scavenge (cleanse) the cylinder of its exhaust gases—forces fresh air into the cylinder above the still descending piston. At the same instant, both cylinder top valves open. Pressured by the blower's scavenging air, exhaust gases are forced out of the cylinder. In their place, the blower forces in fresh air, thus accomplishing in one action both exhaust gas expulsion and air intake, chores requiring two strokes in the four-stroke diesel.

Reaching the bottom of its power stroke (at bottom dead center), the piston now starts upward on the second and last of its two strokes, its compression stroke. As it does so, the blower continues to charge the cylinder above the piston with fresh air and the valves remain open to expel, if possible, the last of the combustive gases. Also expelled is some of the newly taken in fresh air. As the upward-moving piston reaches and once again passes the inlet ports, it seals them shut, both cylinder-top valves closing at the same time. Moving upward toward the top of its compression stroke, the piston compresses the cylinder's air to ignition temperature, fuel is injected and self-combusts, and the cycle begins all over again.

The two-stroke diesel has delivered its promise, seemingly. It has managed in but two piston strokes to do the work of the 4-cycle's four. Doing so, it has powered the crankshaft on every second stroke, not simply on every fourth stroke. Within a cylinder of identical displacement, it apparently has managed to produce *twice* the power of the 4-cycle engine.

Why, then, does your diesel go with a 4-cycle, rather than a 2-cycle, engine? One reason is that the 2-cycle cannot produce two times the horsepower of the 4-cycle diesel. At best, it can produce only about 1.6 times the 4-cycle's power—and that at a fuel cost roughly twice that of its rival. By the very nature of its operation, the stroke of the 2-cycle's piston is shorter than that of the 4-cycle, and the shorter a piston's *effective stroke*—that part of the stroke which actually delivers power—the less power it can deliver. The effective power-producing part of the 2-cycle's power stroke ends the moment it passes and uncovers the intake air ports, for the power which had been driving the piston downward is lost in doing so. For the rest of its way to bottom dead center, the piston merely coasts. Working twice as hard as its counterpart, and exposed twice as often to the sizzling heat of combustion, the piston of the 2-cycle diesel develops nearly twice the heat of the 4-cycle's. This necessitates special oil cooling and, in turn, the cooling of the oil itself through an *oil cooler*. Left uncooled, the hot oil would no longer effectively cool the engine's vital bearings.

Then, too, so short is the *induction period*—the split second in which the blower must both expel exhaust gases and recharge the cylinder with fresh air—that not all of the spent gases of combustion are swept from the cylinder. They linger to dilute the new fresh air charge, and this dilution reduces combustion efficiency. The result is unburnt fuel and higher fuel consumption. The by-product of both is soot which, in time, clogs the intake air ports, further reducing engine efficiency and requiring, for the 2-cycle, generally more and more frequent maintenance than for the four-stroker.

Additionally, the scavenging blower, being mechanically driven by the engine, robs the diesel of considerable power and brings in the problem of noise. With such a huge volume of air and spent gases coming and going, noise increases considerably—meaning more exhaust muffling, more intake air quieting, and more of a number of other noise-suppressing components.

Even the 2-cycle's heavy-duty truck advantages—more power in a more compact engine, greater acceleration and fuel economy for its size—have scant carryover to lighter vehicles and the reason for this is the clincher to the comparison of 2-cycle versus 4-cycle: the 2-cycle diesel, to achieve its heavy-duty advantages, must be operated at relatively slow engine speeds because at really high rpms the *air induction cycle* grows so short that, even aided by its blower, a cylinder can scarcely be exhausted of gases and recharged with air before the next stroke begins. So at high speeds, 2-cycle efficiency falls.

Thus, a typical heavy truck 2-cycle diesel operates in the 1,950-to-2,200 rpm range, fine for a truck, but far too slow an engine speed to give the kind of acceleration that today's diesel and light truck owner demands of his high-speed, 3,000-to-6,000 rpm four-stroke diesel. For all of its theoretical advantages over the 4-cycle, the 2-cycle falls short in light vehicle practice. The "exceptional" acceleration a 2-cycle diesel gives a heavy truck is far from exceptional in an automobile. The "excellent" fuel economy of a 2-cycle in heavy over-road powering—for large truck 2-cycle engines, seldom more than 4–6 mpg—would hardly please the diesel owner reaching for 50, even 60 mpg.

At the heavy end of the vehicular spectrum, the 2-cycle diesel often excels. Probably the majority of dieselized military vehicles, for example, go with 2-cycle engines. And so, as we've noted earlier, do many trucks, buses, and ships. At the light end of the vehicular spectrum—"go" power for automobiles and light trucks—the 4-cycle diesel, turbocharged, manages almost the power of the 2-cycle, but with far better fuel and operational economies.

In time, the engineers may clone a 2-cycle diesel for the average car. But cloning as a practical matter, whether of humans or diesels, seems yet a considerable way off.

### UNDER THE HOOD

On your first look under the hood of a diesel, you might be amazed that so much gadgetry could be boxed in so little space. But as you become a veteran diesel owner and driver, you become appreciative of the orderliness with which the engineers have managed to put everything in its proper place in that little space between the fenders and under the hood—the lid of the package that holds most of the essentials of diesel efficiency and performance. Under the hood, a diesel likely has no more components than a gas engine vehicle and in some respects has fewer. Missing from beneath a diesel's hood is the entire ignition system; self-igniting its fuel by heat of compression within its cylinders, a diesel has no need for external ignition. Under a diesel's hood is a logical arrangement of a half-dozen systems, all of them serving the diesel engine and all of them designed to assuring its long life and high performance.

**Fig. 2.17** Under the hood of a turbocharged diesel. The new International Scout turbo-diesel is first in U.S. production of a four-wheel-drive vehicle.

**Fig. 2.18** Open the hood of a typical full-size sedan with a diesel, and this is the view. This one happens to be a 1980 Pontiac with the GM 350-cubic-inch V-8 diesel. Note the dual batteries, one behind each set of headlights.

**Fig. 2.19**   This is a mechanic's eye view of the VW Rabbit diesel engine compartment. Like its gas engine counterpart, the diesel is installed transversely. The front of the engine is at left, and the injection pump is in the foreground.

### Cooling System

The cooling system continuously circulates the radiator's reservoir of water/ethylene glycol coolant through *water jackets* that surround each cylinder, through the engine's *head* where the valves are, and sometimes also through a *lube oil cooler,* absorbing engine heat and dissipating it through the radiator. Radiator cooled, the coolant is recirculated through the same closed system to absorb more engine heat. Without continuous cooling, the engine would turn red hot— and destroy itself. Within the diesel's cylinders, source of nearly all of the engine's heat, temperatures may soar to 3,000°F and more during combustion. This is far hotter than in a gasoline engine. About a third of this heat is dissipated through energy transformation: Heat energy becomes mechanical energy, driving the engine's pistons, their connecting rods, and the crankshaft. Another third is gotten rid of through the exhaust, where hot exhaust gases may also be used to

**Fig. 2.20**   The fan is belt driven by the crankshaft. On many diesel engines, the water pump is driven by a timing gear, circulating water to cool the pistons and other components that absorb so much heat that they must be cooled to prevent damage.

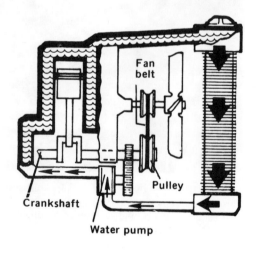

power a turbocharger. The remaining third is dissipated through the cooling system.

Hot coolant, returning from the engine, enters the top of the radiator. Circulating through the radiator's tube-like *core,* which is air cooled by the *fan,* the coolant's excessive heat is transferred to the air. Cooled, the coolant leaves the radiator, circulated by the *water pump* (which is usually driven by a timing gear, also crankshaft powered), and routes once again through the engine.

When the engine is cold (right after starting), radiator cooling is not immediately needed. The engine, in fact, needs to be warmed. Until the engine warms to operating temperature (beginning at about 170°F), a water temperature regulator—the *thermostat*—installed in the top of the coolant line, closes, preventing the coolant's circulation through the radiator. When the coolant warms to operating temperature, the thermostat automatically opens, permitting the now hot coolant to route through the radiator.

To locate coolant system components visually, trace the coolant flow from where, cooled, it leaves the radiator (*bottom radiator hose*), through the water pump (gear or belt driven on the front of the engine), possibly through a *tubular oil cooler,* then into the engine. Leaving the engine, the coolant line goes back to the radiator (*top radiator hose*). The thermostat, generally installed at the point where the coolant hose comes out of the engine, en route to the radiator, will probably not be visible.

## Lubricating System

From the crankcase (oil pan) lube oil reservoir (as much as 7 quarts) every moving part is continuously filmed, sprayed, or bathed with oil. Lube oil plays three vital roles: It lubricates the engine's moving parts; it cleans, carrying away dirt, metal particles, and combustion deposits, including soot, from cylinder walls; and it helps to cool the engine, absorbing some of the heat generated by friction between moving parts. Oil's cleaning function is particularly important in a diesel engine whose fuel and its combustion produce not only abrasive soot but corrosive acids. No matter how good a diesel's lubrication system may be, for automotive diesels there is no substitute for frequent oil changes, as prescribed in the Owner's Manual.

The engine is cleverly designed interiorly to permit oil, pressured by the *oil pump,* and cleansed by filtering, to reach even the most remote, hardest-to-reach moving part. Oil, pumped within the engine under pressure through lubricating arteries called *galleries,* reaches obscure lubricating points through capillary-like *oilways* leading from the galleries and drilled through the block and various engine parts. For example, oilways drilled through the crankshaft lubricate the crankshaft's *main bearings* and the equally hard-to-get-at bearings of the connecting rods. Oil spray continuously lubricates each *piston pin* within its moving piston, the *piston rings* as they slide along cylinder walls, and the *cylinder walls* themselves. If, in a moment of fantasy, you were to become an automotive Lilliputian and could stand beneath the fast-rotating crankshaft, you'd be drenched in a veritable rain of oil, as lube oil circulates blood-like through the engine.

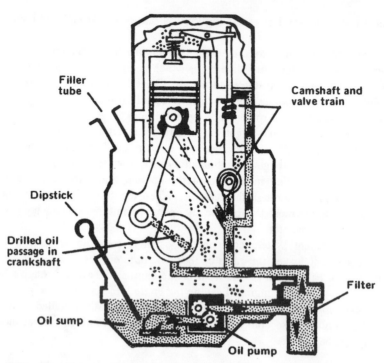

Filler
tube

Camshaft and
valve train

Dipstick

Drilled oil
passage in
crankshaft

Filter

Oil sump

Oil pump

**Fig. 2.21** The oil pump forces oil through the oil filter, where contaminants are removed. Oil, in the form of a fine mist, is forced from these throughout the entire engine.

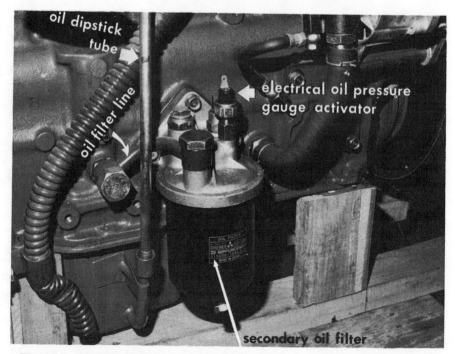

oil dipstick
tube

oil filter line

electrical oil pressure
gauge activator

secondary oil filter

**Fig. 2.22** Many diesel engines have a secondary oil filter (*front center*) in addition to the primary filter. (Photograph by James Joseph)

The force-fed *lubricating pump,* driven either by a *crankshaft gear* or by a *timing gear,* also crankshaft driven, takes in crankcase oil through a *suction bell* located in the lower part of the crankcase called the *oil pan.* From here, oil goes to one or two *oil filters,* a primary and a secondary one. When there are two filters, one may be the full-flow type, which cleans all of the oil (the oil's "full flow") delivered from the pump. The other may be a partial-flow oil filter, called a *by-pass* because it cleans only some of the oil, passing the rest directly to the lubricating points. Excess oil returns to the oil pan to be repumped, refiltered, and reused.

As lubrication is wholly internal, generally visible under the hood are only the oil filter(s), occasionally the lube pump, and an *oil cooler,* if included in the system. To locate lube system components, start at an oil filter and trace the lube system upstream (into the engine) and downstream (to the lube pump, if it's under the hood).

### Fuel System

Drawing fuel through an *intake filter* within the *fuel tank,* the fuel system cleans (through *primary* and *secondary filters*) and conditions (perhaps through a *water separator*) the fuel, delivering it by means of a *transfer (fuel lift) pump* under low pressure (about 30 pounds per square inch) to the working heart of the diesel engine, the *fuel injection pump.* Its fuel output closely controlled by a *governor,* the injection pump feeds fuel under extremely high pressure (some 1,700 pounds per square inch) individually to each cylinder's *injector,* which force-injects fuel directly into the top of the *cylinder* if the diesel is the direct-injection type or into the cylinder's *precombustion chamber* in an indirect-injection type engine.

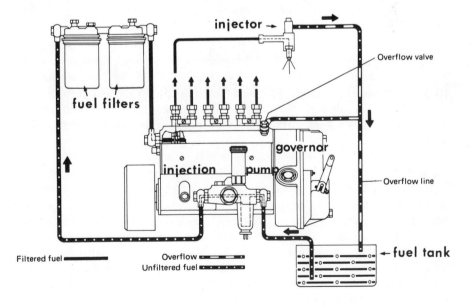

**Fig. 2.23** Schematic of a typical diesel fuel injection system.

**Fig. 2.24** Typical injection pump installed on the engine: (1), injection pump; (2), hand prime pump; (3), high-pressure injection outlets; (4), fuel inlet line from filter; (5), fuel filter; (6), injection pump throttle; (7), governor.

From the fuel tank to the injection pump—the system's low-pressure fuel transfer and conditioning section—fuel is cleansed of dirt and large contaminant particles (through the primary filter) and then rid of any remaining particles, even microscopic ones, through the secondary filter. Fuel delivered to the injection pump must be superclean; anything less risks clogging the injection pump and injectors.

Of all diesel engine components, the injection pump and its governor, which controls the pump's fuel release, are the most complex and sophisticated. Together, they make up a second key section within the fuel system. The injection pump boosts the fuel to high pressure (1,700 psi, or even higher)—pressure needed if the injected fuel stream, atomized to a spray at the instant of injection, is to overcome and successfully penetrate the compressed, high-pressure (430–780-psi) air mass within the cylinder. Within the injection pump is a separate "pump" for each injector. The injection pump of a 4-cylinder diesel contains four miniature injector pumps (each consisting of a plunger and its cylindrical barrel), that for a 5-cylinder engine, five.

**Fig. 2.25** Note the clamps on the metal fuel injection lines to keep them from vibrating against each other. Note also that each injector line is the same length, to keep injection pressures uniform.

A single stroke of the injector plunger within each mini-pump barrel builds fuel pressure from its delivered 30–50 psi to 1,700 psi—injection pressure. When pressure reaches about 1,700 psi, the injector that each mini-pump feeds begins to accept fuel. But not until fuel within the injector itself reaches the injection pressure of 1,700 psi does the injector ''fire,'' injecting its fuel charge into the cylinder's combustion chamber. When it does, injection timing must be precise.

Fuel injection, thus the fuel injection pump, must be synchronized with the engine's speed. Injection of fuel (in a matter of $^1/_{1,000}$th of a second—faster than a blink) must take place when the cylinder's piston, at or near the top of its compression stroke, has reached or come very close to top dead center (T.D.C.), for it is then that, through compression, the cylinder's compressed air charge has reached fiery precombustion temperature.

A set of *timing gears* synchronizes the injection pump and other engine components whose operations must be precisely timed to the position of the pistons within their cylinders. Powered by the crankshaft and thus timed to the pistons' movements within their cylinders, are the timing gears that, located on the front of the diesel within a *timing gear case,* both synchronize and power the various components they drive. One gear of the *timing train,* the *injector pump drive gear,* powers and synchronizes the injection pump's fuel-pressuring plungers.

But merely delivering fuel to the injectors is not enough. it must be the right amount of fuel, for several reasons. First, varying speeds are demanded in driving, which means varying fuel injection. Second, and from the engine's view far more important, there is a maximum top speed at which it can safely operate without damaging its innards. All diesel engines are governed not to exceed a fixed maximum speed. Third, there are times—as when starting cold a diesel whose fuel is directly injected into the top of its cylinders—when better combustion takes place if injection timing is retarded, delayed a split second to allow more compressive heat to build within the cylinder. And there are times when injection should be advanced, begun a split second sooner than normal. Again involved is cold starting, but this time when fuel is injected indirectly into a cylinder's precombustion chambers. The precombustion-chambered VW Rabbit's cold start knob is an "injection advance" device. Finally, there are times when fuel can be saved, starting can be made quickly, or the engine more easily cooled after a long, high altitude climb, for example, if the engine's idle speed can be driver controlled, as with the Audi diesel's manual idle control. Turning the control counterclockwise increases idle speed, which Audi recommends both for cold starting and engine cooling.

**Fig. 2.26** On some diesels, like this Audi 5000S, you can adjust the idle from inside the car. (Photograph by James Joseph)

The *governor* is the essential controller of how much fuel the injection pump sends to the injectors. Governors on most of today's fast-speed diesels are of two basic types: mechanical, which sense engine speed mechanically from a crankshaft or injection pump gear, and pneumatic, responding to varying engine air-intake velocity (some Mercedes-Benz governors are this type). Chances are your car's governor and injection pump are a single unit, such as the combined governor and injection pump of the Oldsmobile 350 V-8 diesel. Whatever its type or housing, the governor's basic job is to limit the engine's maximum speed, never permitting it to exceed the manufacturer's engine speed limit. Within this governed maximum diesel speed, the governor not only responds to your foot on the accelerator, but to a number of other ever-changing conditions—for example, the engine's need for more fuel when starting, for less as you drive to higher altitude, for varying amounts of fuel when, from idling, the engine is suddenly put under load.

A peculiarity of the diesel—due in part to having an unrestricted excess of air in its cylinders—is that no fixed fuel-throttle setting, by itself, will accurately maintain a fixed engine speed. While idling without governor control, the diesel's speed might either "droop" to zero (the engine might stop) or its speed might continuously increase, eventually overspeeding and destroying the engine. The governor ensures that neither of these possible extremes happens; forever sensing the engine's speed, the governor continuously adjusts the amount of fuel delivered by the injection pump, either to maintain some preset speed (idling, for instance), or to vary engine speed, as when you accelerate.

Although it has become increasingly sophisticated, the mechanical governor varies engine fueling one way or another. One way is by mechanically rotating the plungers in the injection pump, changing the position of a fuel orifice in the plunger in relation to a fuel inlet orifice in the plunger barrel, thus forever changing the amount of fuel available to the plunger and the amount of fuel injected into the cylinder. The toothed, mechanical device that physically rotates the plungers is called a *control rod* or *fuel rack*. The control rod's movement itself is controlled by a pair of rotating weights, called *flyweights*. Their ever-changing centrifugal force, in response to engine speed, acts on a spring that moves the control rod backward or forward, rotating the position of the fuel plungers within their injection barrels.

And finally are the fuel system's "big guns," the *injectors,* which, inserted directly into the combustion (or precombustion) chambers, fire their fuel into the cylinders' hot air mass at point-blank range. In the process, injectors atomize the fuel and direct it, under high pressure, in a critical spray pattern. For most effec-

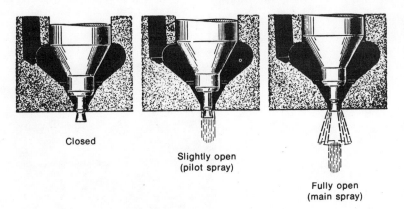

Closed

Slightly open
(pilot spray)

Fully open
(main spray)

**Fig. 2.27**  Injector nozzle operation.

tive combustion, the spray pattern, controlled in some injectors by nozzle-end *spray tips*, should be cone-shaped and rather narrow, its spray arc ranging from 2° to 21°. Figure 2.29 shows a bench test of a defective nozzle with too wide a spray pattern. (Bench-testing, incidentally, is for experts only. An injector's high-velocity fuel stream can cut through an unwary hand.) Diesel injectors may be scarcely larger than a gas engine's spark plugs, as in your car's diesel, or mammoth size in truck diesels.

It is easy to locate fuel system components, as the entire fuel system is usually visible—and obvious—under the hood: from the transfer pump and fuel filters to

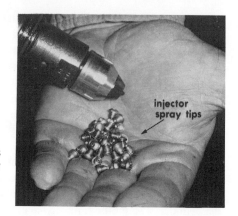

**Fig. 2.28** Some diesels use injectors with replaceable spray tips. (Photograph by James Joseph)

**Fig. 2.29** Injectors can be tested using special equipment. The spray pattern should be as described in the text. (Photograph by James Joseph)

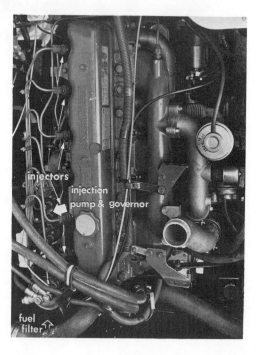

**Fig. 2.30** The Nissan Diesel used by International Harvester shows the important parts of the fuel system.

the injection pump, always close to the engine, and its injectors located in each diesel cylinder. Fuel lines from injection pump to injectors, because of the fuel's extremely high pressure, are always metal. By contrast, the glow plugs, which are sometimes confused with injectors, are actuated by electrical cables.

### Air-Intake System

One reason for its fuel economy is that it burns far more air than fuel; a diesel's consumption of air is prodigious. Whereas a gasoline engine's air intake is carefully restricted and controlled by the carburetor to ensure that no more than fifteen parts of air to one part of fuel reach the combustion chambers—more air, and the air fuel mixture won't ignite—, the diesel's air intake is unrestricted. A 4-cycle diesel may ingest the equivalent of eight railroad tank cars of air in a single hour; and if the diesel is turbocharged, forcing still more air into the combustion chambers, air intake nearly doubles. Dust, dirt, and other contaminants sucked at high velocity directly into a diesel's *intake (induction) air manifold*—the pipe-like engine structure that takes in air and distributes it to the various cylinders—can do serious diesel damage unless removed from the intake airstream.

What removes air's often engine-abrasive contaminants is an *air filter,* sometimes two of them. Of numerous types, the two most common are the *dry* and *oil-bath.* *Dry type air filters* are the most efficient over the widest engine operational range, filtering out upwards of 99.9 percent of contaminants, including microscopic particles as small as one micron in size. They use as their filter medium a paper element that is usually impregnated with resin. *Oil-bath air filters* are also highly effective. Oil in the filter's base, the primary filter, first removes larger contaminants, then secondary filtration through a fine mesh, often steel wool,

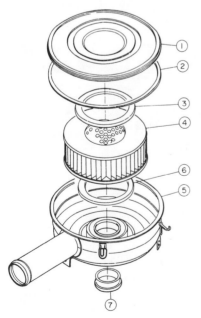

**Fig. 2.31** Typical diesel air cleaner: (1), cover; (2), gasket; (3), sealing ring; (4), air cleaner element; (5), air cleaner housing; (6), lower sealing ring; (7), gasket.

removes the smaller particles before the air enters the engine. Mostly because of the contaminant-holding capacity of its oil, this type can filter out and hold a greater quantity of contaminants than the dry type before becoming clogged—one reason the oil-bath, which predates the dry type, has been the longtime preference among users of heavy equipment, especially off-road bulldozer and construction machinery. The dry type, probably most effective in normal highway driving, is the air filter you'll likely find under your hood. Both, of course, must be periodically cleaned—the dry's filter element changed, the oil-bath's oil drained and replaced and its mesh cleaned or renewed. Changing out an oil-bath filter can be a messy job, but changing the dry type's paper element seldom even gets your hands dirty.

When a diesel is naturally aspirated (not turbocharged), air intake is straight through and straightforward; air enters the filter, is cleaned, and passes immediately and directly into the cylinders' combustion chambers through the *intake air manifold*. Turbocharging vastly increases a diesel's air consumption. Doing so, it may boost horsepower as much as 50 percent and increase torque (pulling power) at low engine speeds almost as much. It may also reduce fuel consumption 20 to 25 percent and possibly more.

But in a world where you seldom get something for nothing, the choice is usually either/or: **either** far greater horsepower and road performance, with little or no improvement in mpg, **or,** a modest horsepower/performance increase, but a significant boost in fuel mileage. Either way, turbocharging's bonuses are considerable. In one respect, turbocharging does hand the diesel owner something for nothing: The turbo is powered by the engine's hot exhaust gases that usually are wasted and lost through the muffler and exhaust pipe.

Turbocharging has brought the diesel to its high level of road performance. As such, it is undoubtedly the most important single remedy for almost legendary

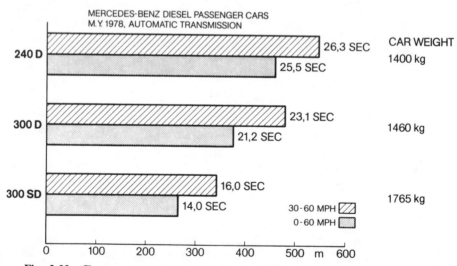

**Fig. 2.32** Chart compares the acceleration capabilities of 1978 Mercedes-Benz diesel models. The 300SD (*bottom*) is a heavier car using the same 5-cylinder engine as the 300D, but with a turbocharger, giving it far better performance.

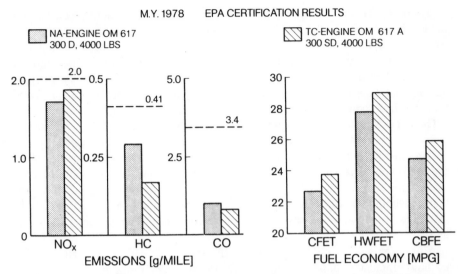

**Fig. 2.33** Comparison of emissions and fuel economy of naturally aspirated (nonturbocharged) and turbocharged 5-cylinder diesels installed in 1978 models.

diesel road-sluggishness in decades. Mercedes-Benz tests show that even though it's 400 pounds heavier than the 300D, which uses the same engine unturbocharged, the turbocharged 300SD goes from 0 to 55 mph in 2.6 seconds' less time. This is no minor feat for an engine of only 183 cubic inches (3,005 cc). Turbocharging raises the engine's efficiency to the point that it produces .601 hp per cubic inch of displacement, the best power-to-engine-size ratio of any diesel car engine. Turbocharging, likewise, will boost the VW diesel Rabbit's 55 mpg/highway into the mid-60s (to about 63 mpg/highway)—a stunning increase in fuel mileage.

By the 1980s, probably under the hood of every diesel vehicle will be a *turbocharger*. And under some may even be a device for turbocompounding, discussed later in this chapter. Together, they could well shove diesel cars into the 70- to 80-mpg fuel economy bracket. Neither turbocharging nor the term "turbocharger" is new. If you follow high-performance auto racing, you're already familiar with the terms "blown" and "unblown" in reference to racing engines; a blown engine is supercharged or turbocharged, an unblown engine is not. What's more, virtually every long-haul diesel truck on the highway is turbocharged, and has been for a decade.

Basically, a turbocharger is simply an air compressor. So, too, is a *supercharger,* but with one considerable difference. A supercharger is mechanically driven by the engine, usually through crankshaft gearing, and even while increasing overall engine power, saps some power. The turbocharger, driven solely by the diesel's hot (1,500°–1,650°F) exhaust, uses no engine power at all. The hot exhaust gases spin the blades of a turbine mounted on a common shaft with an air compressor. The result is an enormous bonus charge of air packed into the diesel's cylinders. A turbocharger may ram upwards of 3.5 times as much air into the cylinders as, an unturbocharged (naturally aspirated) diesel might ingest without turbo-boost. The air is forced via tubing to the air cleaner. It then travels through a funnel-shaped duct to the inlet of the compressor portion of the turbocharger, passing through a flexible tube that narrows like a diffuser as it nears the compressor. From the compressor, the air is forced through an aluminum diffuser into the manifold, then flows into the individual cylinders. The 300SD turbocharger produces about 11 psi of boost pressure, developing maximum boost at about 2,000 rpm, reached about three seconds after accelerating from a standing start.

On a gasoline engine, supercharging and turbocharging, while both aim to increase horsepower, necessarily also increase fuel consumption—again, because an air/fuel mix greater than fifteen parts air to one part fuel won't spark ignite. Supplied with more air, a gas engine must use more fuel. The opposite is often true in the diesel, although turbocharging is not necessarily designed to reduce fuel consumption. Turbocharging increases a diesel's volumetric efficiency, so that a diesel may have the power and road performance of an engine nearly twice its size.

A turbocharger ups diesel volumetric efficiency in several ways. First, no matter how efficient a diesel, on the downward air-intake stroke its pistons cannot take in the full air capacity of their cylinders. On an engine with a 300-cubic-inch displacement its pistons can pull into the combustion chambers only about 85 percent of maximum air volume, or about 255 cubic inches of air; thus, naturally aspirated, a diesel's volumetric efficiency is rated about 0.85, or 85 percent. Turbocharging not only makes up this 15 percent volumetric deficit, but often increases volumetric efficiency far beyond the 100 percent level—to as much as 1.6 (160%) of capacity, nearly doubling volumetric efficiency. On the 300SD, the turbocharger increased the horsepower from 77 to 120 and boosted the maximum torque from 115 to 168 ft/lbs, while adding only 33 pounds to the engine's dry weight.

The greater its air supply, the greater a diesel's efficiency. One outward sign of a turbo-diesel's increased efficiency is turbocharging's virtual elimination of exhaust smoke, the telltale of unburnt, wasted fuel. As little as 1 percent unburnt fuel can cause objectionable exhaust smoke. In doing away with most smoking, turbocharging overcomes one diesel paradox: the fact that a diesel, even with only 85 percent volumetric efficiency, almost always has an oversupply of air, although not necessarily a great enough oversupply to permit every fuel molecule to find sufficient air for combustion.

With more air in its combustion chambers, a diesel can also burn more fuel more efficiently, increasing engine horsepower far beyond the 15 percent power boost indicated, solely through bringing the combustion chambers up to full-rated air capacity.

Turbocharging has many uses. It can significantly increase engine power and performance, it can add a power boost during driving when it's needed, as when passing or climbing a hill, and at high altitudes it can stuff enough air into the cylinders for the engine to have the same performance at 10,000 feet as it does at sea level.

In a typical turbocharger, hot exhaust gases, routed directly from the engine's *exhaust manifold,* turn the turbine blades, which turn a shaft on which the compressor (impeller), a centrifugal air blower, is also mounted. The faster the turbine turns, the faster the compressor turns. Filtered air, from the intake air filter, enters the turbocharger's compressor section, where it is compressed, then routed directly to the cylinders. How fast the turbine turns depends on the heat and velocity of the engine's exhaust stream. As engine speed and power increase, so do the heat and velocity of its exhaust. The turbine blades—eleven of them on the Garrett AiResearch turbocharger, used on the Mercedes-Benz 300SD—are cleverly designed so that the exhaust's hot gases, expanding across the blades, are converted from heat energy to mechanical energy, driving the turbine, which in turn drives the compressor.

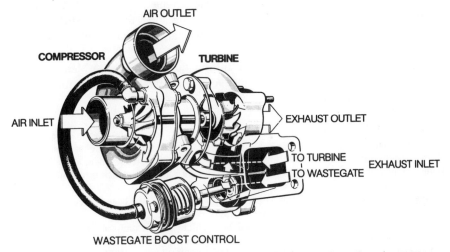

AIR OUTLET

COMPRESSOR

TURBINE

AIR INLET

EXHAUST OUTLET

TO TURBINE
TO WASTEGATE

EXHAUST INLET

WASTEGATE BOOST CONTROL

**Fig. 2.34** Schematic of the Garrett AiResearch turbocharger shows how it operates.

To compress intake air effectively, the turbocharger must spin at all but fantastic speed—anywhere from 10,000 to 65,000 rpm at normal highway speeds, up to 110,000, which makes lubrication critical. The turbo on your diesel is designed to give the diesel a big power and torque boost, even at relatively low engine speeds. Since it does, it must guard against overspeeding as you rev the engine higher. Thus, on the Mercedes-Benz 300SD (and soon on the VW Rabbit diesel), the turbocharger has a *wastegate control*. At high engine speed, boost pressure is maintained at a constant level by the wastegate, which uses pressurized air from the compressor to activate a spring loaded by-pass valve, varying the exhaust gas flow to the turbine wheel. The wider the valve opens, the greater the quantity flowing directly through the exhaust system and the less spinning of the turbine. A three-way valve in the pressure line from the turbocharger to a control unit on the fuel injection pump is activated by a pressure-sensing switch if the wastegate malfunctions and boost goes too high. This vents the line to the atmosphere, cutting down the fuel delivered and preventing engine damage. The reduced quantity of fuel injected lowers temperature and pressure in the cylinders and also results in lower exhaust gas flow, cutting boost. The car can still be driven, but the reduced performance will indicate that the engine should be checked. Despite its high speed, the turbocharger has long life. Still, turning as fast as it does, turbo life can be shortened by contaminants either in its intake air or in lubricating oil (the same lube oil used in the engine). With a turbocharger, air and oil filters and lube oil may have to be changed more frequently.

Turbocompounding, now being tested—among the testers: Cummins Engine Co. and the U.S. Department of Energy—goes a step further and eventually will further boost diesel performance and power. In turbocompounding, a second turbine is added to capture exhaust gases wasted from the turbocharger, and the turbo-boost is applied directly to the vehicle's driveline.

Many manufacturers say turbocharging must not be added to present diesels and declare their warranties may be voided if this is done. One reason is that turbocharging adds considerable stress to the engine. Mercedes-Benz's turbo-equipped diesel, typically, is strengthened, as are some driveline parts, to withstand the turbo's added heat and stress. Turbocharging your diesel engine is not recommended.

The following quote from a Service Information Newsletter to Mercedes-Benz dealers is typical of the attitude of most vehicle manufacturers on retrofitting turbochargers to diesel engines.

The engine has undergone substantial redesign and reinforcement in order to cope with the higher thermal and mechanical stress it is subjected to as a result of its higher power output from turbocharging. . . . Retrofitting of naturally aspirated Mercedes-Benz diesel engines, both current production as well as older engines, is not recommended, for technical as well as administrative reasons.

Beginning with registration year 1975, our diesel engines have been subject to EPA certification pursuant to the Clean Air Act of 1970 as amended. Subsequent installation of a turbocharger on these engines would void the vehicle certification and may constitute a prohibited act under the Clean Air Act Amendments of 1977.

Passenger cars with diesel engines built before registration year 1975 are not covered by the Clean Air Act, but are still affected by the following *technical aspects* which, of course, are also applicable to vehicles of registration year 1975 and thereafter.

Raising the engine power through turbocharging requires an increase in the rate of fuel injected to cope with the higher air charge rate of the cylinders and, of course, the fuel-to-air ratio must be matched throughout the operating range. This condition cannot be met with the fuel injection pumps existing on those engines, as they do not have the capacity for such readjustment. In addition, pneumatically controlled injection pump governors would not function properly as a result of the change in intake manifold pressure characteristics.

Further, most basic engine components such as the crankshaft assembly, cooling and lubrication systems as well as intake and exhaust systems and drive train components would be overloaded by the higher thermal and mechanical stress from turbocharging an engine which was never designed for it.

Most importantly, please note that the retrofitting of a naturally aspirated Mercedes-Benz diesel engine with a turbocharger automatically voids the applicable Emission Warranty as well as any remaining warranty coverage on the engine and power train of the vehicle so equipped.

Nonetheless, some excellent turbo kits are available at about $1,000 for the kit; $1,400 installed. Many who have "kitted" their naturally aspirated diesels, and now revel in their vehicle's new performance, swear they would never again drive unturbocharged, in spite of the warranty risk. One thing is certain: Turbocharging has newly gifted the diesel vehicle with the kind of performance it never had before, a performance which booms diesel as *the* economy *and* performance engine of the eighties.

The list of changes Mercedes-Benz made in its time-honored 5-cylinder diesel to fit it for turbocharging is long. Under the hood, the unturbocharged Mercedes-Benz 300D is quite a different car from the turbocharged 300SD, and not simply because turbocharging raised the diesel's 77 hp to 120 hp and its maximum torque from 115 lbs ft to 168 lbs ft. Here are a few of the changes:

Extended the engine block to make room for a new, high-capacity oil pump system because of the turbocharger's higher lube requirements.

Redesigned cylinders' combustion prechambers to withstand higher internal engine temperatures from turbocharging

Developed new, heat-resistant pistons and a unique new way to lubricate and cool them (oil jets at the bottom of each cylinder direct sprays of oil upward, into the pistons)

Developed new, high-temperature piston rings

Increased oil supply for piston and turbocharger bearing cooling, upping lube capacity by one quart to total nine quarts (which allows extending the 300SD's oil change period to 4,000 miles from the 300D's 3,000–3,500 miles)

Developed new injectors with far higher injection pressure (over 1,950 psi), to assure penetration by their highly atomized fuel spray of the more highly compressed combustion chamber air charge in locating air system components under the hood, the most obvious component of all, aside from the engine, is the air cleaner. Usually directly beneath it, but often difficult to see, is the turbocharger. Close proximity (called *close-coupling*) of the exhaust manifold, the turbocharger, and the air cleaner is vital if the turbocharger is to work efficiently, and all three are about as close together as the engineers can contrive to group them.

## Electrical System

Often the most obvious diesel difference under the hood is the battery; either it's oversized (half again the size of the battery powering a gas engine vehicle), or there are two standard-size batteries instead of the usual one. Greater electrical storage backup is needed to crank (turn over) the diesel fast enough to produce heat of compression in the cylinders sufficient to ignite the fuel for starting—particularly in cold weather when engine oil becomes less free-flowing and more viscous, making starting harder for any engine. Typically, whereas a standard battery may be rated 55 ampere-hours, an oversized battery's rating may be 88, or about 50 percent greater than standard capacity. The larger the diesel and the greater its cubic inch displacement, the higher its cranking and thus battery requirements. Depending on engine size, required battery ratings may go up to 128 ampere-hours for normal starting and driving conditions and to as high as 165 when the same engine is operated in extremely cold weather.

A diesel's electrical system, while quite similar to that of a gas engine vehicle has, aside from more battery capacity, one other distinction: It must power the engine's glow plugs—the heater elements, one installed in each combustion chamber, that quickly warm the chambers' air as a further aid to starting. Although cranking might in time turn the engine fast enough to compress the cylinder's air to the nearly 1,000°F generally needed for spontaneous ignition, it would be a

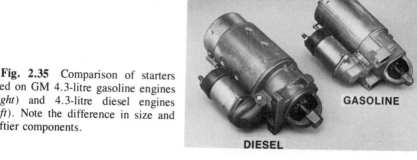

**Fig. 2.35** Comparison of starters used on GM 4.3-litre gasoline engines (*right*) and 4.3-litre diesel engines (*left*). Note the difference in size and heftier components.

GASOLINE

DIESEL

drain on the battery. A glow plug inserted in each cylinder's combustion (or precombustion) chamber does the heating job faster, often in a matter of 6–10 seconds. In a warm engine, glow plug preheating usually isn't necessary; when the ignition key is turned to START, the engine cranks once and starts. Nonetheless, in some diesel vehicles, the glow plugs continue to operate (even though the glow plug dash light flicks off) for upwards of 1.5 minutes after starting, to ensure that cylinder air is at ignition temperature. "Preglow" is the term applied to the preignition glow plug warm-up period. Continued warming after ignition is called "afterglow."

Electrically, diesel and gas engine electrical systems are virtually identical. Both are 12-volt DC (direct-current) systems, and in both, the battery is the sole storage reservoir of electrical energy. In both, an *alternator,* belt driven by the engine, recharges the battery, the charging rate being controlled by a *regulator.* In both, turning the ignition key to START energizes the *starting motor* and an electrical *solenoid* which, through a spring-lever device, mechanically engages the starting motor's *pinion gear* with a *ring gear* that turns the *flywheel,* which is fixed to the *crankshaft.* Battery-powered, the starting motor turns (cranks) the flywheel, turning the crankshaft and moving the pistons in their cylinders. When the pistons have compressed the cylinders' intake air to ignition temperature, injected fuel spontaneously ignites, and the diesel self-starts.

Glow plugs, because they are unique to the diesel engine, deserve a closer look. A glow plug is a simple device, little more than a heating element inserted in the combustion chamber. When battery energized, glow plugs turn red hot, warming the cylinder air to spontaneous ignition temperature. All passenger-car diesels use glow plugs to heat the combustion chamber so the diesel fuel will ignite readily from a cold start. In extremely cold weather a diesel will not start quickly because the heat of compression is lost through the cold engine. Many owners of diesels in cold weather climates park the car inside or use a block heater. (See Chapter 4 "The Minimum-Maintenance Engine" for how to use the block heater.)

The time required to reach ignition temperature depends on the type of glow plugs used. Old-style glow plugs (each of which might draw 6.5 amps) were relatively slow warmers and slow starters, taking upwards of fifteen to twenty seconds, and sometimes longer, to heat cylinder air to ignition temperature. But fifteen to twenty seconds—and far longer in cold weather—is too long, certainly longer than most car owners want to wait before the engine starts.

**Fig. 2.36** Many diesels come equipped with a built-in engine block heater that can be plugged into a wall outlet to facilitate cold-weather starting.

In 1979, Oldsmobile made a major engineering breakthrough in diesel engine technology, by introducing a fast-start system that nearly eliminated the need to wait while the glow plugs warmed the air in the prechamber. The system allowed diesel cars to start in approximately six seconds at 0°F., as compared to about sixty seconds on 1978 models at the same temperature. The system uses an electromechanical device to control glow plug temperature, preglow time, wait/start lights, and afterglow time and has a dual control to prevent glow plug failure. Regardless of the input voltage, a control switch will compensate to keep the glow plugs at the proper temperature. Initial heat-up and sustaining the fast-start glow plug temperature during engine cranking requires less than half the electrical energy necessary to operate the 1978 system.

New, quick-starting *fast glow plugs,* operated with pulsating current, rather than the steady current characteristic of the older type, and using six volts rather than twelve volts, cut the preglow period by half. The newer are also often circuited (and wired into a kind of *harness*) in electrical parallel, rather than in series, as were the older type. Glow plugs wired in parallel behave much like Christmas tree lights similarly wired; even if some burn out, the others remain on, and operating.

Typically, the Olds 350 V-8 diesel's glow plug system uses an electromechanical controller to regulate glow plug temperature, preglow time, the dash's WAIT/START glow plug indicator, and afterglow time. The controller, located in the front water passage of the engine's intake manifold, senses engine coolant temperature and glow plug current to determine preglow and afterglow time periods and signals a lamp control relay to turn off the dash's WAIT light and turn on the START light. It also energizes a fast idle relay to speed up the

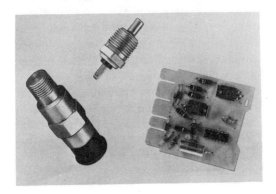

**Fig. 2.37** Starting in 1979, GM diesels use a fast-glow system that greatly shortens the start-up time. The fast-glow component (*left*) replaces the previous system (*right* and *center*).

engine during the initial period just before start-up (idle is automatically returned to normal when, the diesel started, coolant temperature reaches 120°F). The glow plug relay, pulsed on and off by the controller, monitors current to the glow plugs, maintaining their temperature without overheating. Substituting a 6-volt plug for a 12-volt, or vice versa, risks plug burnout.

Other than the alternator (V-belt powered off the front of the engine), batteries and glow plugs, a diesel's electrical system (gauges, lights, relays, printed circuits, and so on) is—like the similar system of a gas engine vehicle—difficult to locate, is complex and hard to trace and even in a vehicle dealership or garage is assigned to auto-electric specialists for repair work. As for the glow plugs themselves, one is located near each cylinder's injector. Because of the cylinders' high internal pressure, glow plugs and injectors must be very tightly installed. Required is usually a *torque wrench* which, when set to manufacturer-specified torque (usually given in ft lbs), automatically adjusts to required tightness. A precision tool, the torque wrench takes the guesswork out of how tight or loose an engine part is—too tight, and an injector or glow plug might be damaged, as might their threads; too loose, and engine pressure might force a part out of the engine.

### Belts, Pulleys, and PTOs

Engine-driven V-belts are the motive power for a number of key accessories—including the alternator or generator, air conditioning, power steering, and sometimes the water pump. Similar accessories are likewise belt driven on gas engine vehicles. Because power belts use engine power, thus reducing any engine's total at-the-wheels go power, the fewer belt drives the better, especially in this era of rising fuel costs. Still, when vehicle owners demand accessories, in particular air conditioning, they are in fact sanctioning the loss of some power at the wheels for more comfort behind the wheel. Mercedes-Benz's 300SD turbo-diesel, for example, powers accessories with four V-belts. Two belts power the water pump and alternator; another, the power steering; and a fourth, the air conditioner's compressor. All V-belts are driven off the front of the engine. In most vehicles, *pulleys* and *V-belts* are virtually synonymous.

Although relatively few pleasure diesel vehicles are equipped with *PTOs*—power takeoffs—they are found increasingly in diesel-powered off-road vehicles and such larger rec vehicles as motor homes. Power takeoffs are gear-and-clutch devices, run by the engine, that give an alternate power source for other than strictly automotive accessories. For one example, suppose you own a diesel motor home and, while camping, want to drive an electrical generator for camp lights. One way to get camp power without installing a separate engine is to run a generator off the vehicle's diesel. But to deliver power through a PTO, the engine, of course, must be operating, usually at high idle. A PTO which, basically, is a gear case fitted with a manual clutch, can also be installed on an off-road vehicle to operate a winch. Engage the clutch, and the gears engage some power component of the diesel—either the crankshaft or gearing powered by the flywheel. This power, through the PTO's gearing, turns an output shaft that can be used to turn a generator, winch, or other piece of power equipment.

**Fig. 2.38** GM diesels use a vacuum pump (1) installed where the ignition distributor would be in a gasoline engine. This ensures an adequate supply of vacuum to run accessories.

The diesel, by the nature of its operation, does not generate engine vacuum, as do its gasoline engine counterparts. However, many manufacturers use engine vacuum to run several of the ever-increasing number of accessories on a modern car. To be able to run the accessories on diesel-equipped cars, Oldsmobile and others have solved the problem by installing a *vacuum pump* in the diesel engine in place of the ignition distributor, which the diesel does not require. The pump is driven by the engine and produces sufficient vacuum to run the required accessories.

### Gauges and Switches

For the diesel two of the most important accessories are the *fuel gauge,* because running out of fuel often requires manual priming of the engine's fuel pump, and the *tachometer.* A *tachometer* (from the Greek word "tachos" meaning speed) measures and records the diesel's rotational speed, its revolutions per minute (rpm). For drivers with manual (stick shift) transmissions, a tachometer is an essential driving aid. The tachometer tells at precisely what engine rpms to shift—at the shift points for engine and transmission—for maximum engine performance. Automatic transmissions, of course, do the shift-point selecting automatically.

When a diesel is turbocharged, as diesels will be increasingly in the eighties, at least one more gauge will become dashboard commonplace: a *pyrometer,* which measures, by means of a heat-sensing device called a *thermocouple,* the temperature of the engine's turbo-powering exhaust gases. Depending on where the pyrometer's thermocouples "read" exhaust gas temperature, a "red-line temperature" is established, beyond which a turbocharger should not be operated. The Owner's Manual, if the diesel is turbocharged and if its dash displays a pyrometer, will indicate the turbo's "red-line" temperature.

A second turbo instrument likely also to become a dashboard familiar is a *manifold pressure gauge,* which shows the turbocharger's pressure boost—precisely how much air-charge boost it is supplying to the cylinders. It's a useful indicator in reckoning how efficiently a turbocharger is operating and can also be a quick indicator of turbo trouble.

Not many diesel owners are "gauge watchers," or care to be. But certainly for manual transmission drivers, the tachometer is worth watching and heeding when shifting. So, too, if the engine is turbocharged, is the exhaust heat indicating pyrometer.

### Sound-Attenuating Devices and Techniques

From the driver's seat, it's hard telling the sound difference in many of today's diesel vehicles, including Oldsmobile's quiet Toronado. Engineers, working overtime to quiet today's diesels, have developed new sound-deadening techniques and put to use new materials that have put the hush on the prime sources of diesel noise: the air intake and exhaust systems, high-pressure fuel feed lines from injector pump to injectors, and the compression-ignition detonation of the diesel engine itself.

Whether you call it "noise" or the sound of a fuel-saving engine at work, two facts remain: First, while much noise can be reduced by sound-deadening and sound barrier materials, it is unlikely that the diesel will ever be as quiet as a gasoline engine; second, whereas sound-quieting materials virtually bar noise from the passenger compartment, diesels outside continue to be noisier than other type engines, and the noise sometimes is objectionable to pedestrians and other drivers. Although its passengers may ride in diesel oblivion and quiet, a "diesel" continues to be recognizable by sound to most within hearing.

In designing its turbo-diesel 300SD, Mercedes-Benz retained some earlier sound-attenuating features, such as its precombustion cylinder design and the acoustical mat fitted to the underside of the hood, and added some antinoise innovations, among them flexible connections between the engine's exhaust manifold and the turbocharger's inlet that prevent noise conduction. A 4-cycle diesel produces low-frequency sound that is hard to deaden. The noise from a 2-cycle diesel is higher pitched, but actually easier to quiet.

Basic sound-quieting materials absorb sound (as do carpeting, porous foam, rubber), bar sound (block or reflect it, as do such heavy materials as sheet lead

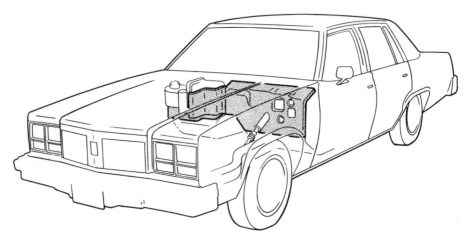

**Fig. 2.39** Most diesel cars have additional sound and vibration insulation (represented by the shaded area on this Oldsmobile).

and asphalt-backed felt), or dampen sound (reduce or eliminate its most objectionable frequencies, including the intensity of vibration noise—mastic and adhesives being two dampening materials).

Asphaltic undercoating below the vehicle's body and floor and overcoating above the floor, but beneath the carpeting, are basic sound-deadening techniques, and foam padding on the hood's underside is another; so, in the case of many diesel vehicles, is use of a lead sheet beneath the usual carpeting. Fuel-to-injector line noise and vibration are often deadened by wrapping the lines in rubber hosing. Firewall acoustical treatment—use of asphaltic sound-deadening material on both sides of the firewall, between passenger and engine compartments—also bars engine noise.

In testing many diesel vehicles for this book, we found diesel noise virtually eliminated from most passenger compartments. For most drivers of a diesel, it's not that a diesel is really nowadays much noisier than its gas engine counterpart. It simply sounds different. It sounds ''diesel.''

## COMPENSATING FOR ALTITUDE

As you drive to higher and higher altitudes, the air grows less dense. Being thinner, it contains less oxygen the higher you drive than a similar volume of air intaken by the engine at lower altitudes.

In a diesel, there are two basic ways to compensate for air's decreased density and oxygen content as altitude increases. One is to cram a greater volume of this thinning air into the diesel's combustion chambers. Even though the air contains less oxygen, so much more air is crammed into the cylinders that the excess air ratio remains about the same as at lower altitudes. What does the cramming is the turbocharger, which also has benefits at lower altitudes.

In the absence of a turbocharger, the other way to compensate for altitude is by fitting the diesel's governor with an altitude compensating device, which senses the decrease in air (barometric) pressure as altitude increases. As air pressure drops, a bellows-like barometric cell expands, mechanically actuating the governor's fuel control rod, which decreases the amount of fuel injected into the cylinders so the fuel-to-air ratio is maintained. Although this method prevents overfueling and exhaust smoking and maintains an efficient air-to-fuel ratio, it usually also causes a loss in power at higher altitudes because less fuel is being combusted.

Many of the newly turbocharged diesel vehicles—the Mercedes-Benz 300SD, for one—employ both methods; turbocharging and altitude compensation. Why both sometimes are needed to ensure diesel efficiency at higher altitudes, particularly on hot summer days, is a matter of atmospheric dynamics: Air's weight decreases about 3 percent with every 1,000-foot increase in altitude above sea level; at 10,000 feet, it's only 70 percent what it was at sea level.

It also decreases as temperature increases; at sea level, air weighs 0.076 pound per cubic foot when the temperature is 59°F and for each 10°F temperature rise above 59°F, its weight decreases about 1 percent through heat expansion. At 90°F, air has lost 3 percent of its weight.

Drive at 10,000 feet, as you can in the West, on one of those unseasonable 90° F days, and the air you're dieseling through weighs 33 percent less than it did at lower altitudes and lower temperatures. Under such abnormal driving conditions, a diesel needs all the altitude and temperature compensation it can get.

# Chapter 3

# Diesel Fuel: Put a Miser in Your Tank

Diesel is a penny-pinching fuel with a walloping power punch. Efficiency is the diesel's trump card and is the single most important feature that gives it the possible means for a manufacturer to meet the federally mandated 27.5 mpg CAFE standard, which takes effect in 1985. Compression ratio, discussed earlier, is the primary determinant of thermal efficiency, so on a strict thermaldynamic basis, the diesel has to be more efficient than a gasoline engine. But the diesel has more going for it.

The energy content of diesel fuel is about 10 percent higher than that of gasoline on a volume basis, allowing it to deliver more work per gallon than an equivalent volume of gasoline.

Gallon for gallon, diesel fuel has more energy—more BTUs (**B**ritish **T**hermal **U**nits), the measure of any fuel's heat content, thus its inherent self-contained power—than gasoline. A gallon of diesel contains some 141,000 BTUs; a gallon of premium gasoline, 125,000. So when you buy a gallon of diesel, you buy more power in the first place. But the diesel engine vastly multiplies this initial advantage by the way it operates; using far less fuel to achieve performance equal to or better than that of the gasoline engine.

Because the gasoline engine's air/fuel charge is spark ignited, the ratio of fuel to air in the gasoline engine's cylinders must be such that it will ignite in the presence of the spark plug's electric spark. To combust spark ignited, the gasoline engine's fuel must be a relatively *rich mix,* usually no less than fifteen parts of air to one part of gasoline—more air, and the mix won't ignite. The gasoline engine operates with a *fixed* fuel ratio, regardless of the engine's work load. Whether it is working hard, perhaps speeding up a mountain grade, or hardly working at all, such as coasting downgrade or idling, the gasoline engine's fuel mix cannot be significantly varied, simply because a *lean mix* (a greater proportion of air to gasoline) won't spark ignite.

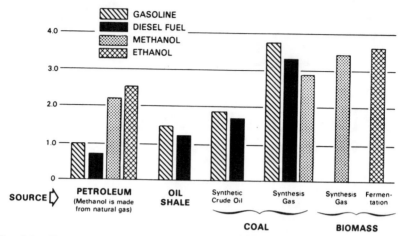

**Fig. 3.1** Comparative amounts of various fuels that can be derived from possible sources. (*Source:* "Automotive Fuels—Outlook for the Future" by Joseph Bidwell, Executive Dept. GM Research Laboratories in Automotive Engineering, November 1978)

But a gasoline engine's so-called "lean mix" (when a mechanic "leans" your carburetor) is a "rich mix" of fuel-to-air compared to diesel's. Generally, a gasoline engine operates with an air-to-fuel ratio of 12–14 : 1 (twelve to fourteen parts air to one part fuel). Floor your gas engine's accelerator and you'll use more fuel, disadvantageously reducing the ratio to perhaps 8 : 1 (eight parts air to one part fuel). But you can't significantly improve it—not and keep your gas engine running. The diesel, by fuel-economizing contrast, does not depend on spark ignition, but rather on ignition by the heat of compression.

In the diesel's cylinders, air alone is compressed by the pistons to precombustion temperatures of about 1,000°F. Any fuel, regardless of quantity, introduced into so hot an air mass would ignite instantly. So ignition, as long as a diesel's cylinders produce their normal heat of compression, is never a problem. A diesel's air-to-fuel ratio can range (when the engine is idling or under light workloads) up to fifty parts air to one part fuel—or as little as one third to one fourth the fuel required, for a given work load, by a gasoline engine.

Even when it needs maximum power (during high speed acceleration, for example), a diesel's air-to-fuel ratio, at worst fifteen to sixteen parts air to one part fuel, is twice as fuel economizing as a gas engine likewise maximum powered. And, unlike the gasoline engine, the diesel can—as when you accelerate—constantly vary its fuel ratio to match power and road requirements. This is because, ignition assured, the diesel's throttle controls only the miserly amount of fuel injected into the cylinders. The gas engine's throttle, to ensure a spark-ignitable air/fuel carburetor mix, controls both the air and the fuel entering the cylinders.

But even while using less fuel, a diesel may, in a given driving situation, produce more power at the wheels. The secret is Diesel's high engine compression. As air is compressed into a smaller and smaller space by the diesel's pistons on their upward compression stroke, air within the cylinder grows both more

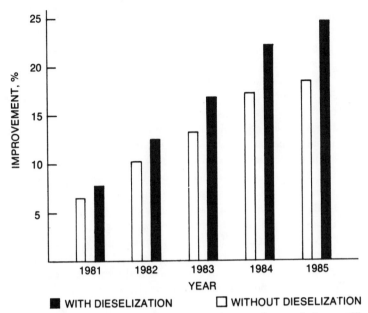

**Fig. 3.2** Fuel economy improvements based on improved transmissions, rolling resistance, lubricants, and aerodynamics for one U.S. automaker.

dense, thus compacting more combustive oxygen into a smaller area, and ever hotter.

Follow, for a moment, this compressive action: When a diesel piston has advanced only one eighth of its way upward on its compression stroke, the air's pressure in the cylinder above it has been increased from atmospheric pressure to 90 pounds of pressure per square inch (psi), and its temperature to some 620°F. As the piston continues to move upward, pressure and temperature rise. At one fourth of its stroke, pressure has built to 155 psi and temperature to 760°F; at the piston's halfway mark, pressure has risen to 320 psi, temperature to 990°F, and at the top of its stroke, at top dead center (T.D.C.), compression reaches some 500 psi and temperature as high as 1,200°F. Depending on the cylinder, the compression ratio may be as high as 25 : 1, meaning the air within the cylinder has been compressed into a space 1/25th its original volume. Inject fuel at this moment, and ignition is almost instantaneous. Combustion, the fuel's spontaneous burning, nearly triples the already fiery temperature of the air mass to near the 3,000°F mark. As does any air rapidly heated, the air mass rapidly expands, forcefully driving the piston downward on its power stroke. From no-cost air the diesel has wrested a tremendous power advantage, the power inherent in compression.

The gasoline engine cannot significantly compress the air within its cylinders or wrest from even its modest compression (compression ratios of 8 : 1 to 11 : 1, only a third to one half that of the diesel) the power latent in compression. It can't for two reasons: First, compressed within its cylinders is a fuel mix, gasoline and air, not simply air, as in the diesel; and second, gasoline, being far more volatile than diesel fuel, self-ignites at very low compression temperatures—at only a few hundred degrees F. Given almost any compressive heat, the gasoline-air mix would self-ignite before the spark plugs fired, resulting in preignition, engine knock, uncontrolled combustion, and power loss. So a gasoline engine can never permit compression temperature to reach the ignition temperature of its gasoline/air mix and thus can never take full advantage of compression, the no-cost "secret" of the diesel's great power and fuel efficiency.

The diesel, however, pays some penalties for such high temperature and compression: To withstand its own internal heat and pressure, it must be built far stronger and heavier than a gasoline engine of equal power, and so the diesel costs more. And it has a special fuel demand. Almost any fuel injected into a diesel's furnace-hot compressed air will burn. In theory, but NOT in practice, an automotive diesel will burn virtually any fuel: from heavy bunker C (the dregs of the "barrel," burnt by slow-moving, massive ship and industrial diesels) to pulverized coal—the fuel Rudolph Diesel initially chose for his first diesel to burn, before opting, on second thought, for more easily ignited fuel oil. In practice, today's high-speed automotive diesels are far more finicky about their fuel. What they burn is Diesel #2 or Diesel #1 (also called 2-D and 1-D)—a clear, oilyish, kerosene-like, and often worse than kerosene-smelling refined petroleum product.

The complex refining process by which diesel fuel—as well as gasoline, kerosene, and many other petroleum products—comes into being is fundamentally simple: A barrel of crude oil (42 gallons in commercial usage) is heated hotter and hotter. Because each of the fuels contained within the oil has a different and distinctive boiling or vaporizing point, at each step-up in temperature one after another product "boils off": vaporizes, is piped to a container and condensed, and again becomes a liquid. Depending on the refinery, approximately 44 percent is gasoline and 36 percent is fuel oil, with other products making up the balance.

The "boiling range" of crude oil progressively yields lighter petroleum products (such as gasoline and butane), then heavier (naphtha, light solvents such as paint thinner), then kerosene, #1 diesel, home heating oil, and #2 diesel. Further up the boiling range are extracted industrial heating oil and lubricating oil. The *end point,* the temperature at which most of the diesel in a barrel of crude oil suitable for high-speed automotive engines has been vaporized out, is between 690° and 725°F.

Diesel's volatility is low, making it a far safer fuel to handle, storage, and tank than gasoline. Whereas regular gasoline releases explosive vapors even at a chill −80°F, diesel gives off almost no vapors at all even at elevated summertime temperatures. A lighted match tossed into a saucer of diesel (but not into a fuel tank) will simply go out. Only when diesel fuel is atomized under high pressure and heat, as in an engine's combustion chamber, does it readily ignite. Diesel's *flash point,* the temperature at which it gives off vapors enough to ignite in an open flame, ranges from 100°F for more volatile #1 diesel to 125°F for #2. Used only as an index of fire hazard, the flash point tells nothing about diesel fuel's ignition quality within the engine.

The most critical parameter of diesel fuel is its cetane number, a measure of the fuel's ignition quality, which influences both ease of starting and combustion roughness of an engine. A cetane number rating is obtained by comparing the given fuel with cetane, a colorless liquid hydrocarbon that has excellent ignition qualities and is assigned a rating number of 100. Alpha-methyl-naphthalene represents the bottom of the scale, with a cetane number of zero. These two hydrocarbons are mixed and matched against the given fuel in a standard research engine, under controlled conditions. The percentage of cetane that requires the same compression ratio for top dead center ignition is the cetane number of the fuel. Diesel fuel's *cetane number* is somewhat analogous to gasoline's octane number. Cetane is an arbitrary number, ranging for most diesel fuels between 35 and 55, which gauges how fast diesel will ignite—specifically, the time lapse between the instant fuel *injection* begins and the instant fuel *ignition* starts. The higher its cetane number, the better a fuel's ignition quality, thus the faster it will ignite, once injected into the combustion chamber.

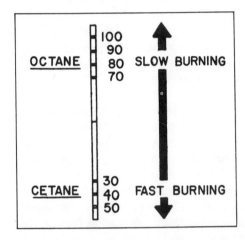

**Fig. 3.3** Relationship between octane (gasoline) and cetane (diesel) fuel ratings.

More critical for diesel owners and drivers is diesel fuel's behavior as winter sets in and as temperatures skid below freezing. Unlike gasoline, diesel first "clouds" and in coldest weather may gel and stop flowing altogether. Diesel fuel's *cloud point* is the temperature somewhere below freezing where wax crystals begin to form in the fuel, turning it cloudy. At still lower temperature lies diesel's no-flow *pour point* at which, winter chilled, it no longer will flow.

Fuel makers produce the two grades of diesel, #1 and #2, to combat the winter-chill problem. Diesel #2 is the automotive diesel's general use fuel—for use, roughly, at temperatures above 20°F. Within its use range, Diesel #2, partly because it is less volatile than #1, gives better fuel economy. To push Diesel #2's use range to lower temperatures—typically, to 0°F and sometimes below—fuel makers "winterize" #2; using various fuel additives and blends to lower both its cloud and pour points. Diesel #1 has a lower cloud and gel point than even "winterized" #2 and can also be used year-around, despite its slightly lower fuel economy. The general rule: Use a fuel whose *cloud point* is at least 10°F *below* the *lowest* temperature you expect to encounter.

Most Owner's Manuals specify the temperatures at which, for their particular engine, you should switch from #2 to #1, if the latter is locally available (often it isn't).

Here's what Oldsmobile tells its diesel owners:

Your diesel engine is designed to run only on diesel fuel. Usually, Number 2-D diesel fuel is the only diesel fuel available. In some areas, however, Number 1-D diesel fuel is also available. Use Number 2-D if you expect temperatures *above* 20°F (−7° C). Use Number 1-D fuel, if available, if you expect temperatures *below* 20°F. During the winter months, "winterized" blends of 1-D and 2-D are available in some areas.

Do NOT use Number 2-D fuel at temperatures below 20°F unless it is "winterized." The cold temperature will cause unblended 2-D fuel to thicken, which may keep the engine from running. Number 1-D fuel may be used year-around, but Number 2-D fuel will give better fuel economy.

Actually, what fuel you use is usually academic. What's served up at the fuel pump is fuel conditioned for local temperatures. The oil company reckons cloud and pour point for you and serves up a diesel fuel—#2, winterized #2, or #1— to meet local temperatures. There are, however, extremes in temperatures where a diesel owner, by "winterizing" his diesel vehicle and at times also its fuel, can largely combat diesel's deep-cold problems (see Chapter 4, "Cold Starting Problems").

At one time or another most diesel owners and drivers ask, "Can I use other than Diesel #1 or #2 in my diesel vehicle?" And virtually every Owner's Manual says "No," based on a number of factors. For one, alternate "fuels" not meant for automotive diesels aren't refined to strict diesel fuel standards. Their cetane numbers may not provide easy starting, and they may contain more corrosive sulphur than permitted by standard diesel fuel specifications. But the primary reason for the Owner's Manual's often stern advice against using any but "diesel fuels" is lubrication and the role fuel plays in lubricating, as well as fueling, the diesel engine. Fuel is the *only* lubricant for such working engine components as the injectors and their injector pump. Obviously, if the fuel you use is not a lubricant, or lacks good lubricating quality, engine damage is almost certain.

Nonetheless, in emergencies, many nonstandard diesel "fuels" can be used, among them kerosene, kerosene-like Jet A aviation fuel (the commercial aircraft turbine fuel available at most airports), and home heating fuel oil, but this book is *not* recommending their use.

Being warned, consider the use of home heating fuel oil, which, produced to fuel your home's furnace, is virtually identical to #1 Diesel. There is one considerable difference: When refined for furnaces, it does not have to pass the tough fuel standard tests required if it's to be labeled #1 Diesel and tanked by your local filling station. But there are times when the refinery turns out #1 Diesel that is also sold to homeowners to fire their furnaces—diesel-grade fuel oil sold under one price tag and brand at the pump and under another when dumped into a householder's furnace fuel tank. The $2,000–$6,000 (price of a new diesel engine) question is: When is home heating oil really #1 Diesel and when isn't it? You don't know and seldom have any way of telling.

Nearly all engine and vehicle makers do grudgingly sanction *mixing* of some of these fuels—notably regular gasoline and kerosene—with diesel, in strict maximum proportions, to improve diesel fuel's winter starting performance should winterized #2 or #1 Diesel not be locally available (see Chapter 5 on diesel driving). None of these alternate fuels, however, will give either the performance or economy of diesel fuel, the miser in any diesel owner's fuel tank.

## DIESEL FUEL SPECIFICATIONS

Available from most oil companies is an analysis of the diesel fuel they serve up at their pumps.

Table 3.1 shows a typical published analysis of an average-grade #2 diesel fuel. Column 1 lists specifications, and Column 2 shows the standard test (as ASTM D975—American Society of Testing Materials test D975) used to get the results in Column 3.

**Table 3.1—Typical Specifications for a "Winterized" #2 Diesel Automotive Fuel**

| 1 | 2 | 3 |
|---|---|---|
| Cetane Index | ASTM D975 | 46.0 |
| Gravity, °API | ASTM D287 | 35.5 |
| Distillation, °F | ASTM D86 | |
|    Initial Boiling Point | | 400 |
|    50% Recovered | | 490 |
|    End Point | | 590 |
| Pour Point, °F | ASTM D97 | −10 |
| Cloud Point, °F | ASTM D97 | − 5 |
| Sulfur, % | ASTM D1552 | 0.2 |

*Cetane number:* This fuel's fairly high cetane number (46, whereas for diesel fuels a cetane number of 55 is often highest, and best) indicates good, but certainly not excellent, ignition quality.

*Gravity number:* Gravity is a measure of a fuel's BTU (heat) content. On the standard API (American Petroleum Institute) gravity scale of from 10 to 44, the *lower* the number the *higher* and better the fuel's heat content. This fuel's 35.5 gravity number indicates only fair heat content—specifically, a heat content of about 139,000 BTU. Highest BTU gravity 10 fuel has a heat value as high as 154,000 BTU.

*Distillation temperatures:* As the table indicates, this fuel was obtained across a fairly low (and desirable) distillation temperature range—beginning at 400°F and with its end point, the temperature at which distillation ended, at 590°F. Since the heat of compression within a diesel's cylinders should be about twice the end-point temperature ($590 \times 2 = 1180$°F), and since compressive heat often exceeds this temperature, this fuel will readily ignite.

*Pour Point:* The indicated − 10° F pour point, extremely good (meaning extremely low temperature) for the pour point of a #2 diesel fuel, most of which stop flowing at far higher temperatures, suggests that almost certainly this is a "winterized" #2 diesel and, as such, is specially formulated for extreme cold weather use.

*Cloud Point:* Likewise, the extremely low (−5°F) temperature before this fuel begins to cloud because of the formation of wax crystals marks this as a win-terized #2, and a good one for cold winter starting and driving.

*Sulfur:* The lower the sulfur content of diesel fuel, the better, since sulfur (and virtually all diesel fuels have some) forms acid that can corrode the engine. Al-though some better-grade diesel fuels have a lower percentage of sulfur (typically, .16%), indicating more refining to reduce the sulfur content, the residual .2 per-cent sulfur here is satisfactorily low.

Table 3.2—Comparison of #1 and #2 Diesel Fuel

| *Requirement* | 1-D | 2-D |
|---|---|---|
| 1. Flash Point, °F minimum | 100 | 125 |
| 2. Cetane Number, minimum | 40 | 40 |
| 3. Viscosity at 100° F, Centistokes | | |
| minimum | 1.4 | 2.0 |
| maximum | 2.5 | 4.3 |
| 4. Water and Sediment, % by volume | | |
| maximum | Trace | 0.05 |
| 5. Sulfur, % by weight | | |
| maximum | 0.5 | 0.5 |
| 6. Ash, % by weight | | |
| maximum | 0.01 | 0.01 |

## FUELING STRATEGIES

"Every week," puns a VW Rabbit diesel owner, "I hop over the border and fill up—for 20 cents a gallon."

That's one fueling strategy. It's a favorite with diesel owners in Texas, Califor-nia, Arizona, and New Mexico. In Mexico, with ample oil reserves of its own, diesel fuel has been selling for as little as 19 cents a gallon at the pumps. But not many diesel drivers can border-hop in quest of bargain fuel prices. That quest, for some diesel owners, has become something more than simply a light-hearted game as diesel prices have climbed to match those of regular gasoline.

Like the border hoppers, some few other diesel drivers have found unusual, low-cost fuel sources not available to most of us—local truck terminal pumps, for example, whose fleet-priced fuel finds its way (at fleet fuel prices) into the diesel tanks of employees and friends of fleet management. But businesses other than truck firms have "company pumps." If you're an employee and drive a diesel that you may also use on company business, it may be possible to fuel at the company pump, and maybe even at no cost, if fuel would normally be billed the company on your expense account anyway. It doesn't hurt either if a friend happens to be a farmer or rancher who lives reasonably close to town; even modest-size farms are likely to have a diesel pump out by the tractor shed.

But for the vast majority of diesel owners and drivers, fueling's No. 1 question remains, "Where am I likeliest to find diesel fuel cheapest?" Where you're *not* likely to find diesel at a bargain is at posh-area filling stations that for years have catered to the Mercedes crowd. These stations, tanking diesel as a favor to their

### Diesel Fuel Additives

Although diesel fuels may contain no additives, listed below are additives that can be used. No single diesel fuel would contain more than a few on the list.

| *Additive Types* | *What They Do* |
|---|---|
| Ignition quality (cetane) improvers | Increase a fuel's cetane number (its ignition efficiency) when the base fuel's natural cetane number is too low |
| Oxidation inhibitors | Prevent fuel deterioration, including rusting and formation of gum when in storage |
| Rust preventives and metal deactivators | Prevent in-storage or handling rusting |
| Smoke suppressants | Minimize exhaust smoking |
| Detergent-dispersants | Keep fuel-insoluble materials in suspension, helping to prevent injection and fuel filter clogging, but also used to maintain fuel cleanliness during handling and storage |
| Pour point depressants | Reduce the pour point of diesel fuel to temperatures significantly below a fuel's cloud point |
| Odor suppressants | Reduce the sometimes objectionable odor of diesel exhaust fumes |
| Moisture preventers | Reduce build-up of moisture and condensation |
| *Additive Types* | *What They Do* |
| Icing preventers | Prevent ice, in very cold areas, from building up, risking fuel line and fuel filter plugging (alcohol is an icing preventer, but only a little can be used, as alcohol lowers diesel fuel's flash point and can also increase corrosive wear of the fuel pump and injectors) |
| Coloring dyes | Color diesel fuel for identification or commercial reasons; have no effect on engine operation |

**Fig. 3.4** You can save at self-serve stations by pumping your own fuel.

customers in years past when diesel pleasure vehicles were rarities, aren't given to dispensing bargains now. Neither are most other metropolitan or suburban filling stations.

You *can* find diesel fuel at its probable lowest price at the truck stops, in town or out. The nation's truck drivers and owners, a no-nonsense lot, are hurting as diesel prices climb. Whereas a dime a gallon more or less seldom adds up to more than pocket money for the diesel pleasure driver, for truckers—their rigs gulping 100 to 200 gallons at every fill—it can add up to profit or loss. Never far from a big rig driver's mind is the current price of diesel at the truck stop he's approaching, and at those all along his route. If a stop hikes prices, truckers shun the place and pass the CB word to their on-the-road buddies. Similarly, word of a truck stop shaving a few cents off a gallon of diesel travels CB-fast, too. Patron pressure like this tends to keep truck-stop diesel prices low—low compared to what's being charged locally at the other places.

The time to tank up at truck fuel stops is when not many trucks are running, as the stops are least busy then. If there is one "best" time to fuel at a truck stop, it would likely be mid-morning on Saturday, when many truck stops are virtually deserted. Worst times to fuel at truck stops are weekday nights (most interstate rigs run at night) and any time Monday, Tuesday, or Wednesday, most stops' busiest days for trucks. Fueling strategy is knowing *when* as well as *where,* with least hassle and greatest savings, to diesel-up.

For where to obtain a directory of diesel fuel stops, see page 204.

## HOME STORAGE OF FUEL

Far less volatile than gasoline, diesel fuel can be safely stored, with proper precautions, at home, although obviously not in your city apartment or condo. Whatever the storage site or container, it must meet local fire and fuel handling codes and, in most states, fuel tax laws that may require posting of a bond ($500 in Arizona), being licensed as a fuel dealer (Michigan, fee: $1), or filing "fuel used from storage" reports to the state, along with remittance of the road tax normally collected at the pumps (Idaho, 9½ cents per gallon). Despite such regulations, storage can be a hedge against scarcity, a convenience for the diesel owner far from a pump, an assurance of high-quality fuel, and can mean sizable fuel price savings through taking advantage of cheaper bulk rates.

Although you should inquire locally about diesel storage local and state regulations and laws, here are some general rules and practices:

Home storage is commonly by bulk tank or by barrel or drum, the latter the commercial 55-gallon size.

Standards of the National Fire Protection Association (NFPA), adopted by most states, rule that *aboveground* diesel storage tanks be at least forty feet from the nearest building, *belowground* diesel storage tanks at least one foot from the nearest foundation or structure.

If home storage presents any real problem, it is maintaining the usually high quality of delivered diesel fuel. Anything less risks clogging your engine's injectors and fuel filters. Water, especially from condensation on inner storage container walls, is one problem. So is the growth of bacteria. Moreover, diesel fuel

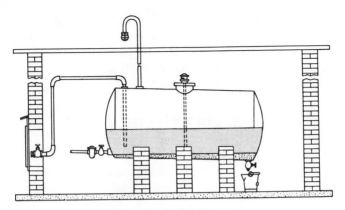

**Fig. 3.5** Fuel oil bulk storage.

can "sour" (polymerize, meaning chemically change) with age. For these and other reasons, your fuel tank must be mounted and fitted, whether aboveground or below, so it can be easily drained of water, rust, microorganisms, and other fuel contaminants.

Some metals, because they react with diesel fuel to form injector and filter clogging compounds (as oxides) should never be used either as storage containers or piping. Don't use copper lines or galvanized tanks. Car fuel tanks, by the way, are plated with terne, a tin-lead formula that is inert to both gasoline and diesel.

Let newly delivered diesel "settle" for at least 24 hours before drawing from storage. This allows water and other contaminants to sink to the tank's bottom, *below* the level of the line or pipe used to withdraw fuel. That line, again to avoid sucking up settled contaminants, should take fuel no closer than four-inches above the container's bottom.

**Fig. 3.6** Fuel oil barrel mounted on trestles.

If additives such as biochemicals to fight bacterial growth, improvers to raise the tanked fuel's cetane rating, or inhibitors to reduce oxidation are used, be sure to add only the amount recommended by their makers.

Finally, every storage tank should be fitted with a filter to filter the fuel *before* it goes into your vehicle's tank. Several commercial models are available.

## MIXING FUELS FOR COLD WEATHER

Temperatures below 20°F demand fueling either with "winterized" Diesel #2 fuel or with #1. Where only standard "summer-grade" #2 is available, it may be necessary to mix the summer-grade #2 either with *regular* gasoline or with kerosene.

Owner's Manuals to the contrary notwithstanding, kerosene is much preferred over gasoline as a diesel fuel mix. First, most diesels will run on straight kerosene; they won't (and shouldn't) on gasoline alone. For another reason, kerosene is compatible with diesel fuel; gasoline is not. Whereas kerosene has fair to good lubricating qualities (and most injector pumps and injectors are fuel lubricated), gasoline lubricates not at all. Gasoline is also volatile; kerosene is not.

### Diesel/Kerosene Mix

A 50 percent diesel/50 percent kerosene fuel mix, the *maximum* amount of kerosene recommended by Mercedes-Benz in any emergency diesel fuel mix, will give close to straight diesel performance, although there may be some power loss. Here is one recommended mixing table:

| Ambient (Outside) Temperature | Diesel #2 Summer Grade | Kerosene |
|---|---|---|
| | percent | percent |
| From +32° F to +14° F | 70 | 30 |
| From +14° F to +5° F | 50 | 50 |

Diesel fuel and kerosene mix best when mixed outside your vehicle's tank. Moreover, with normal precautions, the mix is safe to store.

### Diesel/Regular Gasoline Mix

*Never more than* 30 percent regular gasoline should be mixed with diesel (thus, 70% diesel summer-grade #2). But the mix, while it works, doesn't work too well. Even a 25 percent gasoline-to-diesel fuel ratio causes the engine to fire unevenly and to make a lot of noise. Short-run use of a gasoline/diesel fuel mix should do no permanent harm (although most makers won't pick up the damage bill, even on warranty, if the gasoline/diesel mix *does* cause engine damage). The danger with a gasoline/diesel mix is that hot spots, combustive fuel deposits hot enough to burn a hole through the piston, may form on top of the pistons. But short-run, moderate-speed operation to get you out of a fuel emergency situation should, under most conditions, do no harm. Given the choice, however, opt for a kerosene/diesel mix and leave the gasoline to gas engine vehicles.

## QUICK CURE FOR FUEL FUNGUS

Diesel fuel, unpalatable to humans, is food for fungus, and for a number of microbes that also grow in other hydrocarbon fuels—home heating oil, jetliner turbine fuel, and the bunker oil that fuels many ships. The amount of fuel the microbes eat (not enough for you to notice) isn't what makes them bothersome in your vehicle or home storage tank. What does is a large enough accumulation of microbes to clog your diesel's filters and fuel injectors.

Water, from condensation in fuel tanks, is a breeding ground for fungus. If a service station operator is careless, his fuel tanks may become infested with microorganisms. Fuel up there, and you've got a tankful, too. Fungus is easily spotted. At fueling, you may notice traces of slime (brown, black, or even green) on the fill pipe or fuel cap. To check, swirl a clean stick in the tank and see if it comes out slimy. In advanced fungus attacks, diesel fuel has a distinctive rotten egg smell.

Happily, there's a quick cure for diesel fungus: one of the biocides specially developed to kill fuel microbes. Among the most widely recommended is "Biobar" (made by the U.S. Borax & Chemical Corp. and marketed by various distributors under several trade names, among them "Gemtrete), which for a quarter century has been used world-wide by oil companies, airlines, and ships to control fuel fungus. Biocides have three distinct uses for the diesel vehicle owner who suspects fungus:

*In your vehicle's tank during normal driving.* Usually 1.4 ounces (about three tablespoons) of "Biobar" added to the tank when you fill up will work a cure in two or three fill-ups. After that, taper off, medicating only every other tankful. When fungus signs disappear, stop the biocide treatment.

*In your tank if you store your vehicle for an extended period.* Treatment is precautionary. Never store your diesel without *completely* filling its fuel tank right up to the top. Topping the tank off eliminates the air space where water-forming condensation, necessary for microbe growth, can occur. The same biocide dosage (1.4 ounces, or about three tablespoons) will prevent growth of fuel microbes while you're away.

*In home-storage diesel fuel tanks.* Biocide dosages, listed below for typical fuel-storage tanks, should be administered each time the container is filled.

| Tank Capacity (gallons) | Recommended Maximum Biocide Dosage (ounces) |
|---|---|
| 50 | 1.4 |
| 100 | 2.8 |
| 200 | 5.3 |
| 500 | 13.2 |
| 1,000 | 26.5 |

Never increase these recommended *maximum* dosages. More gives no added benefits; half the listed maximums, in fact, will probably do the job. Biocide is expensive, and too much can cause problems. Never use a biocide in an empty tank, even in one with only a little fuel, or as a tank cleaner. Small quantities of water, almost always present in fuel tanks, will cause the biocide to form crystals that can clog delicate diesel systems.

Tanks very heavily infested with fungus/microorganism, whether your car's or home storage, should be drained and thoroughly cleaned (steam clean or use one of the detergent-type commercial tank cleaners), then completely refilled with fuel and the biocide administered. Cleaning rids heavily infested tanks of the infestation's highly corrosive waste products that remain in the tank even after the biocide has killed the microbes. These waste products, if they become concentrated, can eat through light steel, aluminum, rubber, and through virtually anything else, in time.

Biocides such as "Biobar" (about $15 a quart), long sold in commercial quantity, are only just now reaching the consumer market, and you may be able to find them at your auto parts store. If no luck there, try local diesel fuel, heating oil, pesticide, or industrial products dealers or at local marinas, where the biocides are often used in the diesel fuel tanks of pleasure boats. Also available for fuel microorganisms is a test kit that reveals the early presence of fuel microbes before they are visually evident. Called "Microb Monitor," the kit (about $12.50) is available from Boron Oil Company, 1876 Guildhall Building, Cleveland, OH 44115.

# Chapter 4

# The Minimum-
# Maintenance Engine

The diesel has rightly been called the "minimum-maintenance engine." But Table 4.1—a diesel-versus-gasoline routine maintenance comparison—might well lead you to believe otherwise. Even a quick glance at the table, which shows routine maintenance *required* by International Harvester for both its gasoline- and diesel-powered Scout utility/recreational vehicles, would hardly suggest "minimum" as the maintenance required for the new Scout turbocharged Nissan 6-cylinder diesel. Whereas, for one example, the gasoline engine Scout's oil *must* be changed only every 5,000 miles or every six months, whichever comes sooner, the diesel Scout's oil *must* be changed every 2,500 miles or every three months. Thus, the diesel requires an oil change twice as often as the gas engine.

The fuel filter must be replaced every 15,000 miles on both the Scout's gas engine and diesel, but the diesel's fuel filter must be *cleaned* (although not necessarily replaced) every 2,500 miles. The air cleaner filter has to be replaced every 15,000 miles or eighteen months on the gas engine, the same as for the diesel, but the diesel's air filter must be checked and, if necessary, serviced every 600 miles.

It isn't until you get down to the table's last two items—a change, inspection or cleaning of spark plugs or fuel injectors, and the adjustment of the engines' idle speed—that the diesel's "minimum maintenance" comes into sight. A gas engine's spark plugs, by International Harvester's *required* maintenance scheduling, must be *replaced* every 15,000 miles or eighteen months, but the diesel's injectors need only be *cleaned* and possibly *adjusted* with the same regularity.

The table graphically underscores two facts about diesel maintenance:

1. *A diesel requires MORE routine oil changes and filter replacements than a gasoline engine*. Sometimes the diesel needs twice as many over the same mileage interval. Nor, in the diesel (as often with the gasoline engine) can these maintenance periods be ignored or stretched out. Doing so risks foreshortening diesel engine life.

**Table 4.1—Required Routine Maintenance: Diesel Versus Gasoline**

| Maintenance | Gasoline | Diesel |
|---|---|---|
| | (International Harvester V-304, 8-cylinder, 122 hp, 304 CID) | (6-33T Nissan inline turbocharged, 6-cylinder, 101 hp, 198 CID) |
| Engine oil, change | Every 5,000 miles or every 6 months, whichever comes sooner | Every 2,500 miles or every 3 months, whichever comes sooner |
| Engine oil filter, change | Change every 5,000 miles or every 6 months | Initial, at 2,500 miles, thereafter every 5,000 miles, or 6 months whichever comes sooner |
| Fuel filter, replace, clean | Replace every 15,000 miles, or every 18 months, whichever comes sooner | Initial, replace at 2,500 miles, thereafter every 15,000 miles; clean every 2,500 miles |
| Air cleaner filter, replace | Replace every 15,000 miles or every 18 months | Check/service every 600 miles; replace every 15,000 miles or every 18 months |
| Engine idle, adjust | Initial, at 5,000 miles | Every 30,000 miles, or every 36 months |
| Spark plugs or fuel injectors, replace/clean | Spark plugs: Replace every 15,000 miles or 18 months | Fuel injection nozzles: Clean/adjust every 15,000 miles or 18 months |

2. *A diesel requires far LESS major (and costly) maintenance than a gasoline engine.* What's more, a diesel runs far longer *before* any anticipated major maintenance and equally longer *afterwards.* A little major maintenance often goes a long way, giving the diesel two to three times the natural life of a gasoline engine.

So, when *major* maintenance is considered, the diesel is, indeed, the "minimum maintenance" engine. Fewer critical parts is one reason: A diesel has no carburetor, no spark plugs, no distributor, no points, no ignition wiring, no condenser, and no "other parts" involved with fuel/air mixing and spark ignition. The diesel doesn't need them because it does not mix fuel and air outside the engine, but rather inside. Nor does the diesel ignite its fuel mix with an electric spark. Both—the "mixing" through injection of fuel into the cylinder and ignition, within the cylinder, by the cylinder's own hot compressed air—are wholly automatic. They're achieved by the laws of physics, not by parts subject to regular maintenance.

The same laws of physics and of combustion explain why, when it comes to routine oil and oil filter changes, a diesel often needs twice as many in the same mileage or time span as does the gasoline engine. Inside its cylinders, a diesel burns dirtier than the gasoline engine. Created in this "dirty" combustion is fuel soot, much of it carbon. It is an abrasive which, one way or another, gets into the diesel's lube oil system, usually reaching and contaminating the lube oil through *fuel dilution*—the fact that no matter how sound the piston rings, some fuel and exhaust gases do manage to leak past the pistons and reach the crankcase and its lube oil supply. Sooted lube oil would be reason enough for relatively frequent oil and oil filter changes. But there is another reason: Almost all diesel fuel contains some sulphur. So the burnt gases and unburnt fuel that may slip past the pistons' rings and into the crankcase's oil also contain sulphur that, in solution, becomes sulphuric acid, a notorious high corrosive.

Frequent oil changes, using *only* diesel-grade lube oil that contains anti-acid additives, not only rid the engine of oil containing acid, but puts into the crankcase fresh oil specially formulated to fight the acidic and abrasively sooty by-products of diesel combustion. Very likely a test of the oil drained every 2,500–4,000 miles, depending on Owner's Manual requirements, would show the oil itself to be in excellent lubricating condition (see later sections in this chapter on lube oil). The same test, however, would show it to be acidic and carbon sooted, thus both abrasive and corrosive to engine parts.

And while it is true that carefully managed diesel truck fleets do "extend" their oil/filter-change periods significantly (to many thousands of miles), they can do so only because they frequently submit samples of lube oil from every diesel crankcase to a qualified oil analysis laboratory. That, plus anticorrosive oil additives not usually found in commercial-grade diesel lube oil, permits the trucker to do what *no diesel motorist can ever do safely*. For the average diesel owner and driver, there can be no shortcuts in lube oil and lube oil filter replacements. But these, along with the periodic inspection or replacement of the air cleaner's filter, and change of the fuel filter—jobs most diesel owners can do themselves—are by any reckoning minor, routine engine upkeep.

Far more frequent and costly can be the "routine" maintenance required to keep a gasoline engine efficient and functioning. The problem with the gasoline engine is "parts-itis" resulting from a whole system of maintenance-prone ignition/combustion parts not found or needed in the diesel. At the heart of this problem is the way it premixes fuel and air in the carburetor and then ignites the mixture by an electric spark involving spark plugs, spark plug wiring, distributor, and so on. To cure its endemic "problem," the gasoline engine requires frequent *tune-ups*—at least every 15,000 miles: nothing less than a complete overhaul of its fuel-mix and spark ignition system. In fact, as any owner of a gas engine car knows, older engines past the 25,000-mile mark need a tune-up every six months or so, about every 6,000–7,000 miles on average.

A diesel, of course, never needs a "tune-up" because it has none of the ignition system parts that are tuned up in a gasoline engine. By contrast, the heart of the diesel's combustion system is fuel injection, involving a fuel injection pump and the injectors it supplies. Maintenance can be kept at a minimum if the fuel reaching the pump and injectors is kept clean by frequent, required change of the diesel's secondary and primary fuel filter elements, sometimes supplemented by a water-separator/filter to rid diesel fuel of water. A diesel's injectors, one for each cylinder, may or may not need cleaning and adjustment (this is *not* a do-it-yourself job) at 15,000 miles. The diesel's fuel injection pump seldom needs even a look-see before 30,000 miles, or upwards of 36 months by most Owner's Manuals. Many injectors operate 100,000 miles or more before replacement, longer than the life of many gasoline engines. Once replaced, the injectors—as well as the diesel—are often good for another 100,000 miles.

Do routinely what routinely *must* be done, such as changing filters and lube oil, to rid the diesel of the by-products of its own combustion and to keep its fuel clean, and the diesel under your hood will, in fact, be a "minimum-maintenance" engine.

## OWNER MAINTENANCE: ROUTINE DIESEL CARE

Basic to keeping your vehicle's diesel at peak efficiency is routine, basic maintenance which any owner can do. There are general rules that apply to all diesel engines but because of different components used by different manufacturers, you should have specific instructions for your vehicle, in the form of a "Chilton Repair & Tune-up Guide" or similar service manual.

**Fig. 4.1** The tool kit that comes with some cars will handle routine chores such as tightening loose screws and nuts, but for serious maintenance you'll need a few more tools.

### Lube Oil

Best time to check the oil level is when the oil is warm after driving—during a fuel stop, for instance. But once the engine is shut down, wait about five minutes before checking the oil's level. This gives time for the oil circulated in the engine while driving to drain back into the crankcase, giving you an accurate oil level reading. If checking lube oil level when the engine is cold (say, first thing in the morning), don't run the engine. If you do, and fail to wait for the oil to return to the crankcase, you'll get the same less-than-accurate reading as when taking an oil level reading immediately after driving. Pull the oil dipstick all the way out of its tube. Wipe the dipstick clean, reinsert it, and remove it again for an oil level reading. The oil level should be *between* the two marks, often labeled "maximum/minimum," as on the Mercedes-Benz dipstick, or "add/full," as for the Oldsmobile/GM V-8 diesel. One quart of *diesel-grade* lube oil brings the oil level from "add" or "minimum" to "full" or "maximum."

*Don't* overfill.

*Do* check the oil level with the vehicle level. It's surprising how many owners

**Fig. 4.2** Checking oil level on a Peugeot 504D. (Photograph by James Joseph)

check lube level while the diesel vehicle is on the driveway's incline. The reading will not be accurate.

*Don't,* as a firm although general rule, use any supplemental oil additives, no matter how highly advertised. Diesel-grade lube oil already contains all the additives normally necessary for diesel engines. In some very few cases, high fuel dilution being one, your dealer may recommend an oil additive specially formulated and tested by your engine's maker. Mill-run additives may foreshorten diesel engine life.

*Do* check the lube oil's level at least once a week, and certainly every time you fill up with fuel. Don't, as do many drivers who patronize no-service stations in today's fuel crunch, simply fill up without checking lube oil. Many drivers, whatever their engines, are doing just that—and winding up with big engine overhaul bills. A diesel will not stand oil level neglect.

*Do* use only diesel-grade lube oil.

In many diesel vehicles, unlike most that are gas engine, the lube oil fill cap (and fill port) is located on top of the engine. But not always: *Before* you add any lube oil, read the can's top, which usually specifies whether the oil is designed for

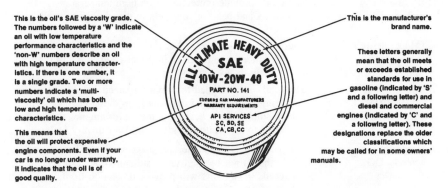

**Fig. 4.3** The top of the oil can will tell you all you need to know about the oil inside.

## Motor Oil Guide

The American Petroleum Institute (API) has classified and identified oil according to its use. The API service recommendations are listed on the top of the oil can, and all car manufacturers use API letters to indicate recommended oils.

Almost all oils meet or exceed the highest service rating (SE), but viscosity should be selected to match the highest anticipated temperature before the next oil change.

| API Symbol (S = Gasoline C = Diesel) | Use and Definition |
|---|---|
| **OIL FOR GASOLINE ENGINES** | |
| SF | SF is a new (1980) improved version of SE oil with improved oxidation stability and anti-wear performance. It will replace SE oils eventually. |
| SE (Severe duty, based on 1972 warranties) | SE represents the most severe service. It is recommended for use in all 4-cycle gasoline engines and cars used for stop and start or high-speed, long-distance driving. It has increased detergency and can withstand higher temperatures, while providing maximum protection against corrosion, rust, and oxidation. Meets all service requirements for classifications SD, SC, SB, and SA. |
| SD (Severe duty) (formerly MS 1968) | These oils provide more protection against rust, corrosion, and oxidation than oils classified SC. They meet minimum gasoline engine warranties in effect 1968–70. |
| SC (Severe duty) (formerly MS 1964) | These oils control rust and corrosion and retard the formation of high and low temperature deposits and meet minimum warranty requirements in effect for 1964–67 gasoline engines. |
| SB (formerly MM) | These oils have antiscuff properties and will slow down oxidation and corrosion. Oils designed for this service afford minimum protection under moderate operating conditions. |
| SA (formerly ML) | These oils have no protective properties and have no performance requirements. |
| **OIL FOR DIESEL ENGINES** | |
| CD (Severe duty) (formerly DS) | These oils provide protection from high temperature deposits and bearing corrosion in diesel engines used in severe service. |
| CC (Moderate/light moderate duty) (formerly DM) | These oils provide protection from rust, corrosion, and high-temperature deposits in diesel engines used in moderate to severe service. |
| CB (Moderate duty) (formerly DM) | These oils are designed to provide protection from bearing corrosion and deposits from diesel engines using high-sulphur fuel. Service is meant for engines used in mild to moderate service with lower quality fuels. |
| CA (Light duty) (formerly DG) | This is a general diesel service classification. These oils should not be used when sulphur content of fuel exceeds 0.4%. Oils will provide protection from bearing corrosion when high-quality fuels are used. |

**Fig. 4.4** Cadillac diesel's oil fill pipe has cap that reminds owner to use only diesel lube oil with "SE/CC" designation. (Photograph by James Joseph)

diesel engines. If in doubt about which diesel grade to use, check your Owner's Manual.

What tells you an oil's *viscosity* is its SAE (**S**ociety of **A**utomotive **E**ngineers) designation, also usually found on the can's top). As a driver of a gasoline engine vehicle, you're already familiar with SAE oil viscosity numbers, such as SAE 30, a *single-grade* (designated by a *single* number) oil, whose "30" viscosity code recommends it for use over a wide temperature range (say, from 32°F to 100°F). You're also familiar with the *multigrade* oils, usually designated by *two* numbers and sometimes also by a letter—such as SAE 10W-30, a so-called "winter" viscosity oil, meaning it will flow and still give engine protection, at low temperatures. In the case of SAE 10W-30, down to -20°F or so. For the diesel engine, the viscosity of the oil you use is especially critical, far more so than for the gasoline engine, because its extremely high compression makes the diesel harder for the battery to start at *any* temperature. Working against a diesel's high compression, a battery has to work harder to crank the engine. That's why diesel vehicles (Cadil-

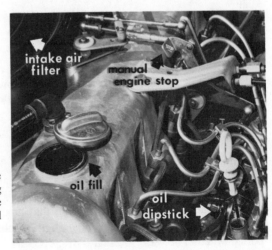

**Fig. 4.5** Under the hood of the Mercedes-Benz 300SD, showing manual engine STOP, air intake filter case, oil dipstick tube, and oil fill port.

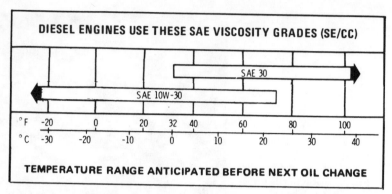

**Fig. 4.6**   Lube oil viscosity chart for diesels.

lac's diesel Seville is typical) have either two batteries or an oversized single. More battery power means more cranking power.

Use a "summer" lube oil (like SAE *30,* whose high viscosity number indicates it does *not* flow well in winter's cold temperatures) instead of a low viscosity numbered "winter" oil, such as SAE *10*W-30, and winter starting will almost certainly be difficult. For now the battery has a double burden: the compressive resistance of the engine plus the physical resistance of the engine's moving parts, working as they are in a tacky, even frozen lubricant.

Later in this chapter (see "Cold Starting Problems"), we discuss in some detail remedies for cold starting problems, including recommended grades of diesel fuel and oil viscosities for cold weather. For now Oldsmobile's lube oil viscosity recommendations for its V-8 diesel can serve as a general guide.

Should you use synthetic lube oil in your diesel engine? The blunt answer: Not until the maker of your engine recommends use of a synthetic and specifies the precise synthetic to use. Thus far, few if any major diesel makers have approved use of synthetic lubricants in their engines. The situation, in time, may change. When it does, your dealer will be able to tell you the approved synthetic for your engine.

### Oil Analysis: Diesel "Blood Test"

Recently, in the morning mail, a diesel car owner received a report saying that the car needed a new air cleaner, that water was somehow (perhaps through water-contaminated fuel) getting into the engine, and that it was time—after only 2,900 miles—for an oil change. If the report had come from the local garageman, it might not have been too surprising. That it came from a laboratory technician who'd never laid eyes on the car, much less peeked beneath its hood, was downright astounding. What the laboratory's technician had seen—and chemically analyzed—was a two-ounce sample of crankcase oil that the diesel owner had mailed the lab in a small plastic bottle. From the same oil sample the laboratory could have diagnosed many other potential engine problems—from piston wear (and reported whether it was "normal" or "excessive") to impending bearing failure.

What's more, the laboratory could have spotted them quicker, and with greater accuracy and impartiality, than many local mechanics. Just as easily, the lab could have given the car's diesel a clean bill of health, saving the car owner unnecessary injector servicing and other routine preventive maintenance, costly in time and money.

There's nothing new about engine lube oil analysis. Thousands of the nation's trucks and buses (probably one out of every five of them) are nowadays regularly "blood tested": have their engine's lube oil analyzed by laboratories specialized to the job. One major trucking company, which operates its own oil testing lab, saves more than $100,000 a year in maintenance bills through monthly oil analysis, to say nothing of more than doubling the lives of its hard-working diesel engines. What is new is the availability of lube oil analysis to individual vehicle owners rather than, as before, almost exclusively to companies operating fleets of diesel equipment.

Here's how lube oil analysis works: You write one of the several laboratories that offer individual diesel vehicle owners lube analysis service. By return mail you'll receive an oil sampling kit. It will probably contain a two-ounce plastic oil sampling container with a screw-on plastic top. Instructions tell you (or your service station worker) how to take the sample. Usually, a lab-bound sample of diesel lube oil may be taken in any of three ways, but always right after the engine has been shut off, so that the sampled oil is as close as possible to normal engine operating temperature. That's important to assure that the lab's tests will be accurate. Oil samples can be taken during normal oil changes, when lube oil is drained anyway. Between oil changes, a sample can be drawn from the engine through the dipstick tube (where you normally check the oil's level). In drawing an oil sample from the dipstick tube, a small suction bulb fitted with a length of disposable tubing is used. The tubing is merely inserted into the dipstick tube, the suction bulb depressed, and the oil sample drawn. The third method of sampling is by loosen-

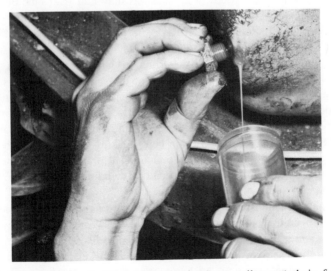

**Fig. 4.7** Taking a lube oil sample from the crankcase (oil sump) drain for analysis. (Photograph by James Joseph)

ing the drain plug on the engine's by-pass oil filter (if your diesel has one). A little oil is caught in the lube sampling container. In all cases, extreme cleanliness is a must, so as not to contaminate the sample with dirt, grease, or other substances not actually found inside the engine. For example, using a rag that contains solvents, metal filings, or other impurities can contaminate the oil sample, leading to false and even alarming lab reports. A bit of technique is required: In taking a sample of lube oil during a routine oil drain, about half of the crankcase's lube oil should be allowed to drain out before the sample is taken. The sample taken, the date, make and model of the engine, its mileage, mileage since last oil change, and sometimes oil type are noted on the container's label, and the container is mailed to the laboratory.

Shortly, you'll receive the lab's report, which, based on a number of tests, including spectrochemical analysis (using a spectrometer, which can detect the presence of virtually all basic elements and contaminants), tells what's in the oil in what quantities and analyzes both the probable source of what was found and whether it indicates trouble. For one example, the finding of more than trace amounts of copper in an oil sample may strongly point to excessive bearing wear in a particular diesel whose bearings contain copper. Some analyses report on as many as eighteen basic elements that may be found in a diesel's lube oil sample, and in the report's "recommendation" may pinpoint their probable source—as, "indicates piston ring wear." Also indicated is the presence of such contaminants as water, solids (the products of oxidation and engine blow-by), and fuel dilution. Noted, too, is the lubricity of the sample—whether, or not, in the lab's opinion, it is still doing its internal engine lubricating job.

*One stern warning, however:* No diesel vehicle owner should ever use lube analysis and a lab's report of "good oil" to extend, beyond the manufacturer's recommendation, the mileage period between oil changes. If your Owner's Manual recommends an oil change every 3,000 miles that's when it MUST be changed, no matter how "good" a lab analysis may find your lube oil. Truckers, admittedly, do use analysis to extend oil use. But truck engines are far tougher than your car's diesel. Repeat: NEVER violate your engine's specified oil change period.

Oil analysis, though scientifically intriguing, has a goodly share of critics. Some say that contamination of the sample, negating the lab's analysis, is far too common and too easy. Others question whether analysis is or can be totally accurate. Still others point to disagreements even between labs as to how, for instance, to take a lube sampling. When draining the engine, some, as we've noted, say to let half of the oil in the crankcase drain before taking the sample. Others recommend that a sample be taken of the "first oil" to drain from the crankcase, in order to include in the sample heavy particles of metal that may settle to the crankcase's bottom.

But oil analysis enthusiasts—including a growing number of ever more sophisticated diesel operators, notably major truck lines—swear more often by oil analysis than at it and often schedule engine maintenance based on a laboratory's lube oil findings. "It's seldom that we consider any really major engine maintenance without first hearing what our lab has to say about the engine's oil," says the maintenance director for a large trucking company. "Contained in a continuing sampling of any engine's lube oil is the whole history of the engine's internal condition. Of course, we take monthly samples of every diesel engine in our fleet. Over a year's time and a dozen lab reports on any engine, we have a pretty good idea what's going on inside that engine.''

This points up one deficiency in sampling by the average owner: the relatively few lube oil samples a diesel owner would take, or care to take, over a year—or, in fact, over the life of his vehicle. The more frequently an engine is lube-sampled, the more accurate and meaningful the lab's reports. Infrequent samplings, although they can spot sudden, unusual changes in internal engine condition, may fail to show the gradual deterioration of engine parts. Ideally, you should have the laboratory analyze a lube sample every other oil change. For most automobile diesels, that's every 6,000 miles. Analysis costs from $7 to $11 per sample. Drive an average 18,000 miles a year and you'd change your diesel's oil six times. In that time, you'd submit three samples to the lab at an annual lube analysis cost of $21 to $33.

One among a number of lube analysis laboratories (see local listings in your Yellow Pages under ''Laboratories'' and the Appendices) is New Jersey-based Ana-Laboratories, Inc. Ana-Laboratories (111 Harding Avenue, Bellmawr, NJ 08030, (609)931-0011) charges $10.50 to analyze a single sample, less if you purchase, in advance, either of two sampling kits. A kit that includes supplies to take and mail to the lab five samples is priced $42.50. A ten-sample kit costs $82.50. Costs are reduced, however, if a number of samples are submitted at the same time. Thus, a neighborhood group of diesel vehicle owners or a car club might sample their vehicles together, and if together they submitted ten or more samples to the laboratory, the cost is reduced to $7.75 per analysis.

Lube analysis? Many diesel buffs insist that lube analysis is any diesel owner's surest guide to preventive maintenance.

But likely the majority of diesel owners, with far less scientific curiosity or interest in their vehicles' engines, will do what all along they've been doing: follow the oil-change recommendation in their Owner's Manual and let it go at that.

### Compression Testing

Compression testing is done with a special compression gauge that registers to 500 or 600 psi. A normal automotive compression gauge will not do the job, because it can't measure high enough. Also, it won't screw into the glow plug hole. A rubber cone gauge won't work either, because you can't possibly hold the gauge in place against 500 psi!

The gauge is inserted in the glow plug hole after the glow plug is removed. But, be careful—some glow plugs, like those on the GM diesel, require a special tool to remove them.

### Maintaining Battery Power

Virtually all diesel vehicles, as we've noted, have either two batteries or an oversized single. Whatever their number or size, battery maintenance—identical

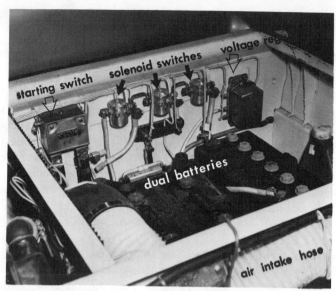

**Fig. 4.8**   View of a diesel conversion, showing dual batteries and neatly wired components. All components are contained in the bed of a pick-up truck. (Photograph by James Joseph)

to that for a gas engine vehicle—can't be neglected. A sluggish battery that may, with luck, start a gasoline engine, can seldom crank a diesel fast enough to produce heat of compression sufficient to start.

If you plan to do basic diesel maintenance, you should buy a simple float hydrometer, available at low cost from any auto supply store, and know how to use and read it.

Your Owner's Manual to the contrary notwithstanding, no battery is "maintenance free." Some, however (GM/Delco's "Freedom" battery, meaning freedom from maintenance), never need water added; in fact, there's no place (no filler caps) to add water. Nonetheless, keeping a diesel's battery maintained is starting insurance. Make sure the battery's water—plain tap water or distilled water, rather than yesteryear's "battery acid"—completely covers the battery plates. Especially for diesel, where crank-to-start battery power *must* be kept high, keep batteries at full charge. A hydrometer reading of 1.26 at 80°F indicates a full charge. Never permit a battery to fall below half-charge, or a reading of 1.225 on the hydrometer. That's doubly important in winter. A *discharged* battery will *freeze* at +20°F. A fully charged battery can withstand temperatures to as low as −80°F.

But what's outside the battery-cables, battery terminals (clamps), and the battery posts to which they clamp—are just as important to keep maintained as what's inside. Inspect battery cables frequently for a build-up of corrosion at their terminals and for frayed, corroded cable ends where cable and its terminal join. Make sure the juncture, an electrical connection subject to shorts, is firm. Keep battery terminals and posts free of corrosion and metal-bright. You want the best electrical connection possible, so that all available battery power can flow to the diesel's starting (cranking) motor. Certainly the majority of all engine starting problems, gasoline engine as well as diesel, are caused by corroded or shorted bat-

**Fig. 4.9**   International Harvester Scout with Nissan diesel and oversized battery.

tery cables and their connections. Clean battery terminals and posts with a stiff bristle brush, using hot water and common baking soda. Brighten contact surfaces, especially terminal posts and inside battery terminals where they contact the posts, with steel wool or a cleaning tool specifically for battery terminals. Then apply a light coat of lubricant, such as Vaseline, chassis lubricant, or even lube oil.

Remember, when working around a battery, that it produces volatile hydrogen gas, explosive to open flame and extremely harmful if inhaled. And also for safety's sake, in disconnecting battery terminals, remember *always* to disconnect the ground terminal *first,* and reconnect it *last* when replacing the terminals.

### Changing the Air Cleaner

How often to inspect/change a diesel's air filter depends on your engine maker's maintenance recommendations (a change every 12,500 miles, at least, for the Peugeot 504 diesel) and on where and how you drive. Obviously, if you operate your vehicle off road or in other dusty conditions, the air filter needs closer attention and more frequent changing. There are two types of diesel air cleaners—the *oil bath,* whose filter element is immersed in a container of oil, and the *dry type,* whose paper element closely resembles that of most gas engine cars—but the diesel engine you have probably has the dry, paper-filter type.

The change-out itself is a 1-2-3 job: (1) unlatch, unclamp, or unbolt the top of the air cleaner holder; (2) remove the old filter element. If merely checking its condition, inspect it, then shake the element, ridding it of dust. If changing the element, refit the cleaner holder with a new filter; (3) replace the cleaner top and reclamp or screw tight the top and its housing.

Some filter elements are girded with a porous, reusable, usually washable prefilter, similar to the filter material used in home air conditioners. But there is one IMPORTANT *caution* in air filter maintenance, and it has nothing to do with the

**Fig. 4.10**  View of typical diesel air filter with top cover removed. (Photograph by James Joseph)

filter itself; it has to do with the diesel engine: *Shut the engine off before removing the filter.* Unlike the gasoline engine, which installs a carburetor between air filter and the engine's innards, the diesel's air intake—an open, unscreened, unobstructed opening—leads directly into the diesel's combustion chambers. And the intake of air, with engine operating, can be as in-sucking as a powerful vacuum cleaner. Virtually anything, from a bolt or nut (the air filter holder's wing nut, for example) or your scarf, can be sucked into the engine. Plainly put, whether run-

**Fig. 4.11**  The reusable prefilter wraps around the air filter. (Photograph by James Joseph)

ning or shut down, a diesel is vulnerable to "drop-ins"—anything dropped or taken in, with air filter removed, through its open air intake.

If the air cleaner element doesn't come clean with shaking or air-blowing (say, with a service station's air hose), replace it with new. Dry-type paper filter elements must never be wetted; that means they must never be cleaned or soaked with any liquid, whether water, gasoline, or cleaning solvents.

### Changing the Fuel Filter(s)

Virtually all automotive diesels have two fuel filters: (1) a *secondary fuel filter,* mounted on or near the engine and (2) a *primary fuel filter,* installed between the fuel tank and the secondary filter, usually upstream from the fuel transfer pump, but generally also found in the engine compartment. The primary fuel filter can be a simple throw-away can (Olds V8) or it can be a cleanable filter such as the ones used by Mercedes-Benz. Sometimes incorporated into the primary fuel filter is a *water separator.* Or it may be installed separately in the fuel system. The separator, as its name implies, removes water and condensation that may be in the fuel. The step-by-step procedure for removing the old fuel filter and replacing it with a new element cartridge differs from filter to filter. But whatever the procedure (and it is simple), first *shut off the engine.*

Change-out of the VW Rabbit diesel's secondary fuel filter element (at 15,000 miles) is an ABC-easy procedure. The Audi 5000 diesel's fuel filter change-out is identical:

1. Unscrew the filter canister (the cartridge that contains the filter element).

2. With the old canister removed, apply a thin film of diesel *fuel* (there should be plenty in the old canister) to the new canister's filter gasket.

3. Screw the new filter canister in the place of the old tightly by hand.

4. Start the engine.

5. Visually check for leaks, especially around the filter's gasket.

Change-out for the Peugeot 504 diesel's secondary filter is quite similar. For change-out details of your own particular diesel's secondary (and primary) fuel filters, see your Owner's Manual.

**Fig. 4.12** Secondary fuel filter showing priming pump.

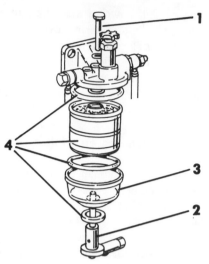

**Fig. 4.13** Replacing the fuel filter cartridge (secondary fuel filter): 1. Loosen securing screw (1). 2. Remove lower union (2), the glass bowl's base (3), and the fuel filter and its gaskets (4). 3. Clean the bowl with diesel fuel. 4. Inspect seals, gaskets, and seating and replace, if necessary. 5. Reassemble, as in Step 2, installing new fuel filter cartridge. 6. Start engine and check for leaks.

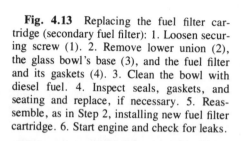

**Fig. 4.14** Remove the main diesel fuel filter on a late-model Mercedes-Benz after removing the center attaching bolt (1); (2) is the bleed bolt.

**Fig. 4.15** Diesel engines use a prefilter in addition to the main fuel filter. Finger points to prefilter; arrow indicates hand primer.

### Priming the Fuel System

The fuel system must be "bled" of air when you change fuel filters, run out of fuel, or periodically, should your Owner's Manual recommend it, and the fuel recirculated through the now air-free system by "priming." For perhaps the majority of automotive diesels, cranking the engine automatically reprimes the fuel system and rids it of air. But the cranking cycle can be relatively long to do the job right, risking wearing down the battery. So most diesel fuel systems include a hand priming pump, with manual priming preferred over cranking, especially in cold weather or if the battery is weak.

Some primer pumps are installed atop the secondary fuel filter, some are separate and include both priming and air bleeding in a single operation, and others have a separate primer pump and an air bleed screw or port. The Mercedes-Benz 240D, 300D, and 300SD fuel systems, for example, are primed and bled in one operation using a single primer/air-bleed pump.

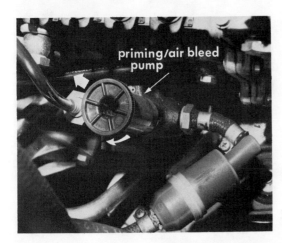

priming/air bleed pump

**Fig. 4.16** Mercedes-Benz 300SD's fuel system priming pump.

To prime and bleed a fuel system with pump and separate air bleed screw, first give the primer pump handle a few strokes to begin recirculation of fuel through the system. Then turn the air bleed screw counterclockwise until you hear air escaping. Continue priming until all air is out of the system, retighten the bleed screw, and push the primer pump handle in to its nonoperative position.

### Changing the Lube Oil Filter

Although the lube oil filter on virtually every diesel can be changed without first draining the crankcase, the filter should be replaced with a change of lube oil, either at every oil change or every other one, as your Owner's Manual specifies. Lube oil filters generally are either the *bolt-on* type, removed with a common open-end wrench, or the *spin-on* type, requiring (as with similar gasoline engine filters) the use of a special filter wrench to loosen it.

In cold weather, run the engine to warm the oil before draining. Warmed, and

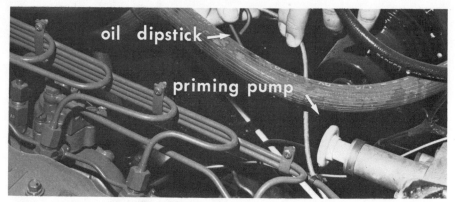

**Fig. 4.17** The fuel priming pump and oil dipstick of the International Harvester turbocharged diesel Scout Terra.

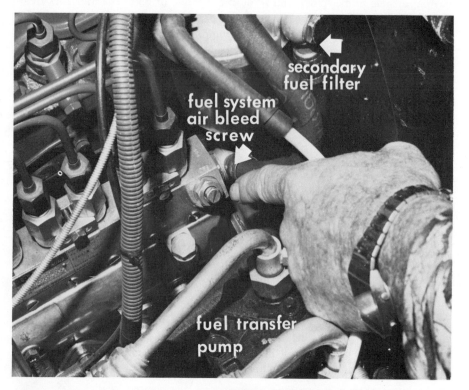

**Fig. 4.18** International Scout's Nissan turbocharged 6-cylinder diesel, showing fuel system's air bleed screw, secondary fuel filter, and fuel transfer pump.

**Fig. 4.19** International Harvester Scout's Nissan turbodiesel's fuel system.

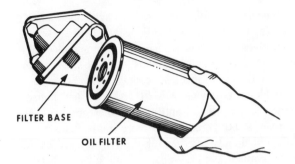

**FILTER BASE**

**OIL FILTER**

**Fig. 4.20** Changing a spin-on type oil filter.

thus free flowing, oil will drain from the engine's interior galleries. Make sure the replacement filter is the proper one (check its model number against the old, or see your Owner's Manual). Having at hand the right-size filter seal or gasket can save time, as the old one may need replacing. Merely as insurance against leaks, a new filter seal is worth its small cost.

For the spin-off type loosen the cartridge with a filter wrench, spin it off by hand, and inspect the seal. If it's OK, lightly film the new filter's seal with oil. Properly seat and screw in the new filter cartridge until the seal just contacts the crankcase. Then *hand* tighten. Finally, replace and tighten the crankcase's oil drain plug and refill through the oil fill port with diesel-grade lube oil of the right viscosity for the weather.

### Checking/Replenishing Radiator Coolant

A diesel's engine combustion, far hotter than gasoline's, is already provided for by an oversized radiator and more internal engine cooling. To make this heftier cooling system work, you must keep the radiator's level and its coolant (antifreeze) to proper antifreeze/water proportion. The antifreeze container specifies the mix, usually no less than 50 percent ethylene glycol (antifreeze). The mix for optimum freeze protection is 68 percent antifreeze, 32 percent water. Typically, General Motors recommends for its V-8 diesel—although obviously dependent on where you live and drive—that "engine freeze protection should be maintained to −34°F/−37°C, or the lowest expected outdoor temperature."

radiator coolant fill pipe

**Fig. 4.21** Hotter running diesel engines, although radiators are oversized (as this Cadillac's), need close attention to radiator coolant level. (Photograph by James Joseph)

At least one diesel maker (Peugeot) absolutely requires, to keep its warranty valid, that *only* Peugeot's own antifreeze be used. While Peugeot's is likewise ethylene glycol based, it contains additives to prevent engine corrosion and electrolysis, both possible problems because the Peugeot diesel is the wet-sleeve type, meaning the cylinders "sleeves" or liners are in direct contact with the coolant. For this particular engine, Robert Flock, editor of *Diesel Car Digest* and himself an automotive engineer, recommends year-around antifreeze use (a good suggestion for any diesel), no less than a 60 percent antifreeze ratio (using only Peugeot's special antifreeze) to avoid unduly overheating the engine, and an annual drain, flush, and refill of the coolant system—again, good advice whatever the diesel coolant system.

With few exceptions, radiator check-out and coolant level maintenance are as routine for diesel as for gasoline engines.

So, for that matter, is most diesel owner-maintenance.

### DIESEL TIMING

A diesel has valves operated by a camshaft, just the same as in a gasoline engine. There is no ignition timing, because the diesel does not use a spark ignition system. But there is a timing setting on the injection pump. When the pump is installed, its drive must be timed and, once the basic timing is established, the final timing adjustment is done by moving the injector pump slightly on its mounting.

Making the injector timing adjustment is easy. All you do is move the pump. The problem is in measuring what the timing is or how much you have changed it. Available are timing lights that will hook into an injector pressure line with a transducer. Every time the injector opens, the timing light is triggered. You can then read the timing on the front pulley, just as on a gasoline engine. Unfortunately, the cost of diesel timing lights is high. Sun's DTL light (which includes a tachometer) has a basic price of $610, with one transducer (different engines require different transducers, depending on the size of injector line fittings).

Volkswagen solves the problem of measuring timing on its diesel Rabbit by doing it with the engine dead. A dial indicator is used to measure the position of the pump piston with the engine at top dead center. This method works OK. But it doesn't tell you what the timing is with the engine running. Mercedes-Benz uses a difficult and imprecise system of hooking up a reservoir of fuel to the pump and turning the engine. When the pump stops dripping, the timing is considered correct. But there's nothing to keep you from overshooting the correct position when turning the engine. Oldsmobile and some other diesel engines use a very simple system. A scribe mark on the pump must be aligned with a mark on the mounting. When the two marks are lined up, the pump is in time.

### Diesel Tachometers

Setting idle speed on a diesel is similar to setting the idle on a gasoline engine, but an ordinary tachometer won't work. Tachometers for a spark ignition engine measure the speed of the engine by counting the sparks or the number of times the distributor points open. On a diesel, there are no sparks or points, so diesel idle speed setting presents a special problem. On the Volkswagen Rabbit there is a vibration pickup that senses the revolutions of the engine and converts them into electrical impulses for use with an ordinary engine-speed tachometer.

Probably the easiest way to get diesel engine speed is through the dashboard tachometer or with a mechanical tachometer connection. Mercedes-Benz uses a connection to the oil pump drive. This method could be used on any engine that had a place to hook up a mechanical tach. But few of them do. Sun's DTL timing light has a tachometer built in and does the job in fine style. But the high initial expense for this unit makes it prohibitive to do the job yourself.

## COLD STARTING PROBLEMS

The bulb is down to $-10°F$, or perhaps merely to $+10°F$, as you slip shivering behind the wheel. You turn the ignition key to preglow position and the glow plug panel light goes on, along with the "WAIT" signal. It's a considerably longer preglow wait than in less frigid weather—thirty seconds, perhaps, by count—before the "WAIT" light finally flicks out and you're ready to start. You turn the key to the START position. Under the hood, the starter motor slowly cranks the engine. Nothing happens. Absent is the comforting throb you've come to expect as, on other starts, the diesel fired and revved to idle's 600–700 rpm. The engine won't start. Sitting there in the chill, you know it won't—not with another ten cranks, or another twenty.

Cold starting problems plague the diesel as well as the gasoline engine. But with diesels, winter hard starts are more common, and they needn't be. Providing you anticipate cold weather, your diesel should start almost as easily at $-10°F$ as at summer's $+70°F$. First is the matter of fuel. Summer-grade diesel #2, as we've explained, "clouds" (forms wax-like crystals) and virtually stops flowing at about $+20°F$ (its "pour point"). "Winterized" #2 diesel fuel, blended to have a lower cloud and pour point, generally works well down to about $+3°F$. Below that—in fact below the normal nonwinterized temperature range of #2 (below $+20°F$)— switch to diesel #1, if available. Obviously, if the fuel you're using won't flow, or if it does flow but forms filter- and injector-clogging wax particles, fuel isn't reaching the combustion chambers.

But let's assume that your engine is properly fueled for winter, that long before the onset of cold you switched to a winter-grade lube oil and that, last night, your engine's block heater was plugged in, warming the block and crankcase. These assumptions made, the problem is likely the battery. Cold has sapped its vitality, and precisely when it must crank your diesel at least as fast as it did at more moderate temperatures. A battery fully charged at 80°F has lost 35 percent of its power at freezing temperatures (32°F) and 60 percent of its power at 0°F. Yet it is in cold weather that a diesel needs fast cranking if it is to start. For, unlike the spark-ignited fuel charge of the gasoline engine, the diesel's fuel charge, ignited solely by the heat of compression, requires within the cylinders about 725°F for combustion. A slowly cranked diesel (as when a battery is weak) simply can't develop compressive heat enough to ignite the fuel charge. Moreover, the cold metal of the engine itself acts as a "heat sink," absorbing in its chill mass some of the heat created even by slowly cranked pistons.

Thus, while any engine—gasoline or diesel—is harder to start in cold weather, the diesel is especially so. Normally, say down to 0°F, the block heater is enough to warm the engine to a quick start. Subzero temperatures may call for something more. Available are a number of cold-weather warmers designed to maintain engine and component temperatures close to what they were in summer. Thus maintained, a diesel will start as readily in winter as in summer. Most diesel warming devices are adaptations of similar gasoline engine devices. Before buying any such device, be sure it's designed to fit your particular engine.

Here are a few of the most used engine-warming aids:

*Block heater:* Warms crankcase, its lube oil and, if properly sized to the engine, takes some of the chill off the rest of the engine as well. Factory-installed block heaters, standard equipment in most new diesel engine vehicles, are sized to the engines they warm. See "How to Use Your Diesel's Block Heater."

*Dipstick lube oil heaters:* This immersion-type heater, used either as a primary or auxiliary (to block heater) engine oil and crankcase warmer, replaces the engine's usual dipstick to keep engine oil warm overnight. Figure 4.22 shows how it works. Low-cost and often quite efficient, the dipstick heater plugs into any convenient electrical outlet. It fits most diesels, including diesel conversions, but not factory equipped with block heaters. The 90-watt heater element fits engine oil stick openings of ¼-inch diameter or larger. The element's stainless steel flexible tube (much like the oil dipstick it replaces) heats oil and air in the crankcase. To install, remove the engine's dipstick, insert heater's element in its place, and plug into any 110-volt electrical outlet. It is important to begin operating heater when engine oil is still warm. Check for heater hood clearance before closing the hood,

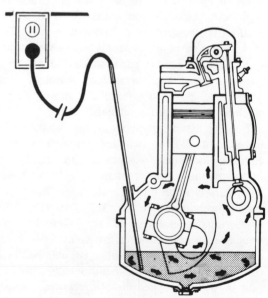

**Fig. 4.22** Operation of dipstick engine oil heater. (Courtesy Five Star Mfg. Co.)

and also make sure no wires come into contact with the heater element. The heater may be plugged in and left operating all night. *Before* starting engine, remove the oil heater element and wipe clean of oil or sludge. Replace engine's normal dipstick.

*Battery warmers:* They maintain battery temperature at near summer temperature, preventing loss of battery, thus cranking, power. There are several types of battery warmers, all of them wired for 110 volts. One type is an *electrically warmed plate* (plate-type battery heater) on which the battery sits. A kind of automotive "hot plate," it is probably most effective in moderate cold temperatures,

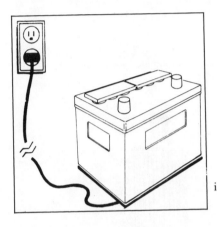

**Fig. 4.23** Battery warmer aids diesel starting in winter. (Courtesy Five Star Mfg. Co.)

say down to −10°F. Plate warmers are available in various wattage models, usually from 50 watts up. *Blanket-type battery warmers,* somewhat akin to an electric blanket, wrap around the battery. Most common are 80–160-watt models (higher wattages for oversized batteries). Blanket warmers are generally more efficient than the plate type, keeping batteries to fast-crank temperature even in extreme subzero weather.

**Fig. 4.24** An electric blanket type battery warmer. (Courtesy Phillips Temro, Inc.)

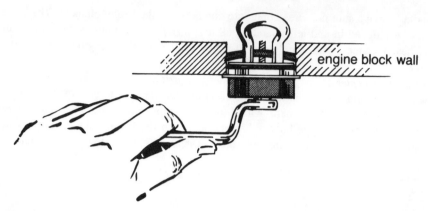

**Fig. 4.25** Installing frost plug type coolant heater in engine block. (Courtesy Phillips Temro, Inc.)

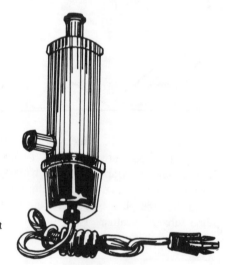

**Fig. 4.26** External tank type coolant heater. (Courtesy Phillips Temro, Inc.)

**Fig. 4.27** Lower radiator hose engine heater. (Courtesy Phillips Temro, Inc.)

*Coolant (water) system heaters:* Easily installed on most diesel engines, these immersion-type heaters warm coolant, preventing water pump and radiator freeze-up. Most are designed to be threaded or bolted into one of the coolant system's engine block plugs, usually as replacement for a freeze or frost plug. More popular, but sometimes less efficient, are the external types, inserted into one of the coolant system's hoses, generally the lower radiator or heater hose. The best of these hose-inserted heaters do a good job, but seldom as well as the freeze plug-inserted coolant heaters. The worst of the hose-inserted are a waste of your money and the time it takes to install them. Whatever their quality, most must be installed at least four inches *below* the point from which coolant is taken from the lower radiator; if one is mounted higher, coolant system circulation may be impaired. External coolant heater ratings begin at about 750 watts.

*Diesel fuel warmers:* Designed to keep diesel fuel warm, fuel heaters permit year-around use of "summer" #2 diesel, which is somewhat lower priced than either winterized #2 or #1, and gets about 5 percent better road mileage. In extreme cold (far north and Alaska), fuel may be warmed by fuel-tank warm-

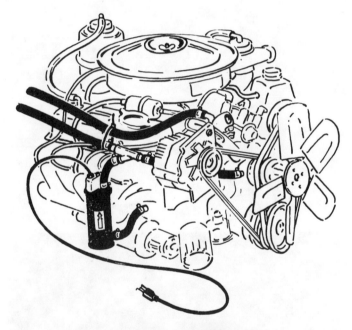

Heaters recommended (by watt/amp rating)
for various cooling system capacities

| VOLTS | WATTS | AMPS | COOLING SYSTEM CAPACITY |
|---|---|---|---|
| 120 | 500 | 4.16 | Up to 18 qts. |
| 120 | 850 | 7.00 | Up to 18 qts. |
| 120 | 1000 | 8.3 | 16 - 25 qts. |
| 240 | 1000 | 4.16 | 16 - 25 qts. |
| 120 | 1500 | 12.5 | 26 - 40 qts. |
| 240 | 1500 | 6.25 | 26 - 40 qts. |

**Fig. 4.28** Externally mounted engine heater. (Courtesy Phillips Temro, Inc.)

ing/circulating devices. Elsewhere, fuel returned from the injection pump to the tank (surplus fuel that wasn't injected), helps warm the fuel tank. Available, too, are pour-point depressants, fuel additives that lower the temperature at which diesel fuel begins to "gel" (form wax-like crystals). Most popular, however, is the fuel-line warmer, inserted between the fuel tank and the engine's fuel pump. Warmed by heat from the engine's coolant system, the best of the fuel-line warmers can keep #2 diesel to near summer temperature (and viscosity) down to perhaps as low as −40°F.

*Starting fluid:* Every Owner's Manual warns DO NOT USE STARTING FLUID to start your diesel engine. Even the packagers of starter fluids caution (usually on the product's can) that the fluid should not be used in engines equipped with glow plugs, and *that* includes *every* passenger car and light truck diesel. Many truckers, whose diesel engines are far heftier than the average car or pickup diesel, use them, and do many diesel car owners. Risky to user and to engine as the "starting aids" are, they often get a diesel going where virtually nothing else will, because starting fluid—most are ether or ether based, sometimes

**Fig. 4.29** Cold start fluid injection kit (*above*) and installed (*bottom*). (Courtesy Kold Ban International, Inc.)

mixed with heptane and Arctic-grade oil—ignites at a far lower temperature (a mere 360°F or so) than required to ignite diesel fuel (725°F). Even a weak-batteried, slow-cranking engine often develops heat of compression enough to ignite the starting fluid, which in turn ignites the diesel fuel to start the engine, almost invariably.

But simply squirting or spraying the fluid into your diesel's air intake (usually located inside the air cleaner's filter) risks more than premature glow plug ignition resulting in a fire or explosion that can seriously injure the sprayer; it risks damage to the engine in a number of ways. Too great a "slug" of starting ether, and the resultant detonation (nothing less than an explosion) can crack pistons or piston rings and even bend connecting rods. Sometimes, too, the fluid reaches only one or two cylinders, starting them, but not the others. Whereas the least that can happen is irregular running and diesel knock, the worst is serious damage to those few cylinders detonated by a super charge of fluid. In short, you can ruin your diesel trying to start it in cold weather.

If, against all Owner Manual warnings (and this book's admonition, as well), you either must use a starting fluid (say, block heater or no, your engine simply won't start), or you occasionally elect to do so in sub-subzero weather, here are two methods, one of them quite safe, one only fairly safe, that are better than unmeasured ether administration:

*Fairly safe:* With the starter engaged and the engine cranking, inject only a *minute* amount of the starting aid—administered in a measured, "safe ratio"—into the engine's air intake. A "safe" ratio can be figured in several ways. If you know your engine's intake air volume (how much air, by volume, it ingests when cranking), then the ratio is 91 parts starting fluid to every 1 million parts of intake air. For most aerosol cans in which most starter fluid comes, that probably means one quick, *partial* squirt, no more. Better, knowing your engine's cubic inch displacement (it's given in your Owner's Manual), administer only a mere 3 cubic centimeters (3 cc) of starter fluid for engines of 500 CID or less. Don't guess whether or not one squirt or half a squirt from the starter can adds up to 3 cc; measure it. Into a flask marked in cubic centimeters, measure how much fluid is

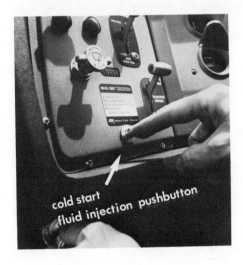

cold start
fluid injection pushbutton

**Fig. 4.30** The cold start fluid injection system is operated by dash-mounted push button. (Courtesy Kold Ban International, Inc.)

released with one squirt, how much with half a squirt. Manual injection of starter fluid has one major drawback. Two are required to do the job—one person injecting, the other inside the vehicle to turn the ignition switch to START.

*Quite safe:* Safer, surer, wholly automatic, and a driver-only operation, the new starter fluid injection systems do the measuring and injection for you. The best of these systems automatically inject the proper amount of starter fluid based on the actual volume of air being ingested by the engine during cranking. Automatic injection virtually assures that all cylinders will be started, not just a few. A dash-mounted push button initiates a single, measured starter fluid injection. Even here, the system's advantages can be overridden by an impatient driver who pushes the control button two or three times, instead of the prescribed once. Do that and a "quite safe" system becomes as engine risky as an unmeasured injection.

Certainly the majority of diesel car or light truck owners will never need more aid in starting than their diesel's own factory-installed block heater. Nor does it make sense investing time or money in auxiliary heaters and warming devices you don't need. For those few who may need them, the warmers can ensure a warm start, even in coldest weather.

## BLOCK HEATERS

The block heater built into many diesel vehicles is designed to warm the engine's block area, including the crankcase. Block-warming at temperatures below freezing (32°F) warms lube oil to near normal, warm-weather fluidity, making diesel starting easier. While primarily warming the diesel's block and crankcase, block heaters take some of the chill off the engine's cylinders as well. Less heat is absorbed by the engine during glow plug preheating, and the engine starts sooner, reducing the usual winter prestart wait.

Under the hood you'll find the plug-in end of the electrical cord that powers the block heater. Plug it into any 110-volt electrical outlet—your garage's, or one of those provided by many cold-area motels, ski, and winter recreational resorts—and your engine stays warm overnight, ready for morning's start-up. The usual three-prong, heavy-duty heater cord installed in most diesel vehicles is far too short to reach any convenient electrical outlet. You'll need an extension, often three-prong, heavy-duty (not flimsy lamp-type) extension cord fifty feet or longer.

Block heaters factory installed in most diesel (as well as gas engine) vehicles are sized to warm the block over a wide range of cold-weather temperatures, often down to −40°F. If you buy an immersion or other type block heater, its rated wattage must be sized to the cubic inch displacement of your engine and to your locality's anticipated lowest temperatures. The larger your engine and the lower local temperatures, the higher-wattage heater you'll need. To reduce utility bills, some diesel owners buy two of the immersion-type heaters—one, of fairly low wattage, for use in usual winter weather and another, of higher wattage rating, for winter's coldest temperatures. Low-wattage block heaters draw only modest current, reducing utility bills except on those few days when the higher-wattage heater is required.

Table 4.2 shows recommended block heater wattage ratings for various-size engines and various winter temperatures.

#### Table 4.2—Sizing an Immersion-type Block Heater to Your Engine

| Engine's Cubic Inch Displacement | Recommended Wattage at Various Temperatures | | | | |
|---|---|---|---|---|---|
| | 0° F | −10° F | −20° F | −30° F | −40° F |
| 100 | 100 | 150 | 200 | 250 | 300 |
| 200 | 200 | 300 | 400 | 500 | 600 |
| 300 | 300 | 450 | 600 | 750 | 900 |
| 400 | 400 | 600 | 800 | 1,000 | 1,200 |

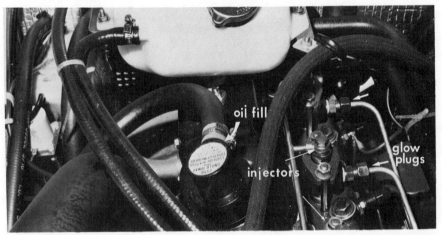

**Fig. 4.31** The Peugeot 504D is laid out under the hood for easy owner maintenance. (Photograph by James Joseph)

Following are charts based on manufacturers' recommendations for diesel and diesel-related maintenance.

#### Peugeot 504 Diesel
##### Diesel/Diesel Related Maintenance

| | |
|---|---|
| *Regular Maintenance Intervals* (by mileage/ kilometers) | After first 600 miles (1,000 km) <br> After 3,000 miles (5,000 km) <br> Thereafter, every 12,500 miles (20,000 km) |
| *Oil Change* | Every 3,000 miles (5,000 km) |
| *Oil Filter Change* | After first 3,000 miles (5,000 km) <br> Thereafter, at every other oil change, thus every 6,000 miles (10,000 km), or more frequently in dusty and other severe driving conditions |

**Peugeot 504 Diesel (continued)**

*Diesel/Diesel Related Maintenance*

| | |
|---|---|
| Recommended Viscosity Types of Lubricating Oils | *Year-around use oil: SAE 10W-40* or following special temperature recommendations: If temperature above 32°F, SAE 30 Prolonged freezing range (32°F to 14°F/), SAE 20 Below 14°F, SAE 10 |
| Air Filter Change | Every 12,500 miles (20,000 km), sooner under dusty conditions |
| Recommended Diesel Fuels and Fuel Winterizing | Only commercial-grade #2 or #1 diesel fuel In extreme cold weather, in absence of #1 diesel or if only summer (nonwinterized) #2 available, may add up to 20% kerosene to #2 summer fuel; see your dealer for possible other approved mixes, such as regular gasoline added to diesel #2 fuel |
| Special coolant-use (antifreeze) caution | *Use only Peugeot #9730-70 antifreeze;* use of any other antifreeze may void warranty |
| Recommended or Required Special Maintenance | Fuel filter must be replaced every 12,500 miles (20,000 km), sooner if poor fuel causes clogging Fuel lines must be bled every 12,500 miles; see your Owner's Manual or elsewhere in this book for procedure |

## A.D.S.: THE CERTIFIED EXPERTS

Logically, if you suspect trouble with your diesel's injection or fuel system, with injectors, governor, or turbocharger, you should take your diesel back to the dealer where you bought it. Hopefully, your diesel car, pickup truck or motor home will still be under warranty. Hopefully, too, the dealer who sold you the vehicle will have on premises the equipment and know-how to repair what's wrong. Things, however, don't necessarily work that way or that logically. Nor, when problems occur (your car begins to smoke excessively, let's say), will you necessarily be within easy, warranty-covered reach of a diesel dealership. At times like that you'll be thankful for A.D.S., the unique, now 700-member Association of Diesel Specialists whose members specialize in the precision work of diesel engine maintenance. Among A.D.S. member specialities are the testing, repair, calibration, and rebuilding of fuel injection equipment, including injectors, governors, turbochargers, and other precision diesel systems and components.

Any good mechanic, or even the diesel owner, can remove a suspected injector and replace it with a new one. Testing an injector for leaks, proper spray pattern, and fuel delivery is quite another thing. The "other things"—most of them precision chores—are what A.D.S. shops, big and small, in more than 200 North American towns and cities, do best. Many dealerships, in fact, send out their precision diesel work to local A.D.S. member shops. And while A.D.S. members have grown up with big diesels—engines powering highway, construction, and farm and industrial equipment—many are now geared to handle precision work on smaller diesel components.

## Chevrolet Cheyenne Diesel Pickup

(with 350 CID, V-8 diesel, and other GM pickups, including GMC light-duty trucks using same diesel):

### *Diesel/Diesel Related Maintenance*

| | |
|---|---|
| *Regular Maintenance Intervals* (by mileage/ kilometers) | *Note:* Virtually identical to maintenance for Oldsmobile Toronado Every 3,000 miles (4,800 km) |
| *Oil Change* | Every 3,000 miles (4,800 km) |
| *Oil Filter Change* | Change with every oil change |
| *Recommended Viscosity Types of Lubricating Oils* | Use only engine oils labeled SE *and* CC<br>Do NOT use an oil if labeled only SE or only CC<br>Do not use an oil if designation *CD* appears anywhere on the can<br>Do not use any supplemental oil additives<br>*Year-around use* (at temperatures above 32°F)<br>  SAE 30 SE/CC<br>  from 75°F to below −20°F: SAE 10W-30 SE/CC |
| *Air Filter Change* | Every 30,000 miles (48,000 km); sooner, if dusty or sandy driving environment |
| *Recommended Diesel Fuels and Fuel Winterizing* | Only Diesel #2, winterized #2 or #1<br>Use Diesel #2 if you expect temperatures above 20°F; use Diesel #1 if you expect temperatures below 20°F<br>Do not use #2 below 20°F unless it is "winterized" |
| *Fuel Filter Change* | Every 24,000 miles (38,600 km) |
| *Recommended or Required Special Maintenance* | Engine idle speed adjust: at first 3,000 miles (4,800 km) check; at 30,000 miles (48,000 km); thereafter, every 30,000 miles |

The logo designating a local A.D.S member (the letters A.D.S. superimposed with a diesel injector) signifies a certified expert—the certification by A.D.S. international headquarters in Kansas City, Missouri. Membership in A.D.S. anywhere in the world (members are now on all continents) signifies that a shop has met the association's increasingly tough Minimum Service Standards. Almost always those standards imply special schooling and technical updating through A.D.S. or local instructors trained by A.D.S.

Since 1972, moreover, most A.D.S shops have participated in the association's Reciprocal Inter-Shop Warranty program. If one A.D.S. member repairs your diesel engine's injector pump and a failure occurs within the warranty period, repair will be made by another A.D.S. member, should you and your car by then be beyond the territory or easy reach of the member originally doing the work. Although the Inter-Shop Warranty isn't as codified as warranties offered by the major car manufacturers, generally it is being increasingly recognized and honored by A.D.S. shops.

If, symptomatically, what ails your diesel lies within the component specialities of this coast-to-coast network of independent precision-component repair specialists, an A.D.S. member shop is often the place to go.

The association has published a directory, included at the end of this book and is available to nonmembers at $15, that lists current A.D.S. members in the United States and Canada. For names of new members not listed or for A.D.S. members in Mexico or abroad, contact A.D.S. international headquarters:

Association of Diesel Specialists
1719 West 91st Place
Kansas City, MO 64114
Phone: (816) 444-3500
Executive director: Betty Puckett

# Chapter 5

# Driving the Diesels

All diesel vehicles have their own peculiar traits and idiosyncrasies. Although these test drives do not include every diesel available, they are a representative sampling of what's available from subcompacts to luxury diesels to trucks. Ride with us while we sample the world of diesels.

## VOLKSWAGEN RABBIT DIESEL

*Description:* Front-wheel drive, four-door sedan with manual five-speed transmission

*Diesel engine:* Transversely mounted, in-line, 4-cylinder, 90 cubic inch displacement, with 23:1 compression ratio, rated 48 hp at 5,000 rpm, developing 56.5 ft/lbs of torque at 3,000 rpm

*Fuel economy:* EPA: 41 mpg city/55 mpg highway

With an EPA 55 mpg highway, the diesel Rabbit is far and away the road's fuel economy miser. The turbocharged version, already in the works and EPA tested, will up the payoff to at least 63 mpg highway—making any other car a mileage tortoise by comparison. The fact is, for high mpg there's really nothing available anywhere in the world the match of the Rabbit, a true international car, with sales (under its outside-North American name: Golf) in some 130 countries. Like the Beetle it replaced, the Rabbit is a wonderfully put together, utilitarian, fun car.

Although soon to be turbocharged, the five-speed manual diesel Rabbit, in this tester's opinion, gets up and goes fully as hippity-hop as its gas engine hutch counterpart, a supreme compliment in itself. Some gas engine Rabbit owners, having driven the diesel Rabbit, find it less hippity—but the difference, if any, is piddling in the diesel's five-gear version. The four-speed manual diesel Rabbit, however, definitely lags in road performance, especially uphill. The dieselized

121

**Fig. 5.1**   The highway fuel miser—the VW Rabbit diesel.

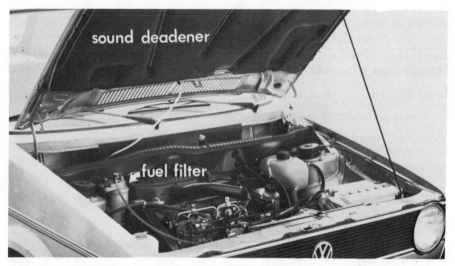

**Fig. 5.2**   VW Rabbit's diesel fits neatly under the hood. Most maintenance chore areas are easily accessible. The knob on the bottom of the fuel filter makes it easy to purge the filter of trapped water.

Rabbit is full of pleasant surprises—like quick acceleration (0 to 50 mph in a bit over eleven seconds), a top speed (which it can apparently do effortlessly all day) of better than 85 mph, and torque enough, if you drop from cruising overdrive fifth gear down to fourth, to get up most grades lickety-split. In the five-gear box, the first three gears are direct drive, the final two (fourth and fifth), overdrive, as a fuel-economizing diesel transmission should be.

The Rabbit isn't the road's quietest diesel, but it is scarcely noisier than gas

### Volkswagen Rabbit Diesel

(named GOLF outside North America):

#### Diesel/Diesel Related Maintenance

| | |
|---|---|
| *Regular*<br>*Maintenance*<br>*Intervals*<br>   (by mileage/<br>   kilometers) | After initial 1,000-mile (1,500-km) servicing: every 7,500 miles (12,000 km) or every six months, whichever comes first<br>*Note:* The VW Rabbit diesel's maintenance intervals and those of gas engine Rabbits are identical—a rarity for diesel vehicles |
| *Oil Change* | Every 7,500 miles (12,000 km)<br>But oil level should be checked, by dipstick, *at every fuel filling or once a week;* VW warns that oil consumption in normal operation can be "up to 2.5 quarts per 1,000 miles or 1.5 liters per 1,000 km" |
| *Oil Filter*<br>*Change* | At every *other* oil change, thus every 15,000 miles (24,000 km); sooner for extremely dusty driving conditions<br>*Note:* Pre-1980 models (before oil pressure was reduced) require torque (not just hand) tightening of replacement oil filter (to 18 ft/lbs torque) with special wrench<br>Dipstick-check oil level weekly |
| *Recommended*<br>*Viscosity*<br>*Types of*<br>*Lubricating*<br>*Oils* | Only single- or multigrade diesel lube oil labeled "For Service API/CC or Mil-L-46152"; letter-code "CC" should appear on oil can alone or in combination with other letters<br>*Year-around use* (from 14°F to 77°F: SAE 20W-50, SAE 20W-40; above 68°F: SAE 40<br>   *Some other approved diesel viscosities:*<br>      from 14°F to 50°F, SAE 20W-20<br>      from 32°F to 77°F, SAE 30 |
| *Air Filter*<br>*Change* | Replace or clean every 15,000 miles (24,000 km) or sooner if dusty driving; if cleaning, shake or air-blow clean only |
| *Recommended*<br>*Diesel Fuels*<br>*and Fuel*<br>*Winterizing* | Diesel #2, winterized #2 or #1; although use of Diesel #1 not mentioned in most Owner's Manuals, VW recently OKed its use<br>Warns against use of home heating oil or gasoline<br>OKs mixing maximum 30% regular gasoline with nonwinterized #2 diesel fuel at low ambient temperatures, but mix reduces power |
| *Fuel Filter*<br>*Change* | Every 15,000 miles (24,000 km) or one year, whichever occurs first (see note below) |
| *Recommended*<br>*or Required*<br>*Special*<br>*Maintenance* | Drain fuel filter's water separator, by hand turning filter bottom petcock, every 7,500 miles at least, more often if water in fuel is a problem in your area<br>*Note:* Owner's Manual to the contrary notwithstanding, many VW shops wrench (not just hand) tighten fuel filter—and say it's necessary |

engine Rabbits. Nonetheless, you know you're driving diesel. To us, at least, that's reassuring. And when you pull into a pump station (something diesel Rabbit owners do only about half as frequently as most), you can almost feel the other car owners turn green with envy—envy at the green you keep in your pocket, thanks to the Rabbit's 55-mpg highway economy.

The Rabbit diesel's Owner's Manual advises you, no matter what the outside

**Fig. 5.3** The 1980 Dasher, Dasher Wagon, and Rabbit Pick-up all use the same diesel engine as the Rabbit model. The Dasher Wagon is EPA-rated 36 mpg city and 49 mpg highway with manual transmission.

temperature, to start things right by pulling out the cold-start (injection advance) knob on the steering wheel's left. But we habitually forgot to follow instructions—not that we advise you to do the same—with no starting problems whatever. One gas engine habit most first-timers to the diesel Rabbit should get out of is pumping the accelerator when starting at normal temperatures, although at abnormal times (below 32°F), you should fully depress the accelerator when starting, as the manual instructs. And a habit worth acquiring after a long, hot engine excursion is to remember not to switch off the engine immediately. Rather, keep the engine idling for upwards of two minutes to let it cool. That's good advice for any diesel, not merely the Rabbit.

The Rabbit diesel gets nearly all of the experts' votes as the sturdiest, most-for-your-money, best buy among all cars, diesel *or* gasoline powered. We add our vote. Moreover, the price premium for the diesel is only $250 or so, up from its original $175 price differential when the diesel Rabbit was introduced into the United States back in 1977. For no-frills road economy and zestful go, the diesel Rabbit is in a class by itself. Nothing else on the road even comes close.

### CITROEN CX PALLAS 2500D

*Description:* Front-wheel drive, four-door, four-passenger sedan, with five-speed manual transmission

*Diesel engine:* In-line, four-cylinder, water-cooled, mounted transversely up front, rated 75 hp at 4,250 rpm, with 151 cubic inch displacement, developing 111 ft/lbs of torque at 2,000 rpm

*Fuel economy:* Approximately 33 mpg gallon combined city/highway driving (not yet EPA-tested)

A new, luxurious, brash and beautiful diesel star (with a not quite down-to-earth price: about $18,000) and on U.S. roads, where it meets federal standards in all fifty states, the French automaker's first production diesel—if you can find one.

### Citroen CX Pallas 2500D (diesel)

#### *Diesel/Diesel Related Maintenance*

| | |
|---|---|
| *Regular Maintenance Intervals* (by mileage/ kilometers) | First 600 miles (1,000 km)<br>Thereafter, every 3,000 miles (5,000 km)<br>   Every 6,000 miles (10,000 km):<br>     a. fuel filter change<br>     b. oil filter change<br>   Every 12,000 miles (20,000 km):<br>     a. air filter change<br>     b. gearbox/transmission lube change |
| *Oil Change* | Every 3,000 miles (5,000 km) |
| *Oil Filter Change* | Every 6,000 miles (10,000 km) |
| *Recommended Viscosity Types of Lubricating Oils* | *Year-around use oil:* (all diesel grade)<br>   to 21°F, 20W-40<br>   from 32°F to 5°F, 10W-30<br>   below 8°F, special brand S10-W (see your dealer) |
| *Recommended Diesel Fuels and Fuel Winterizing* | Only #2 or #1 diesel |
| *Engine Break-in Caution* | During first 600 miles (1,000 km), do not exceed these gear speeds:<br>   first, 18 mph; second, 34 mph; third, 52 mph; fourth, 74 mph; fifth, 80 mph |
| *Recommended or Required Special Maintenance* | Recommends strict maximum/minimum dipstick (lube oil) readings<br>Warns it is "imperative to stop immediately" if any engine monitoring<br>   warning light goes on |

The waiting list is understandably long for this stellar performer that is almost too quick to be diesel, which can get to 60 mph in under twenty seconds, to its top 100 mph shortly thereafter, as you slip smoothly into the highest gear (fifth) of its five-speed front-wheel-drive transaxle transmission. Smooth getaway and road-holding stability are due partly to front wheels wider apart (by 4-½ inches) than the rears, a width difference not readily discernible at casual glance. Nor, for that matter, is this quiet engine new Citroen discernibly diesel, it runs so quietly.

**Fig. 5.4** The "D" in the Citroen CX 2500 Pallas is the only giveaway to the diesel under the hood. (Photograph by James Joseph)

**Fig. 5.5** Under the hood the Citroen CX 2500D Pallas is all diesel. The transversely mounted engine powers front-wheel drive.

Combined with road alacrity and gas engine performance, the Citroen CX (the "CX" for "coefficient of drag," denoting a minimum-wind-drag, four-door body design) still manages typical, although not as yet EPA-tested, diesel fuel economy: in the 33 mpg range. With its eighteen-gallon (68-liter) diesel fuel tank, the range between pump stops is a comforting 550+ miles. Comforting, too, is the diesel CX's glow plug warm-up (fast), engine warm-up (almost as fast), and all but smokeless getaway. A dash-panel cluster of seventeen instrument warning lights, plus engine oil pressure gauge—and a kind of cockpit environment, what with the molded U-shape dashboard and the steering wheel dead center of the U—gives the CX's driver quick insight into diesel and road performance.

The Citroen CX, while exotic in body, is also a strictly functional diesel machine. For example, the engine's air intake grill is flush mounted into the hood, well to the right (passenger side) of the hood's centerline, a not unpleasing off-center arrangement. Since that's where the diesel's intake is, that's where the grill is, and there's no design nonsense (like concealed intake air piping) to camouflage the fact. The Citroen CX Pallas 2500D is road proof that you can have gas engine (and perhaps better) performance without turbocharging—and diesel fuel economy, too.

### MERCEDES-BENZ 300SD TURBODIESEL

*Description:* Four-door, five-passenger sedan, with automatic four-speed transmission

*Diesel engine:* Turbocharged 5-cylinder, water-cooled, rated 120 hp net at 4,350 rpm, with 183 cubic inch displacement, a 21.5-to-1 compression ratio, developing 170 ft/lbs of torque at 2,400 rpm

*Fuel economy:* Approximately 26 mpg EPA combined city/highway

This is unquestionably, Mercedes-Benz's diesel masterpeice. That's a first impression as the turbocharged 300SD responds to your first nudge of the accelerator. The impression lasts to become a conviction in less than a handful of miles. With its new Turbodiesel—at 3,785 pounds, the heaviest in the Mercedes passenger diesel line—Mercedes has achieved gasoline engine road performance (and then some) plus fuel economy, with seeming power to spare and in .656 horsepower per cubic inch of displacement has produced the highest power ratio for any diesel engine its size. And turbocharging (this is, you'll remember, the world's first turbo production automobile) makes the difference.

There's no sluggishness on the getaway here: Acceleration from a standing stoplight start will beat virtually anything through the intersection. And there's barely any diesel noise—virtually none from inside and not much from outside, ei-

### Mercedes-Benz 300SD Turbodiesel

#### *Diesel/Diesel Related Maintenance*

| | |
|---|---|
| *Regular Maintenance Intervals* (by mileage/ kilometers) | *Note:* Chart shows Mercedes-Benz' NEW extended maintenance schedule<br>Initially, at 800–1,000 miles (1,300–1,600 km)<br>Then at 5,000 miles (8,000 km)<br>Thereafter, every 15,000 miles (24,000 km) except for lube oil and lube filter changes every 5,000 miles |
| *Oil Change* | Every 5,000 miles (8,000 km), but at least once a year if using year-around multigrade oil; otherwise, twice a year (in spring and fall)<br>*Special note:* Every 4,000 miles/6,400 km in severe operating conditions when filter *not* changed at every oil change |
| *Oil Filter Change* | Every 5,000 miles (8,000 km) at time of regular oil change or more frequently under severe operating conditions, including poor roads, dusty/muddy conditions; heavy in-town/short distance driving |
| *Recommended Viscosity Types of Lubricating Oils* | Diesel-type lube oil grades approved by Mercedes-Benz; see your dealer<br>*Year-around use oil:*<br>to −4°F, SAE 10W-40, 10W-50<br>below 14°F, SAE 5W-20, 5W-30<br>*Some other approved viscosities:*<br>Where temperature constantly exceeds 32°F, SAE 30, 20W-40 and 20W-50<br>to 23°F, SAE 15W-40, 15W-50 |
| *Recommended Diesel Fuels and Fuel Winterizing* | Commercial (filling station) #2 or #1 diesel<br>Commercial winterized #2 should give no trouble as low as 3°F<br>If below 3°F, and no #1 is available, and only summer (nonwinterized) #2 is available, kerosene or regular gasoline may be mixed with summer #2, at mixing ratios no more than 30% regular gasoline or more than 50% kerosene<br>Not recommended: premium diesel fuels, heating oil, marine diesel fuel, etc.<br>Change main fuel filter every 30,000 miles |
| *Recommended or Required Special Maintenance* | If car runs out of fuel, fuel system must be bled of air bubbles, using primer pump under the hood; see Owner's Manual or elsewhere in this book for procedure<br>*Special maintenance service:* Every 15,000 miles |

**Fig. 5.6**   The Mercedes-Benz 300SD is the state of the art in diesel passenger cars.

**Fig. 5.7**   The 300SD's manual stop button is for emergency shut-off of the engine. It's a bright red label you can't miss.

ther, even though under the hood the turbocharger (built in the United States by the Garrett AiResearch Division) may at top engine speeds be whirling at better than 100,000 rpms. But it's on the open road—we tested for miles on the freeways—that the Turbodiesel 300SD surprises. It gets quickly to legal (and even a bit illegal, in the mid-60s) road speed, stays there, and hardly works at all doing it. Not once in our testing at legal speed and over did the 300SD's dashboard tachometer nudge above the 3,000-rpm mark. That's virtually half engine top speed. It would have been fun to have played Autoban (Germany's famed highways have no speed limit) and pushed the 300SD to its speedometer's maximum: 200 km an hour, or about 125 mph. Yet even with the speedometer showing 64 mph, the tachometer's pointer stayed below 3,000 rpms.

The 300SD has that heavy car feel that many a sized-down Detroit product has sacrificed for mileage. Mercedes gets both, the luxury car feel plus fuel economy, with its Turbodiesel. A lovely road machine, you tell yourself (and, if you're testing, your tape recorder), and one whose true diesel (not a gasoline engine remade to perform like a diesel), with proper care, should take the average owner a decade of miles (150,000 at least) before it needs any serious looking at.

With the automatic transmission selector in the "S" (for "Slope") position, the transmission upshifts only to as high as third gear, not to fourth, drive. It's the gear position Mercedes suggests for so-so (but not really steep) slopes, particularly if they're continuous. With the selector lever in "S" position—and we tried it—and with the accelerator depressed to nearly full throttle, second gear covers a wider speed range than when in "D" (for "Drive"). With the automatic selector in L (for "Low"), the transmission upshifts only to second, the gear Mercedes suggests for steep mountain going, especially if you're pulling a trailer. The same gear is suggested for any severe operating condition, including snow going, and as the braking position on extremely steep downgrades.

But even on the downgrades, the turbocharged 300SD is strictly upbeat—a car that is all luxury and all diesel, and delivers the promise of both.

## OLDSMOBILE TORONADO DIESEL

*Description:* Front-wheel drive, four-door sedan with automatic transmission

*Diesel engine:* Oldsmobile's V-8, 5.7-litre, water-cooled diesel, rated 120 hp at 3,600 rpm, with 350 cubic inch displacement and a 22.3:1 compression ratio, delivering 220 ft/lbs of torque at 1,600 rpm

*Fuel economy:* EPA: 21 mpg city/29 mpg highway

The Oldsmobile front-wheel-drive Toronado, which earns a rave rating from this tester to add to bushels of raves from satisfied (one magazine survey called them "ecstatic") Toronado diesel owners, is perhaps the most owner-satisfying diesel anywhere on world highways today.

The Toronado's V-8, which powers many other General Motors diesels, is the most powerful (at 120 hp) and biggest (at 350 CID nonturbo) diesel in production automobiles. Although as yet unturbocharged, its eight cylinders gift the Toronado with gas engine quick acceleration and with road performance as good as or better than a gas engine, and for its heft (more than two tons of luxury) with superb fuel economy. Moreover, unlike that of some other diesels, the diesel Toronado's fuel economy can be compared directly with the same size engine (also a V-8, also 350 CID) which powers gas engine Toronados. The diesel, in fact, is a rework of the gas engine 350 CID, and both are from GM/Oldsmobile engine works.

The gas engine Toronado in 1979 had an EPA rating of 16 mpg city/22 mpg highway, against the diesel 350-CID V-8's 21 mpg city/29 mpg highway—a 35–40 percent diesel mileage bonus. Once behind the Toronado's wheel, you find yourself making another diesel-versus-gasoline comparison, which goes to prove

**Fig. 5.8**  The Oldsmobile Toronado Diesel was introduced in 1979.

## Oldsmobile Toronado Diesel

(350 CID V-8 diesel). Applies also to *all other GM cars and pickups using this engine:*

### Diesel/Diesel Related Maintenance

| | |
|---|---|
| *Regular Maintenance Intervals* (by mileage/ kilometers) | Every 3,000 miles (4,800 km)<br>*Special lubrication maintenance interval:*<br>  Unless performed sooner, chassis lubrication at maximum 7,500 miles or twelve months, whichever first (relay and tire rods, idler arm, upper and lower ball joints, etc.) |
| *Oil Change* | Every 3,000 miles (4,800 km) |
| *Oil Filter Change* | Change with every oil change |
| *Recommended Viscosity/ Types of Lubricating Oils* | *Special notice.* "Use ONLY engine oils labeled SE *and* CC. Do not use any other type of oil. *DO NOT use an oil if the designation CD appears anywhere on the oil can.* Using any type of oil other than SE/CC may affect your warranty."<br>*Year-around use* (at temperatures above 32°F<br>  SAE 30 SE/CC<br>*Some other approved viscosities:*<br>  below 32°F, SAE 15W-40 SE/CC<br>  below 0°F, use block heater, or if vehicle not equipped with block heater, use SAE 10W-30 SE/CC |
| *Air Filter Change* | Every 30,000 miles (48,000 km); sooner if particularly dusty driving conditions |
| *Recommended Diesel Fuels and Fuel Winterizing* | Only Diesel #2, winterized #2 or #1<br>  Unless "winterized," do NOT use #2 at temperatures below 20°F<br>*Special notice:* "Do not try to use home heating oil or gasoline in your diesel engine. Heating oil may cause engine damage. Use of any fuel other than diesel fuel may affect your warranty" |
| *Recommended or Required Special Maintenance* | Change diesel fuel filter every 30,000 miles (48,000 km)<br>Does not recommend that engine be washed; but if you must, never except when engine is cool—washing even a warm engine may damage fuel injection pump |

what diesel insiders have been saying for years, that substituting the same CID-size diesel for a gas engine will give you acceleration, pickup, and performance equal to that of the gas engine, plus fuel economy. And the Toronado proves yet another point of diesel contention, that a diesel engine need not intrude audibly, given enough careful attention to engineering and "barriering" against sound. The Toronado's V-8 is scarcely audible, inside or outside the car.

Five minutes in the driver's seat, and it's as though you've driven this car a lifetime. There's very little "diesel" that requires either getting used to or adjusting to. With its new fast glow plugs, part of what Olds dubs its "fast start system," the Toronado's dashboard WAIT light flicks out and START comes on, even with the temperature outside hovering near the 0°F mark, in less than ten seconds—six seconds, says Olds. That's one tenth the previous sixty-second wait at the same chill temperature required of Olds' pre-1979 slowpoke warming plugs.

If the Toronado and other GM cars and pickups going with the same powerplant

**Fig. 5.9** The Oldsmobile Diesel Cars use a dual battery set-up for required cranking power. The 5.7-litre (350 cu. in.) V-8 GM diesel is used in Oldsmobile, Buick, and Cadillac passenger cars and Chevrolet and GMC trucks.

have one drawback, it's GM's trailer towing restriction, limiting trailer weight to a mere 2,000 pounds, a considerable limitation for economy-minded owners who want to tow a roomy bed-and-board trailer at low diesel mileage cost. Even with trailering aside, the Toronado is what a diesel sedan ought to be: performance, luxury, *and* fuel economy. And its price—$10,000–$15,000 less than many other luxury diesel cars—is definitely right.

**Fig. 5.10** The GM diesels have a heater cord and plug, and a warning on the air cleaner against the use of starter fluids. (Photograph by James Joseph)

### INTERNATIONAL HARVESTER TURBO-SCOUT (TERRA)

*Description:* Two-door, half-ton pickup with four-wheel drive and four-speed manual transmission

*Diesel engine:* Turbocharged Nissan 6-33T, 6-cylinder inline, rated 101 hp at

**Fig. 5.11**   The International Scout Terra, Scout Traveler and Terra Pick-up are all available with a turbocharged 6-cylinder Nissan diesel.

3,800 rpm, with 198 cubic inches displacement, a 22 : 1 compression ratio, developing 175 ft/lbs of torque at 2,200 rpm

*Fuel economy:* EPA: 22 mpg combined; 24 mpg highway

A driver's first impression of the Terra pickup is "Pick up . . . and go." The Terra is a handsomely sturdy half-ton sports/utility vehicle introduced in 1980, along with International's similarly powered Scout Traveler and Scout II utility wagons, with the first turbocharged version of Nissan's dependable 6-cylinder diesel engine. The new International family scores a sizable first: first four-wheel drive (it's standard in all models) production vehicles with turbo-diesel.

Pickup buffs who commute via the expressways will find the Terra a more than satisfactory choice for any family's first or second vehicle. But Terra's name ("terra" is Latin for "earth") suggests its true territory: the recreational "out there"—or wherever rough going goes best with the twin goodies of high diesel torque at low (2,200) rpms and four-wheel drive engaged with a second stick alongside the Terra's four-speed manual shifter. The turbo-diesel Terra skittles with typical turbo alacrity into high-speed expressway traffic and reaches 55–60 mph in a jiffy. But we doubted, although we didn't go the maximum, that any amount of floorboarding would actually get Terra to its speedometer's new top reading: 85 mph/137 km/hr, down from its previous year's 100 mph/160 km/hr.

We found the turbo-Terra a fun vehicle, but with some attributes best appreciated by longtime pickup fans: Terra is definitely noisy, inside and out; it's a muscular shifter (you *drive* this one), and it is quite "trucky" in handling and performance. The standard power steering makes parking as easy as with the family car. One Terra test we didn't anticipate was a diesel no-no: We ran out of fuel (despite the fact that the fuel gauge was still a wink above Empty). If nothing more, tanking-out put to test Terra's fuel system priming ritual, required of it, although not of all diesels. To bleed air from the system, once you've tanked up again, you merely give the pump handle a couple of strokes and then turn the bleed screw counterclockwise until the hissing of air escaping from the system tells you entrapped fuel-air has been ousted. That done, you're ready to go again.

## International Harvester Scout II

turbocharged diesel; also IH's Scout Traveler (wagon) and Scout Terra (pickup truck)

### *Diesel/Diesel Related Maintenance*

| | |
|---|---|
| *Regular Maintenance Intervals* (by mileage/ kilometers) | Every 2,500 miles (4,000 km), or every three months, whichever occurs first<br>*Special maintenance intervals*<br>High and low engine idle: check/adjust every 30,000 miles or 36 months |
| *Oil Change* | Every 2,500 miles (4,000 km), or every three months, whichever occurs first<br>Check oil level daily |
| *Oil Filter Change* | First, at 2,500 miles (4,000 km), or within three months of vehicle's purchase, whichever comes first<br>Next, at 5,000 miles (8,000 km), or within six months, whichever comes first<br>Thereafter, every 5,000 miles or six months |
| *Recommended Viscosity/ Types of Lubricating Oils* | *Year-around use* (at temperatures 20°F–120°F:<br>CD/CC diesel grade SAE 30, 10 W-30, 10 W-40, 20 W-40, 20 W-30<br>*Some other approved diesel viscosities:*<br>0°F–90°F, SAE 20W, SAE 10 W-30, 10 W-40, 20 W-40, 20 W-30<br>to −10°F, SAE 10W, 10 W-30, 10 W-40<br>below −10°F, SAE 5 W-20, 5 W-30 |
| *Air Filter Change* | Check/service element every 600 miles; change every 15,000 miles/eighteen months |
| *Recommended Diesel Fuels and Fuel Winterizing* | Only diesel #2, winterized #2 or #1<br>*Special fuel component servicing:*<br>Fuel injection nozzles: clean/adjust every 15,000 miles (24,000 km)/eighteen months<br>Fuel injection pump timing: check/adjust every 30,000 miles (48,000 km)/36 months |
| *Fuel Filter Change* | First, 4,000 miles (2,500 km), or at three months, whichever comes sooner<br>Next, 15,000 miles (24,000 km) or eighteen months<br>Thereafter, every 15,000 miles/eighteen months |
| *Recommended or Required Special Maintenance* | Above service intervals based on average *highway* use; more frequent maintenance required for off-highway, dusty, etc. use conditions<br>Valve lash: check/adjust every 15,000 miles (24,000 km), or every eighteen months |

The whole process, priming to start-up, takes less than three minutes. Fast glow plugs make normal weather Terra starting a short wait of ten to fourteen seconds. On the Terra, you press and hold in a dash button until the red preglow light flicks out. To kill the engine, you pull an engine-stop knob.

Turbo-Terra has a lot going for it. Ruggedness is one of its plusses, another is good high-ride visibility above traffic, turbo-diesel get up and go is a third, and topping them all is fuel economy: at about 22 mpg, at least 6 mpg better than gas engine Terras and in all likelihood the best fuel economy of any four-wheel drive pickup in its weight (4,117 pounds) class.

## MERCEDES-BENZ 300D

*Description:* Four-door, five-passenger sedan with four-speed automatic transmission

*Diesel engine:* Water-cooled, in-line, 5-cylinder, 183 cubic inch displacement with 21:1 compression ratio, rated 77 net hp at 4,000 rpm, developing 115 ft/lbs of torque at 2,400 rpm

*Fuel economy:* EPA: 23 mpg city/28 mpg highway

Mercedes-Benz's 300D, the most popular of all M-Bs sold in North America, is a lifetime car—one reason why some 70 percent of Mercedes-Benz sales in the United States are diesel and among the most fuel saving of luxury diesel automobiles. The 300D's 5-cylinder diesel (the first in a production automobile when the 300D was unveiled back in 1975) should go at least 200,000 miles before any serious engine work. But this kind of engine longevity isn't due to its five cylinders. Odd-numbered cylinders are no oddity in the diesel world, although Mercedes was first to go odd cylindered in a passenger car. In opting for more cubic inch engine capacity, thus more power than possible from four cylinders, but loath to add the extra weight of six cylinders, engineers compromised on the Mercedes 5-cylinder diesel. Its long road life, however, can be credited to something far more basic than the number, odd or even, of its cylinders: the simple fact that the 5-cylinder, like all Mercedes-Benz diesels, is a *true* diesel, built that way from the crankshaft up. It is not merely a beefed-up gasoline engine remade to perform like a diesel, as is the case of some of its diesel competitors. If one word—other than "luxurious," "elegant," or "efficient"—describes the 300D, it is "substantial." The feel is that of a heavy car, although the 300D weighs only 3,530 pounds, some 200 pounds less than the sporty two-door hardtop Mercedes-Benz gas engine 450SL.

Our test drive proved a point not many 300D owners themselves fully appreciate: The engine hardly exerts itself at all from standstill idle (at 700 rpm) right up

**Fig. 5.12** Mercedes-Benz 300D's 5-cylinder diesel—the first in a production automobile.

## Mercedes-Benz 300D

(also 240D, 300CD and 300TD)

### *Diesel/Diesel Related Maintenance*

| | |
|---|---|
| *Regular Maintenance Intervals* (by mileage/ kilometers) | *Note:* Chart shows Mercedes-Benz's NEW extended maintenance schedule. Same as for 300SD. Initially, at 800–1,000 miles (1,300–1,600 km) Then at 5,000 miles (8,000 km) Thereafter, every 15,000 miles (24,000 km) except for every 5,000-mile lube oil and lube filter change |
| *Oil Change* | Every 5,000 miles (8,000 km), but at least annually if using year-around multigrade oil; otherwise, twice a year (in spring and fall) *Special note:* In severe operating conditions, if filter *not* changed at every oil change, change oil every 4,000 miles/6,400 km |
| *Oil Filter Change* | At every oil change: Every 5,000 miles (8,000 km), more frequently under severe operating conditions, including poor roads, dusty/muddy conditions, heavy in-town/short distance driving |
| *Recommended Viscosity/ Types of Lubricating Oils* | Diesel grades, but for specifics (M-B's most current brand-name recommendations), see your dealer *Year-around use (multigrade):* SAE 10W-40, SAE 10W-50 *Some other approved diesel viscosities:* 14°F and *below:* 5W-20, 5W-30 68°F–23°F: 20W-20 |
| *Air Filter Change* | Clean at 15,000 miles (24,000 km) Change at 30,000 miles (48,000 km) Change thereafter every 30,000 miles |
| *Recommended Diesel Fuels and Fuel Winterizing* | Diesel #2, winterized #2 and #1 Winterized #2 should give minimum problems to 3°F. Below this, use #1 Diesel. If unavailable, nonwinterized ("summer") #2 may be mixed with regular (*not* premium) gasoline, not to exceed 30% gasoline; or with kerosene in following proportions: to 14°F: 70% diesel, 30% kerosene; to 5°F maximum 50/50 mix |
| *Fuel Filter Change* | Change every 30,000 miles (48,000 km) |
| *Recommended or Required Special Maintenance* | *Special maintenance:* Every 15,000 miles (24,000 km): air filter cleaned, valve clearance adjusted, V-belts checked/retensioned if necessary Lubricate battery terminals with acidproof grease Antifreeze coolant should ensure minimum coolant system protection to −4°F |

to and well past the highway's legal 55-mph mark. Not once in our cruise tests to 65 mph did the 300D's tachometer flick past 3,000 rpms (yes, the 300D has not only a tachometer, but likewise real instruments, not idiot lights). At 55–65 mph, the engine's rpms (and tach's needle) habitually stayed within the 2,500–2,700 rpm zone. At 22 mph, normal traffic speed, the diesel purred along at 1,600–1,800 rpm. High torque pull and low engine speeds bolster fuel economy. Nonetheless, the 300D, underpowered despite its five-cylinders, is sluggish on the getaway—a fault which turbocharging the same engine in the 300SD spectacularly corrects. The 300D's "purring," although muted to those within the passenger

**Fig. 5.13**  The Mercedes-Benz 300TD shares the same engine with the 300D sedan and is EPA rated for 23 mpg city and 28 highway.

compartment, is definitely "diesel"; step outside and you can't mistake that a diesel lurks under the hood.

As the first among modern diesel passenger cars, the 300D's popularity tells you more about its owner reverence than any bundle of statistics: Those who can afford virtually *any* car have made the 300D the most vaunted in its luxury-price, mid-size class—a diesel of elegant prestige and, for many, a kind of automotive annuity.

Chapter **6**

# Driving Tips from the Experts

Granted, the diesel differs. But does a diesel also drive differently from a gasoline engine vehicle? The answer is no. Half an hour behind the wheel of your new diesel car, pickup truck, or motor home and you'll feel you've driven it a lifetime. Still, there are things worth knowing if you want to get the most from whatever diesel you drive—how to put to use the diesel's high pulling power (torque) at low engine speeds, how to use the high engine compression and fuel-saving combustion process to advantage, how maintenance affects the diesel engine.

Here, from old-hand diesel owners and diesel pros—the latter including factory experts, off-road diesel race drivers, and others who make diesels and diesel vehicles their life work—are tips worth knowing and remembering. Almost all are simple "tricks" used by the most knowledgeable of diesel drivers, technicians, and engineers—"tricks" that become tips, saving you fuel (and its rising cost), making winter starting as easy as summer, lessening your chance of violating your owner's warranty, and more.

### DRIVING IT RIGHT

#### Engine Performance Curves

Understanding any diesel engine's performance curves—its performance potential displayed in graph form—will help you to get better mileage, to drive better and with more confidence, and to increase your diesel's performance where it counts: on steep grades, when pulling a trailer, or when mired in mud, slush, or snow. A performance curve is a graphic engineering analysis of engine performance. Typically, dozens or even hundreds of engines of any particular model are tested and the data of their individual performances plotted on a graph. The data

137

may show any of numerous criticals in engine performance: horsepower output in relation to engine speed, torque in relation to speed and horsepower, or perhaps fuel consumption in relation to engine or vehicle speed. With test data plotted on the graph, a line or "curve" is drawn, averaging the performance of all of the tests and resulting in: a performance curve. For every model of engine the curve of performance is apt to be different, sometimes strikingly so.

Figures 6.1 and 6.2 show typical performance curves for two popular diesel engines. Figure 6.1 is the performance curve for the Volkswagen Rabbit Diesel, and Figure 6.2 is for the Nissan turbo-diesel that powers International Harvester diesel Scouts. Both performance curves, somewhat simplified here, show the same things: engine speed (in rpms) required to produce the full horsepower output range of each diesel and torque (also in rpms), particularly its relationship to engine speed. A quick glance shows that although giving the same performance information, the graphs for the VW diesel and for the Nissan are quite different. This means a corresponding difference in the performance of the engines.

Consider Figure 6.1, the Rabbit Diesel and note how nearly proportional horsepower output is in relation to engine speed. In engineering terms, the curve (engine speed in rpms versus horsepower output) is virtually *linear*, meaning that throughout much of this engine's entire speed range, an equal increase in engine speed (when you step on the accelerator) results in a nearly equal proportional increase in horsepower. The engine speed versus horsepower curve for the Nissan turbo-diesel is somewhat less linear. While an increase in engine speed results in a nearly equal proportional increase in horsepower from about 1,200 rpm up to 2,800 rpm, after this point proportionally less horsepower is produced with every increase in engine speed.

Fine, you may say, but what has all this to do with driving? The answer: Everything. Driving "by the curves" can save fuel, reduce engine wear, help you to shift more efficiently—in a word, drive better and get better performance from your diesel vehicle.

Consider the Nissan's horsepower versus engine speed curve: The engine produces some 90 horsepower (almost 90 percent of its maximum power) at 2,800 rpm, but requires another 1,000 rpm (25 percent of total engine speed) merely to produce the final 10 percent of maximum power (101 hp at 3,800 rpm). The fuel cost to produce this final increment of horsepower (a mere 10 hp) is obviously high. The question the Nissan driver must ask, based on this diesel's performance curve, is "Is that extra 10 horsepower really worth the fuel cost?" The answer is likely to be no. Driving the Nissan "by the curve," you'll save considerable fuel and increase mileage if you keep the tachometer's needle (assuming the vehicle has a tachometer) at or below 3,800 rpm. Nudging that final 10 horsepower means revving the engine up another 1,000 rpms, and that consumes fuel—a lot of it. Driving the Nissan turbo-diesel, you can achieve 90 percent of the engine's potential full-power output with the engine turning a modest, fuel-saving 2,800 rpm. Economy-wise, you've bought a driving bargain: gotten 90 percent of the engine's power while holding the engine to only 75 percent of its top governed speed.

The Rabbit Diesel's power curve, by contrast, shows that the engine delivers 90 percent of maximum power at 80 percent (4,000 rpm) of full speed (5,000 rpm). Squeezing the final 10 percent of potential engine power requires another 1,000

# GOLF Diesel (VW RABBIT)

## Engine output, torque

Output  ▬ ▬ ▬       <u>Rating:</u> 48 hp at 5000 rpm
Torque  ▬ ▪ ▬ ▪ ▬              56.5 ft/lbs torque at 3000 rpm

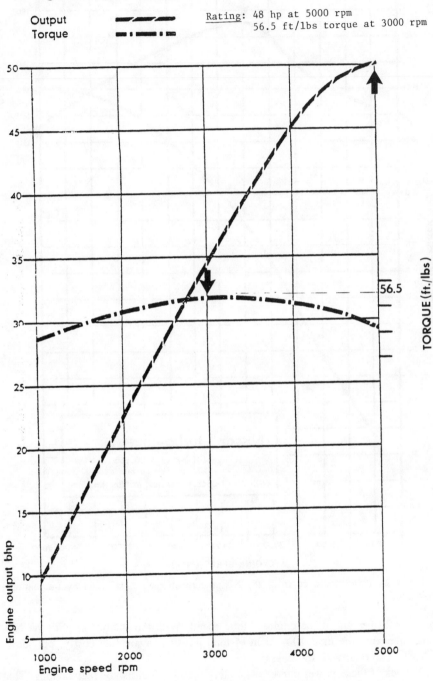

**Fig. 6.1**  Performance curve of the VW Rabbit diesel engine.

## ENGINE PERFORMANCE CURVE

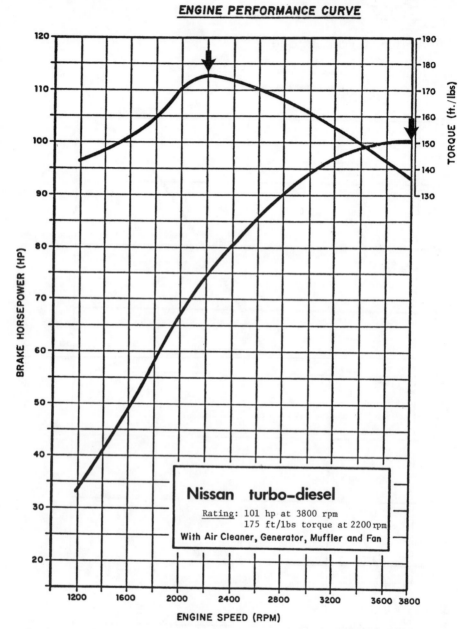

**Fig. 6.2**  Performance curve of the Nissan turbocharged diesel used by International Harvester.

rpm, or 20 percent of the engine's total speed. With the Rabbit, as with the Nissan, squeezing the final 10 percent of total power is again fuel costly, but somewhat less so than with the Nissan.

Neither of these power curves accurately predicts fuel use or fuel savings. That requires yet another set of curves, not shown here, but available (as are all performance curves) from your dealer or directly from the engine or vehicle maker, at no cost. Performance curves are not shown in the Owner's Manual simply because most owners aren't all that interested, even though they should be. Still, while the power curves shown here don't specifically indicate fuel consumption at various engine speeds and horsepower outputs, they predict fuel consumption. For, as a general rule, any time you've got to increase engine rpms proportionally *more* to get proportionally *less* power, you're using proportionally more fuel.

The two graphs, of course, chart vastly different diesels. The Rabbit's is four cylinder; the Nissan's, six. And the Rabbit's highway mileage is a lofty 55 mpg, contrasted to the Scout's good, but not extraordinary, 25 mpg or so. The mpg difference lies not merely in their engines' fuel-consumption performance, but in the total vehicular package—the vehicles' respective weights, gear ratios, and the like. Actually, despite the more than 25-mpg difference between VW's Rabbit Diesel and International's Scout's, both show far above ordinary gasoline fuel economy, for the kinds of vehicles they are. The Scouts are four-wheel-drive pickups and wagon-type vehicles. Their 25-mpg highway fuel economy rating is extremely good for their type and weight class, and especially so for a 6-cylinder vehicle.

Just as significant for diesel drivers is the torque curve shown for each of these engines. The curve of any diesel's torque is unique, and uniquely "diesel." For torque, pulling power, is developed at very low engine speeds in a diesel. Low-revved, a diesel often develops nearly maximum torque—more torque, usually, than a similar gasoline engine revved to far higher engine speed—which means higher fuel consumption. One of the diesel's fuel-saving secrets lies in its developing high torque at low, fuel-economizing engine speeds.

But again, the torque curves for the Rabbit Diesel and for the Nissan are quite different, and so are their torque outputs. Note the Rabbit Diesel's almost flat torque curve. Maximum torque is developed at only 3,000 rpm, 2,000 rpm below the engine speed of 5,000 rpm required for maximum horsepower output. Because the Rabbit's torque curve is flat, indicated is the obvious: The Rabbit Diesel develops very nearly its total torque across virtually the entire span of its speed range. Torque for the Rabbit at a mere 1,000 rpms, just above engine idle speed, is not significantly less than the torque at far higher rpms. So the Rabbit develops high torque at nearly all engine speeds. At 1,000 rpms it has practically the same pulling power as at 5,000 rpms, top engine speed. If it's pulling power you want (as contrasted to road speed), you can get it using very little fuel—because pulling power is there in the fuel-economizing low-rpm range.

Not so, however, with the Nissan. Its torque curve, rather than being flat across all engine speeds, is humped. With the Nissan, there is a definite point of "peak torque"—175 ft/lbs developed at 2,200 rpm, climbing rather rapidly up from 1,200 rpm and falling afterwards almost as rapidly from 2,200 rpm to this engine's maximum 3,800 rpm. Thus, in the Nissan, if you need maximum *pulling* power, keep engine speed somewhere at or just below 2,200 rpm, because above that engine speed, you'll have *less* pulling power, despite higher fuel consumption.

The Rabbit Diesel's nearly flat, across-all-rpms high torque helps account for its swift getaway. Right from the start, at just above idle rpms, its got high getaway torque. The Nissan Scout's acceleration is less hippity-hop, because peak torque is not developed until the engine reaches 2,200 rpm.

How important to driveability and fuel economy are performance curves? When many major truck executives buy whole fleets of trucks based on their canny reading of engine performance curves, no equally canny car or pickup buyer should plunk down his down payment without careful study of a vehicle's performance curves.

### Downshifting for Torque

The torque curve (Figs. 6.1 and 6.2) predicts a diesel phenomenon: Often, especially once at highway cruise speed, you can downshift—actually drop down a full gear—without any appreciable dip in actual road speed. The reason is torque. Because diesel torque pulling power is highest in the lower rpm ranges, torque maintains your speed even though the engine itself is running slower and using less fuel.

But there are many other instances when downshifting, either manually or by easing your foot on the accelerator and letting the automatic transmission drop a gear, gives you a power boost—uphill, for instance, and especially on steep, slow-go back roads, or should you become mired in mud or snow. Whereas the gasoline engine driver guns his engine to boost power in situations such as these, the experienced diesel driver revs his diesel hardly at all, knowing that the diesel's secret pulling power—its torque—lurks at low rpms, not high up on the rpm curve.

Downshifting has other uses, too: Some still underpowered diesel cars fairly zip through and around traffic—if you downshift, up-powering through torque, where the engine's own power may in itself be insufficient. This is particularly true of some small European diesels (but definitely *not* the gee-whiz VW Rabbit). Downshifting these underpowered models, especially when passing on the highway, is often absolutely essential; without a downshifted power boost from torque, passing can be faltering, if not perilous.

### Lugging

Does all this downshifting and torque-jockeying in the lower rpm ranges risk lugging? This is a fair question. And the answer is yes. A more basic question, however, is "What *is* lugging anyway?" Even if you've never driven diesel, you've probably heard the term. And almost always the connotation has been bad.

Lugging, although not even all diesel old hands agree precisely when it occurs, is the overloading of the engine, especially at low rpms, causing the engine to run roughly and, obvious to any ear, to be overworking. But, since operating at low rpms is a fuel saver, many of today's "fuel-squeezing" truck diesel engines operate in the 1,400–1,600-rpm range (down from yesteryear's 2,100–2,200 rpms). Many of these fuel-economizing big rigs run the road a hair's-breadth above "lugging," and some actually lug on the upgrades.

Truck diesels, of course, are far stronger and heftier than that in your car or light truck. Still, short-term lugging shouldn't harm your diesel, although extended low-range, overload operation *can* cause diesel damage—in a couple of instances:

1. If you have a manual transmission that is directly coupled to the driveshaft, lugging can put such strain on the crankshaft that eventually it can break.

2. If, besides, your crankshaft's flywheel is lightweight, as are many today, the chances of crankshaft damage increase when a manual transmission and engine are extensively lugged—run at low, overworked rpms.

But, if your transmission is automatic or otherwise fluid coupled (not directly coupled) to the driveshaft, it is all but impossible to lug the engine.

Typical lugging situations are typical overload situations: You're pulling a heavy trailer in too high a gear; you're laboring uphill in high, rather than in third or second gear; you're mired in mud, or driving a steep road, and are purposely in low gear and low rpms to gain the advantage of high torque, but the load and road are working together to pull engine rpms down even lower than you'd anticipated. Suddenly, the engine is lugging and "rattles," intermittently varying its output (if you could see the drive wheels, you'd notice they are alternately slowing and speeding up). And, in extreme lugging, the engine threatens to quit. The solution is readily apparent: Shift into a lower gear or speed up the engine's rpms, or both, depending on the situation.

Whatever the debate over lugging's causes and effects, hold lugging to an absolute minimum. A little lugging isn't all that unusual in abnormal driving situations; but a lot of lugging, any time, is to be avoided for the physical health of your engine and for your own fiscal well-being, thanks to lower repair bills.


## Shift Points

If yours is an automatic transmission, at specified engine rpms it shifts automatically at the proper shift points. But if your transmission is manual, selecting the proper shift points is up to you. Finding at what rpms to upshift or downshift comes easily to most drivers and soon becomes a habit. You may find that shifting into third gear and leaving it there much of the time gets you best through town traffic, as higher gears merely cause you an undue amount of downshifting. But there are times, even with an automatic transmission, when you should limit the venture into higher gear. For instance, in climbing you rein in gear by presetting the automatic's selector lever. For moderate ascents or descents, Mercedes-Benz recommends presetting the gear lever to "S," which prevents the transmission from shifting any higher than into third gear. For really steep going up or down, or when trailering in the same terrain, Mercedes recommends putting the automatic transmission into low ("L"), which limits the transmission's upshift any higher than second gear.

Precisely at what rpms to shift up or down varies with every vehicle, its engine, and where on the gear range you are at any particular time. The important thing is to observe the maximum permissible speeds recommended in your Owner's Manual for any gear and often indicated by "gear limit marks" on the speedometer.

The speedometer markings (one dot for top speed in first gear, two dots for top speed in second, three for top speed in third on the Mercedes-Benz 300D, typically, indicate the *permissible top speeds* for any particular gear. Thus, for the 300D:

| Gear | Permissible Top Speed |
|------|-----------------------|
| 1st  | 22 mph (35 km/h) |
| 2nd  | 37 mph (60 km/h) |
| 3rd  | 61 mph (98 km/h) |
| 4th  | 90 mph (145 km/hr) |
|      | (max. speed) |

These charted limits tell the 300D driver not to exceed 22 mph while in first, 37 mph in second, 61 mph in third, and 90 in fourth. "Natural" shift points for any engine come much earlier than these top gear speed limits. A few hours' driving will give you the feel of the gears—and of engine performance in response to your shifting. For the diesel, as for most manual-shift vehicles, it's almost as simple as that.

Geared to go, with an eye on torque, and in your mind's eye a recall of your particular engine's performance curves, you'll find driving diesel no different from driving gas engine—but fuel-wise, far more economical.

## THE PROS SPEAK FOR THEMSELVES

### Downshifting for Torque: What I Learned in the Baja 1000

By Jimmy Jones, professional off-road driver and a diesel finisher in 1979's Baja 1000

The Baja 1000 has got to be off-road's toughest race on drivers and their machines.

I drove the 1979 Baja 1000 in an International Harvester four-wheel drive Scout Terra half-ton pickup, fitted with the new turbocharged Nissan 6-cylinder diesel. I learned a lot in that race, my first with a diesel vehicle—for one thing, the importance of downshifting, which works as well in typical city traffic as running cross country in the Baja 1000. Downshifting (dropping down one gear when you feel power dropping) increases your power and boost, without any slowdown in the speed you had at the higher gear.

Downshifting, of course, is an old diesel driving trick for pulling maximum performance power when it's needed, whether in traffic or off road. Since nearly full torque comes early on a diesel's rpm curve, you can reach down for torque without any slowdown in speed—by downshifting. As an example of how low on the power curve torque is developed, consider the Nissan-6 diesel I was driving in the Baja 1000. The diesel idles around 600 rpm. By 1,400 rpm, you've got torque ("boost"). And from there on up, torque rises rapidly. So when you feel torque

**Fig. 6.3** Off-road pro driver Jimmy Jones made Baja 1000 run in turbo-diesel International Scout Terra, seen here.

slacking off, a quick downshift gets boost back up and keeps you rolling at the same speed you were before the downshift.

The turbocharged Nissan proved, on the Baja 1000, to be a very fuel-economizing engine. On the Baja 1000, I got thirteen miles to the gallon, which was 2½ to 3 mpg more than I'm used to off road in a gasoline engine rig. To me, the diesel economy was outstanding and something of a surprise, this being my first off-road race with diesel. Coming back by highway, the turbo-diesel averaged 18 mpg. The whole round trip, something like 1,954 miles—1,000 of them racing off road, the rest by highway—used just 127 gallons of diesel fuel at a total cost (in Mexico, where diesel fuel is 18 to 19 cents a gallon) of just $22.86.

Upshifting or downshifting, you can't very well beat that in a four-wheel drive vehicle.

### The #1 "Must": Regular Oil and Filter Changes

*By Darel Davenport, service manager, Dixon Cadillac Co., Los Angeles*

Changing lube oil, oil filter and the fuel filter, as the Owner's Manual prescribes, is an absolute must. For Cadillac's diesel, the lube oil and lube filter change comes at every 3,000 miles; the fuel filter change, every 6,000 miles. To change the oil filter, the crankcase must be drained and the filter changed, a procedure identical to that of changing oil in a gasoline engine. The gasoline engine, of course, has no fuel filter that needs frequent maintenance; the diesel does. In Cadillac's case, the canister-type fuel filter sitting right behind the fuel injection pump is the only filter in the fuel system that must be changed. There's another filter, called a pickup filter, in the fuel tank, but there is nothing to change there.

To change the fuel filter, you don't have to drain the fuel. All you're doing, really, is disconnecting two fuel lines that run to the fuel filter and replacing the filter canister. Anyone can make the change with a few tools, but you do need the right-size wrenches for the fittings on the filter's two fuel lines. These are brass fittings, which means they are relatively soft metal, and using the wrong wrench to remove them can pretty well tear them up. With the few right tools, fuel filter change-out is only a few minutes' job, but one of the most important in diesel engine care.

### Coming: Oil Filters That Obsolete Oil Changes?

*By Robert Gibbons, president, Diesel Automobile Association*

Electrostatic fluid processing is a technology of promising importance to diesel car owners. It is a technology that we of the Diesel Automobile Association have been working on in conjunction with its patent holders. The technology looks toward development of a compact electrostatic filter unit that will do away with the necessity for ever changing the engine oil of a diesel automobile or truck. As diesel car owners and drivers, we of DAA are interested in doing away with the need for every 3,000–4,000-mile oil changes. Oil changes are dirty, messy, and expensive, and it is all too easy to let a change period pass. Letting that happen today, with a diesel's standard filter, is inviting very major and very expensive engine trouble. We feel, however, that today's standard filters represent an outmoded technology and that there are better ways to ensure clean engine oil, one of which is electrostatic processing, which continuously cleanses the engine's lubricating oil, making oil changes unnecessary. With electrostatic processing, engine oil would merely need to be topped periodically with small quantities of lube oil added to keep the system full.

Electrostatic processing has been in operation in several critical fuel and fluids areas, so its feasibility has been proved. Electrostatic lubricating oil processing has already been used in diesel locomotives with a great deal of success, and the technology has also been used by NASA and by the U.S. Air Force to "ultra-purify" missile fuels and other aerospace liquids, including hydraulic fluids.

We are anticipating the development of the electrostatic lube oil technology to the point where, for the first time, it will alleviate a diesel car owner's need to change his engine's lube oil. When that time comes, eliminated from diesel car maintenance will be one of its most bothersome, frequent, and expensive maintenance chores.

### Trailering/towing: 2000 Pounds Are Maximum for Some Diesels

*By Robb Henry, Chevrolet assistant manager of truck merchandising*

Owner's manuals rather routinely contain a disclaimer, warning car owners against heavyweight towing or trailering. Generally, these warnings restrict towed weight to 2,000 pounds maximum, the restriction applying to gasoline as well as to diesel engines.

For the Oldsmobile/GM 350 CID V-8 diesel that powers Chevrolet's light pickups (notably the half-ton C-10 series), as well as many other GM pickups and cars, the 2,000-pound towed-weight restriction is *absolute*. If you do pull greater towed weight with this diesel, you will shorten the life of the engine. And the reason is obvious: With a net horsepower rating of only 125 (compared to upwards of 170 net hp for the 350 CID gasoline engine), the diesel will be strained and its life foreshortened if required to pull more than the maximum 2,000 pounds of towed or trailered weight.

Within this 2,000-pound maximum you can safely pull a small boat or tent trailer. You very definitely can*not* pull a full-sized trailer. But overheating the engine is not the problem or the reason for the 2,000-pound towed-weight restriction, as the engine is equipped with heavy-duty cooling, including engine and transmission oil coolers. The problem is simply a lack of horsepower for anything but modest and light towed loads.

Pull more than the 2,000-pound maximum, and you risk more than merely violating our Owner's Manual recommendation. You risk the life of the diesel itself.

**Fig. 6.4** International Harvester is one of the few manufacturers to OK towing of trailers up to 5,000 pounds—but only when diesel vehicle has special tow gear.

### Changing Air Filters: Shut Off The Engine

*By a veteran diesel mechanic*

With a gasoline engine, you can leave the engine running when you replace air filters, or even when you're adjusting the carburetor. Mechanics routinely do carburetor adjusting and fiddling with the air cleaner while the engine is running. One reason they can is that in a gasoline engine the carburetor effectively acts as a barrier between the worker and the engine's interior.

But a diesel, which has no carburetor, consequently has no barrier. In a diesel, once you remove the lid of the air cleaner holder, you expose the engine's open air intake, which leads directly to the diesel's precombustion chambers and cylinders. Remove the air cleaner's lid to replace the air filter with the diesel running, and you risk having something sucked into the engine; or inadvertently you might drop something in—a nut, a wrench. Who knows? Either way, you can ruin an expensive diesel engine.

Rule No. 1 when changing a diesel's intake air filter: First, shut off the engine. *Then* change the filter.

### A Simple Equation: A Little Maintenance = Many Trouble-Free Miles

*By Robert Gibbons, president, Diesel Automobile Association*

In general, other than routine injection inspection or service at 100,000 miles or so, there is relatively little that needs to be attended to in the average car diesel. But these few things are critical.

One, of course, is the engine lubricating oil. Most car makers require (as stipulated in their warranties and in the owner's manual) that lube oil *and* filter be changed every 3000 miles. We at DAA (Diesel Automobile Association) would like to emphasize the importance of doing just that . . . because diesel combus-

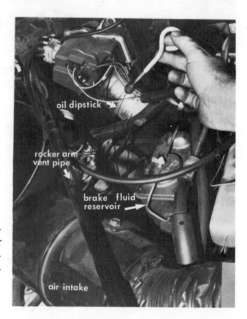

**Fig. 6.5** The oil dipstick's white handle makes it easy to find among other components under Cadillac diesel Seville's hood. (Photograph by James Joseph)

tion produces *extreme* amounts of carbon which contaminates the lube oil, is an abrasive, cuts down on the oil's lubricity (its oiliness) and can clog the fine oil passages in the engine. So it is very important to change the oil *exactly* as the Owner's Manual calls for—every 3,000 miles in the case of some diesels, as Peugeot; every 4,000 miles for most General Motors diesels; every 5000 miles (under its now extended oil drain interval) for Mercedes-Benz. Doing that, a diesel car owner should have reliable service from his vehicle for more than 100,000 miles.

Another maintenance item of importance involves the air cleaner filter. Whether it is the oil bath or dry element type, it must be kept clean. Exactly when to change the air filter varies with the manufacturer of car and engine. Some of General Motors' cars call for changing the air cleaner element every 25,000 miles. The older Mercedes oil-bath type filters should also be looked at and the filter element and filter unit oil replaced at least that often.

A third maintenance item of considerable importance in diesels other than General Motors is adjustment of the intake and exhaust valves. We recommend that this be done at least every 25,000 miles. The procedure is not an expensive one; all that's involved is removal of the valve cover and adjustment of the valves when the engine is cold, to assure optimal combustion. And it is an adjustment that is particularly important in winter. If valves become tight through loss of adjustment, compression leaks may occur, and winter starting will be much more difficult.

Finally, the use and misuse of fuel can be considered a maintenance procedure—and for diesels, especially as an aid in cold weather starting, an important one. As cold weather sets in, we recommend use of a winterized #2 diesel fuel. We don't recommend using diesel #1 fuel unless the temperature drops below zero, when #1 diesel is pretty much the only fuel that will flow. Admittedly, General Motors recommends that #1 fuel be used below 20°F, which is very considerably above the 0°F switchover point (from winterized #2 to #1) recommended by DAA, but we think that General Motors' is a conservative recommendation. The fact is, of course, that diesel #1 fuel is hard to find; it is certainly not as plentiful or as readily available as #2. In some colder parts of the country, however, diesel #1 is routinely available. Generally, you can find #1 in those areas where you need it if you look for kerosene, for stations or other fuel outlets that advertise kerosene. *Kerosene and diesel #1 are identical*—absolutely identical and reliably so. The only difference is that kerosene may not have the state and federal road taxes included in its price. We leave it to the diesel owner to decide (if the tax decision is his) what to do in that situation. On the other hand, we do *not* recommend that owners of diesels substitute heating oil for #2 diesel, because home heating oil is usually *not* identical with #2 diesel fuel.

### No Fuel? Your Fuel Cap May Be the Culprit

*By a GM diesel expert*

Depending on the diesel you drive, its fuel tank cap (what the non-diesel driver calls a "gas cap") may or may not have a tiny vent hole in it. If there is a vent hole, it's meant to be there. Fitting your tank with a standard "gas cap," which has no vent hole, will permit creation of a low, even negative pressure in the diesel fuel tank, often making it impossible for the diesel's fuel pump to send fuel to the injector pump. So you "run out of fuel" even though your tank may be full. This problem arises because the average driver of a diesel whose fuel tank is fitted with a vent hole cap doesn't realize there's a purposeful difference between his cap and any other. One day he loses his fuel tank cap and goes into an auto parts shop for another. What he's likely to get is an unvented gasoline tank cap, and his fuel problems are apt to begin right there.

Gas caps aren't vented for a reason: to prevent escape from the gas tank of evaporative hydrocarbon emissions, gas fumes. Diesel fuel emits no such fumes. Nonetheless, when a diesel tank cap has a vent hole, it too is with reason: to provide, in the absence of any other in the diesel fuel system, a vent preventing a low-pressure situation in the fuel tank. Often this necessary vent is provided somewhere other than in the fuel tank's cap—in the neck of the fuel tank fill pipe, for instance, or perhaps in the fuel filter. But when the system vent is that tiny vent hole in the fuel tank's cap, it is likely the system's only vent and, as such, is necessary to the satisfactory operation of the fuel system. Use an unvented gas cap (which, unfortunately, will usually fit the diesel tank) in place of the vented cap that came with the diesel vehicle, and your diesel's operation is likely to be anything but satisfactory.

### Injection Service Life: 100,000 Miles

*By an injector service specialist*

It is true that injection units in fuel injectors are more expensive than spark plugs. But if a diesel car owner is running with clean fuel and doesn't have water problems, he should not have to touch his injectors or have his service people do anything to them for 100,000 miles. Injectors cost more than spark plugs, but their life may be five times longer. At the 100,000-mile mark, however, it's a very good idea to have the injectors checked or replaced.

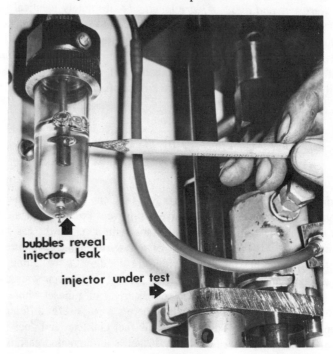

**Fig. 6.6**  Injector "bubble test" reveals faulty injector. But many injectors go 100,000 miles before checking.

### Save Money—and Pumps: NEVER Wash Your Diesel Engine

*By Brian R. Wilson, resident instructor, General Motors Training Center, Burbank, Calif.*

We caution the buyer never to wash his diesel engine. The caution is aimed at keeping from hitting a hot injector pump (the Roosa Master injection pump, common to all Olds 350 CID V-8 diesels) with cold water. Hit a hot pump with cold water—or even with hot water, as when steam-cleaning an engine—and you can ruin the pump. The tolerances and workmanship of that pump are so close, as they must be, that the parts can seize up once you've thrown them out of tolerance with a dose of water. Once the damage is done, you know it soon enough—right off the wash rack when you attempt to start up. The pump seizes and is ruined. I know of at least one instance where it *did* happen, in a steam-clean situation. Even hot water hitting a hot engine and a hot pump can do the damage.

Although we're definitely not recommending it, if you feel you must clean your diesel engine—and there are some owners who do—let the engine cool down *completely*. If you must have the engine washed or steam-cleaned, have it done with a *cold* engine—one that, let's say, has cooled overnight.

### There's Plenty of Fuel in the Boondocks—If You Know Where to Look

*By a ten-year diesel owner*

Say it's Sunday, you're way out in the boonies, every gas station is closed tight, and your fuel gauge is dropping perilously toward EMPTY. You're better off, really, than the driver of a gas engine car in the same situation. Just about every farm has diesel for its machinery and electric generator's diesel engine, so does every small trucking outfit (try a local terminal or service garage), and so do county and state road maintenance district yards and offices. And don't forget the local hospital; most have emergency generators run by diesel. Some towns make their own electricity, at a town-owned diesel-electric plant—plenty of diesel fuel there. There's plenty, too, at numerous local agri-plants, the kind that process fruits, vegetables, and other farm crops. In season, they work Sundays and every other day of the week, too. And you will probably pass plenty of homes whose furnaces are fueled with home heating oil. Your diesel will burn that, nicely, even though car makers frown on extended fueling with heating oil (it is not as highly refined). And if it comes to worst, there's a good chance the local airport has Jet A fuel (which some call "aviation diesel"). Your engine will burn Jet A, and even seem to like it, and get you on your way to the next open station with diesel.

### An Electric Hair Dryer as a Cold-Starting Aid

*By a North Dakota Mercedes diesel owner*

With the thermometer *really* bottoming the bulb, as during a few days each winter, I've had trouble cranking my diesel to start, despite its being equipped with a block heater.

What often works on sub-cold mornings like that is the family hair dryer. I simply remove the air cleaner and insert the dryer's nozzle end into the Mercedes's air intake. Then I go in for breakfast. Fifteen minutes later, the engine's cylinders warmed, I remove the dryer, put back the air cleaner—and we're usually on our way.

### Quick Test for Watered Fuel: A Clean Measuring Cup

*By a longtime diesel car owner*

Sooner or later you're going to get "watered": You drive in, fill up, and what you get is water along with the fuel.

When I suspect a station, usually one of those sleazy ones where a diesel car owner now and again finds himself forced to fuel, I haul out my clear plastic measuring cup, the sixteen-ounce, two-cup size your wife uses around the kitchen to measure things. *Before* filling the tank, I fill my cup, then just let things sit awhile—three to five minutes, or so. If there's a lot of water coming out of that pump along with the diesel fuel, my cup tells me right off I'm about to be "watered": The fuel rides on top of the water, and it's pretty plain to see.

It's worth a five-minute wait before fueling rather than be stalled a whole lot longer somewhere down the road. Twice in the last several months my cup test showed water, in one case a lot of it. I said, "Thanks anyway, buddy," and fueled at the next diesel stop.

### Save $7,500 Just for Fuel: The "Payback" in Conversion Costs

*By Ray Prussing, Jr., Isuzu Diesel of North America*

Economically, you can go about twice as far on a gallon of diesel fuel as on gasoline, and that in itself initially cuts the diesel driver's fuel bill in half. Consider even the current price per gallon of diesel fuel and gasoline, roughly about the same; let's call it $1 a gallon for both. The advantage remains with the diesel owner, and the saving for the diesel driver becomes greater, in fact, as the price of diesel and gasoline rise, as almost surely it will.

Let's consider a diesel conversion, costing—to install a diesel engine in place of the gasoline one you have—in the neighborhood of $5,500; that's for the diesel and its accessories, including adapters to mate the new engine to your vehicle's existing transmission. Let's say you drive 20,000 miles a year, a little more than the now over 15,000 annual miles for the average driver. With gasoline last year (1979) at $1 a gallon, the same price as diesel fuel, you saved $2,000 alone, because of twice the fuel mileage with diesel. In 1980, with fuel prices projected to go to $1.25 a gallon, you'll save another $2,500. By 1981, based on $1.50 a gallon—a price optimistically low, I'm afraid—you'll save $3000. So, driving 20,000 miles a year, you'll save $7,500 just for fuel and in just three years. And that doesn't even consider a possible differential in fuel prices, diesel versus gasoline, the diesel hopefully costing less per gallon than gas.

So the payoff for a $5,500 diesel conversion, a diesel swapped for a gasoline engine, should come somewhere between the second and third year. Nor does it matter, our figures show, what set of years you're talking about, whether 1979–1981 or 1982–1984. Whatever the years, as long as you drive at least 20,000 miles a year, you should recoup most of the cost of a diesel conversion by the end of the second driving year—and all of it, and more, by the third.

But for the payoff to work for you, you've got to drive a bit higher than average mileage—not a lot higher, just a little.

### Downhill Fuel Economy: Deceleration Trick Saves Fuel

*By the editors, Diesel Car Digest*

Believe it or not, at engine speeds above 1,200 rpm on a full downhill deceleration, your Mercedes's Bosch in-line pump injects *no* fuel at all into your engine! Under these conditions, the engine is acting as an air compressor only and uses no fuel. Seasoned Mercedes-Benz diesel drivers know this, and are not surprised at a sudden increase in fuel economy on trips where long downhill grades are encountered.

### Calculating Fuel Economy: Don't Measure MPG with a "Hot" Fuel Tank

*By Tony Capanna, diesel conversion specialist*

I test fuel mileage on many of the cars, pickups, and motor homes I convert from gasoline to diesel, and on my own Oldsmobile diesel 98. One mistake I don't make, but one which many diesel owners do, is to make my miles-per-gallon check with a "hot tank" when the fuel is warm, as on a trip. It's a common mistake and, I suppose, a natural one, since most diesel owners still think in "gasoline" terms. What they don't know, or forget, is that diesel fuel, when warmed, expands. And it expands quite a bit. So let's say you're on a trip, eager to check your fuel economy, and you pull into a service station to fill 'er up and use that figure, the amount of fuel the tank will hold, to calculate how many miles you got per gallon. Right?

No, wrong. Unlike gasoline-fueled cars, in diesels the warm fuel is circulated back to the fuel tank. Return fuel heats what's in the tank, expanding it. So when you fill up with a "hot tank," it won't take nearly as much fuel as, say, the next morning when the fuel has cooled and contracted. It may, in fact, take another gallon or so—changing, obviously for the worse, your "hot tank" miles-per-gallon calculations of the day before. When you check for mileage, check when the tank is cold, at least several hours after you've stopped for the night or, better, the next morning before you start out.

### A Problem Easily Solved: Water in Diesel Fuel Is Serious

*By a diesel fuels specialist*

Water does seem to be a problem in diesel fuel around the country at the moment, and probably it will continue to be for some time. Largely, I think, it is caused by allocation problems of the Department of Energy, by certain supply and delivery problems, and also by the fact that many service stations are converting their gasoline tanks to diesel fuel and that in those tanks is sometimes an ac-

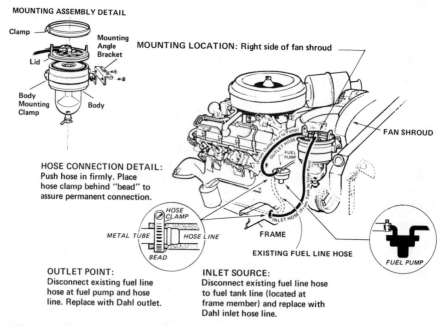

**Fig. 6.7** Installing a water separator (this one is combined with fuel filter) makes sense in some areas.

cumulation of water. One of the best ways for a diesel car owner to protect himself against water, of course, is to ask directly at the station, "Are you having a water problem?" Direct questioning isn't foolproof, as any diesel driver knows, but it's helpful.

More nearly foolproof is installation of a water separator, which is a simple centrifugal filter. This filter-separator should be installed upstream—ahead of—the engine's standard fuel filter and should not be used as a replacement for, but rather as an addition to, the regular fuel filter. The water separator has a glass sediment and water collection bowl, at the bottom of which is a petcock device. This petcock should be drained as often as necessary to get rid of collected water; as long as water problems seem to exist, it should be drained at least twice a week in areas where fuel watering is common.

It's worth emphasizing that water problems in fuel are not universal, but tend to be spotty and regional, seeming to exist, in the main, in southern California,

Texas, some other southwestern states, and also in Mexico, where quite a few near-border diesel owners tank up because of the low fuel prices there. In these areas, certainly, a diesel owner would be wise to install a filter-separator (either a fuel filter combined with a water separator, or the separator alone). The separator costs approximately $50–$60, plus another $35–$40 for installation. By venting the separator's petcock a couple of times a week—or more often, if necessary—a diesel owner can fairly effectively cure the water problem where it exists.

# Chapter 7

# Diesel Conversions

If your recreational vehicle (RV—pickup truck or motor home) is now getting eight to ten miles to a gallon, you can expect sixteen to twenty—*at least double* your present mileage. If start-up power, especially on grades, is something you now lack, you can have nearly full torque at start-up, pulling power when you *really* need it. If you're bugged by frequent tune-ups or worse (at 50,000 miles, your RV's engine has already lost its zip), forget it. This engine can go 125,000 miles, often 250,000 and more, before major overhaul—and, throughout those quarter-million miles, with scarcely a mechanical looksee. This is not because of a "miracle" engine for your RV. It's the diesel, of course. Diesel engines are scarcely new—except to RVers, who seem just now to be discovering them. But a few, having made the happy diesel discovery years ago, have experienced the kind of diesel economy unknown to owners of gasoline engine recreational vehicles.

Take the diesel-run experience of RVer Sam Thompson, a retired auto mechanic from Ojai, California, who over the years has owned three pickups, all of them diesel powered and two of them turbocharged. "Some years ago," remembers Thompson, "I pulled a 22-foot Airstream trailer to Guatemala, 11,000 miles round trip, with a half-ton Ford F100 pickup powered by a little 99-hp English-made Perkins 6-cylinder diesel. That trip was an eyeopener. I swore then I'd never go with anything but diesel again." And Sam Thompson hasn't. He has, moreover, made all of the gasoline-to-diesel conversions himself, even to installing turbochargers. "Turbocharging," he says with the enthusiasm of a veteran mechanic turned backyard do-it-yourselfer, "ups diesel economy and mileage another 20 percent, at least."

What opened Sam Thompson's sharp eyes during his Central American diesel junket were his own carefully kept mileage and cost records—the costs, admittedly, in an era of low-priced diesel fuel. Thompson's records show that during both the Central American trip and afterwards across much of the United States,

156

**Fig. 7.1** If your motor home now gets 8–10 mpg, it can get at least double the mileage, fitted with a diesel. (Photograph by James Joseph)

the diesel managed 22 miles per gallon towing his Airstream at 50 to 55 mph. Mileage like that, plus low-cost fuel (Sam bought #2 diesel for a rock-bottom 15.5 cents a gallon in parts of South America; it is currently selling for only 20 cents a gallon in Mexico) let him pull his trailer for around 1½ cents a mile. And he has the sales slips to prove it.

Thompson has since turned that pickup over to his son George, who commutes sixty miles each day to work. George Thompson says he was getting 22 mpg in normal 55–60-mph freeway commuting (sans the trailer, of course) until, the diesel having racked up 180,000 miles and not a quarter's worth of any but routine maintenance, Sam pulled the little engine and replaced it with a slightly heftier diesel of the same make.

Son George promptly went back to commuting, dieselized as before, but this time with higher horsepower (130 hp). The somewhat larger engine, in terms of fuel economy, did almost as well as the smaller: It racked up an average of 21 miles to every gallon in high-speed freeway traffic. It has done even better since Sam turbocharged it. And now its odometer, not all that many years later, shows more than 250,000 miles, all without major maintenance.

As is obvious from these high mileage figures, Thompson's are the kinds of conversions, vehicles certain to put a lot of miles under their wheels, that benefit most from diesel's long-run economies. Obviously, too, ex-mechanic Sam Thompson is a diesel buff. What proves it is what he did some dozen years ago when he bought a new 26-foot Airstream trailer and a new Ford three-quarter-ton pickup to pull it: He drove his spanking new Ford Ranger pickup the fifteen miles home from the showroom, hauled out its showroom-new V-8 gasoline engine and in its place slipped in a 130-hp "little" diesel. "Sure," he recalls, "I tried my darnedest to buy a pickup installed with a diesel; or, failing that, one with no engine at all. But every dealer I asked, including the zone people for most major

U.S. makers, said, 'No, you can't buy a pickup truck factory installed with diesel. And we won't sell you one without an engine, either.' ''

Today, of course, you *can* buy a number of pickups and motor homes with standard or optional diesel engines. But it's doubtful, should you wish to convert a pickup truck without optional diesel, whether even now you could order one fresh from the factory without any engine at all.

Sam Thompson is typical of car and RV buffs who over the years—and often long before the present rush to dieselize—quietly made the switch. Once addicted to diesel, they almost never break the habit. Many, in fact, disdain driving anything less.

## THE DOLLARS AND SENSE OF CONVERSION

Converting a pickup truck to diesel is often significantly less expensive than buying new. For one analytical example, consider Russ Field of San Antonio, Texas. A U.S. Air Force retiree, Field in 1977 had his 1971 GMC half-ton pickup truck, with only 42,500 miles on its 350 CID V-8 gasoline engine, converted to diesel. His decision to go diesel was based on a number of factors: His gasoline engine truck, used to pull a family 5,000-pound fifth-wheel trailer, was a fuel hog; buying a factory-new diesel pickup of the same size and power would have cost around $10,000: and Field liked his 1971 rig—he thought it better built than some newer models.

Recently, in *Diesel Car Digest,* Field added up the cost of the conversion, in which a Chrysler-Mitsubishi 6-41, 6-cylinder diesel with 243 cubic inch displacement, the engine later turbocharged, was substituted for the pickup's former 350 CID gas engine:

| *Conversion costs* | |
| --- | --- |
| Diesel engine | $2,850 |
| Installation (parts and labor) | 2,350 |
| Turbocharger and gauges | 1,050 |
| Automatic transmission with torque converter | 287 |
| Rear axle ratio change | 250 |
| Cost | $6,787 |
| Less sale of old engine | 450 |
| Total conversion cost | $6,337 |

Towing Field's trailer, the gas engine GMC pickup had averaged 7–7½ miles per gallon. With diesel engine, it gets 13½ mpg. Empty, the gas engine pickup's "best" fuel average had been 11 miles per gallon. Today, dieselized and running empty, it averages 18–22 mpg.

## BUYING A USED DIESEL ENGINE

Buying used, what with the diesel engine's long, long life, often makes considerable sense. And especially if you'd like to "get into diesels"—convert your car, pickup or motor home to diesel—at rockbottom cost. A 100,000-mile "old" diesel is still "young" and may well have another 100,000 miles of life even before overhaul—and after that, another 200,000. At 100,000 miles, a gasoline engine, if still running at all, is in its latter years. Buying used, you can expect to save at *least* 30 percent and sometimes half the cost of the same engine purchased factory-new.

Typically, old hand used-diesel expert George Soderlund asks only $1,250–$1,450, depending on condition, for a used Perkins 6-354, a favorite automotive conversion 6-cylinder British-made diesel that's rated 124 hp at 2,800 rpm; new, the same engine is priced around $5,500. Says Soderlund, a Los Angeles-based, seventeen-year veteran to the used diesel scene, "The buyer of a used diesel has got to buy in cheap—get his used engine for a whole lot less than he'd pay new, because having picked up a used diesel, he will almost certainly want a mechanic to go through it." "Going through" a diesel can be expensive, because what's involved, although not a complete overhaul, is something close to it.

Thus, roughly, on top of the engine's used price you should figure another $500–$600 for a mechanic's go-through labor, plus parts, which for a thorough go-through generally average about $100 a "hole" (per cylinder). So for a complete engine go-through, which restores the engine to virtually like-new life, parts will add another $400, $600, or $800, depending on the number of cylinders. In the case of Soderlund's 6-cylinder Perkins—selling, let's say, for $1,450 used— you'd probably need to add $600 mechanic's labor and $600 for parts ($100 for each of those six cylinders) for a total bill of around $2,650, or about one half the cost of that $5,500 Perkins new.

Nor need you be anything like an expert to judge a used diesel's probable condition, both on the used sales lot before you buy and after you've bought and trucked it home. Here are some tests Soderlund suggests any used diesel buyer should make:

1. *Give it a walk-around test.* Give the engine a careful inspection, being alert for potentially expensive missing parts (such as injection pumps or starter motors) and for obvious damage—cracks in the block, a patched hole where a rod once punched through, or impact damage that may have occurred when the engine was removed from its former vehicle and trucked to the sales lot. Advises Soderlund, "Look for completeness, for everything that is supposed to be on the engine. Replacing major missing components like the alternator, injection or fuel pump, or starter motor can be expensive and make a 'bargain' used engine something less than a bargain."

2. *Have the compression tested.* This test involves turning (cranking) the engine's crankshaft manually, though it can be quite a chore to overcome several hundred pounds of compression pressure. Turning the crankshaft moves the engine's pistons in their cylinders. On a diesel, if cylinders and pistons are in

good shape, you'll hear a distinctive "pop" (it's called a "compressive pop") as you manually crank the engine. To do it, you need a wrench that fits the hub on the crankshaft pulley directly beneath the engine's fan. Turning the hub turns the crankshaft to which it is fitted. Soderlund adds, "A better test for compression that takes only a little more doing is to pull (unscrew) either a glow plug or an injector (some engines like GM's V-8, require a special puller), and in its hole insert a special diesel engine compression gauge. Then hook a car battery to the engine's starter motor and let the motor crank the engine a few times. The gauge should show at least 300 pounds of compression."

3. *Give it the finger test for evidence of exhaust pipe oil.* Oil should not show up in the diesel's exhaust, and its presence is a nearly sure sign that engine rings are worn. Insert a finger in the exhaust pipe, and if your finger comes out oil smudged, be very suspicious. Diagnoses Soderlund, "It's a thirty-second test that can tell you a surprising lot about a used diesel engine."

4. *Finally, give it an oil analysis.* Take a small sample (two ounces are usually enough) of the used engine's crankcase oil for lube analysis by a competent laboratory. Often a used engine's crankcase will still contain the diesel's original "running oil." Most legitimate used engine dealers will permit you to take a crankcase oil sample. Mail the sample to one of the several engine oil analytical laboratories (see page 96 for the "how to" of taking and mailing an oil sample for analysis). In a week to ten days you'll have the lab's report, and often seemingly uncanny insight into the used diesel's innards. The $7–$10 cost of an oil analysis is an engine buyer's cheapest assurance of getting full dollars' worth.

After you have acquired a used engine: *Give it an insider's look.* If you have the equipment to do so safely (a simple A-frame rigged with a block-and-tackle will do), turn the engine on its side. That done, unbolt and pull out the crankcase's oil pan, exposing (on most diesels) the crankshaft, main, and rod bearing locations and, in diesels that have them, the cylinder liners. What you're looking for is obvious scoring and wear, the telltale as to whether the used engine you've just purchased requires a complete go-through or something less, and less expensive. You need not be an expert to look-see a diesel's insides, from the bottom up. "Wear is wear," says Soderlund, "and it's pretty obvious to anyone with decent vision who's not afraid of dirty hands."

With the engine on its side, its crankcase oil pan removed, and a friend manually cranking the engine (turning the crankshaft, causing the pistons to move up and down in their cylinder liners), you're ready to get down to visual business. As first one, then another piston reaches the top of its travel, you can easily see the bottom of the liner and the liner's interior, where the piston travels. If there's wear, it's pretty obvious. So, usually, is wear on the crankshaft's wear-prone surfaces and bearing wear itself. To check main and rod bearings visually, remove the caps that protect them. Inspection of a few of the main bearings and a few of the rod bearings should give you pretty good insight not merely into their condition, but into the engine's general condition as well. That done, and with things put back, the engine set upright, and your hands washed, you're ready to call a mechanic to fix what *really* needs fixing.

But even if you do no more than the four-step salesyard inspection above, you'll buy smarter when you buy used.

## BUYING A USED DIESEL VEHICLE

Tire kicking gives precious little insight into the condition of a gas engine car, pickup truck, or motor home, and it gives you even less into the condition of a diesel vehicle and its engine. What *can* be informative are these ten guides to buying used:

1. *Check the vehicle's odometer.* Even if it shows close to 100,000 miles, the diesel may still be good for again that many miles. But if the condition of the vehicle—such natural wear areas as the seats, floor covering, rubber moldings around doors and windows, obvious repainting, and so on—does not match the odometer's reading, suspect more diesel miles than the odometer shows.

2. *Demand to see—and carefully check—the engine's maintenance record.* Routine maintenance prescribed by the Owner's Manual—change of oil and oil filter every 2,500–4,000 miles, for example—during the used vehicle's *entire* road life is your tip-off to the engine's probable condition. If the maintenance record shows neglect, or if there *is* no maintenance record, suspect engine abuse; and in a diesel that means an engine which, at 100,000 miles, may shortly need major and costly overhaul.

3. *Start the engine, then look and listen for signs of trouble.* If the engine is difficult to start (must be cranked too often or is too long to start), if the glow plug period is excessive (count the seconds before the "WAIT" light goes off), or if the engine, once started, knocks or runs roughly, suspect trouble—with glow plugs, injectors, or the injection or fuel pumps.

4. *With engine running, give the vehicle a walk-around.* Often from the outside you can hear engine roughness that you can't detect from behind the wheel. Look especially at the exhaust for the telltale signs of smoke and the *big* trouble that smoke color can indicate: *white,* poor cylinder compression; *blue,* worn piston rings, cylinders, or valve guides; *black,* faulty injection pump and injection system problems. (See the smoke guide, p. 193.)

5. *Give it a drive test.* See how the vehicle climbs hills, how it gets up to speed, how it handles on the open road. Unless it's turbocharged, it is not likely to have the performance of the gas engine vehicle you now drive (but there are exceptions, among them the VW Rabbit diesel and virtually all vehicles powered by GM's nonturbo 350 CID V-8). Nonetheless, certainly the majority of pre-1978 diesel vehicles tended to be underpowered.

6. *With engine stopped, check for exhaust pipe oil.* If a finger, poked into the exhaust pipe, comes up smeared with oil or sludge, suspect piston ring wear.

7. *Give the engine and engine compartment a careful inspection.* A dealer's engine grooming can hide *some* signs of trouble, but seldom the most obvious, such as patched cracks or holes in the block, wiring that has obviously been burnt (or frayed from inattention), signs of fuel leaks around the injectors or injector pump, or deteriorating hoses. Be alert for indications of quick-grooming, such as a spanking new air filter (when you unlatch its holder) when most other parts under the hood seem drab and neglected.

8. *With a short piece of tubing, siphon out some fuel from the tank and inspect it in a clear glass or plastic container.* If you see stringy or clumpy black indications of fuel bacteria, you can be pretty sure the vehicle has been garaged and not

162 CHILTON'S DIESEL GUIDE

run for quite awhile (had the fuel been heavily contaminated by bacteria, it is unlikely you could have gotten the engine started).

9. *Ask to see receipts showing maintenance work done on the vehicle, especially other than routine engine care.* Get complete maintenance records if you can, at the least one covering the last 20,000 miles or so. Any dealer has them, and any private owner should. Be suspicious either of too little or too much maintenance, especially on the engine.

10. *Finally, before you buy, ask if you can have a competent diesel mechanic check out the vehicle.* The $25–$75 you may spend for the few minutes it'll take a seasoned diesel hand to confirm your own appraisal is worth the cost, and then some.


## TONY CAPANNA ON CONVERSIONS

With gasoline priced at $1.25 and more a gallon, and likely headed skyward, you've winced as you fueled your gas-guzzler and concluded what you need is an engine swap: a fuel-economy diesel for that gas gulper. Plainly, but not necessarily so simply, you have decided to convert: gas to diesel. But then questions arise: Does conversion make sense for you and your car (or pickup or rec-vehicle)? Will promised diesel economies permit you to recoup, any time soon, the considerable cost of conversion? Will a diesel engine stuffed under the hood in place of your gas engine fulfill the promise not merely of better fuel mileage, longer engine life, and lower maintenance costs, but also of performance?

Dollar-and-sense questions as these can be answered only by a conversion expert—the likes, for instance, of Tony Capanna, the acknowledged dean among the handful of specialists who make diesel conversion their business. Capanna and his busy, but modest Wilcap Company in Torrance, California, have likely swapped more diesels for gas engines than any other converter in the United States—and, probably, anybody else in the world. Largely unheralded are some astounding Capanna conversion successes.

A Capanna conversion—not, as many believe, the vaunted high-mileage Volkswagen diesel Rabbit—remains the top-ranked fuel miser among nonexperimental cars thus far tested by the Environmental Protection Agency. (The experimental Integrated Research Volkswagen (IRVW) ranks above both Capanna's conversion and the VW Rabbit diesel as the top EPA economy performer tested to date.) The conversion, a Ford Pinto powered by a 61-hp Nissan/Chrysler 4-cylinder turbocharged diesel, scored a heady 46.1 mpg in city driving, 60.3 mpg on the highway. The same conversion, fresh from capturing fuel economy top honors in 1974's much-publicized Inter-Collegiate Reduced Emission Devices Rally, made headlines (and a fuel-misering record) during the 1,400-mile Student-Engineered Economy Design Rally held in 1975. That time it drove away with economy honors by achieving an average 73.03 miles per gallon. By contrast, the EPA fuel economy measure for the Rabbit diesel is 41 mpg city, 55 mpg highway. Still another Capanna conversion—a Mazda 1200 fitted with a 37-hp, 4-cylinder English Leyland diesel—achieved 84 miles per gallon during General Motors testing. And, like many Capanna diesel conversions, made its mark virtually without fan-

**Fig. 7.2** Still hanging around Tony Capanna's shop as a daily errand car is his 84-mpg Mazda conversion. (Photograph by James Joseph)

fare. The Leyland conversion, incidentally, still hangs around Tony Capanna's shop, an errand car used daily by shopmen.

To answer that weighty question "Should I convert my car, pickup, or recreational vehicle to diesel?" here is a characteristically plainspoken and frank-answer interview with the dean of diesel converters, Tony Capanna.

### High-Mileage Drivers Likeliest Candidates

*Question:* Who are the likeliest candidates for diesel conversion?

*Tony Capanna:* High-mileage drivers—drivers who put, or plan to put, a lot of miles on their vehicles. That would include salesmen, folks who plan to retire and

**Fig. 7.3** Says Capanna, "The likeliest candidate for diesel conversion is the high-mileage driver." (Photograph by James Joseph)

spend a lot of their leisure time on the road, business drivers who shuttle around town most of the day and, of course, those stuck with real low-mileage motor homes and heavy-haul light vehicles, as the three-quarter-ton pickups.

*Question:* Is there any one "typical" driver who comes in for a diesel conversion?

*Capanna:* Yes, the guy with a recreational vehicle who's just a few years away from retirement and figuring to be on the move. Fellow like that plans to put on a lot of miles over the next five to six years. That means, with a conventional gasoline engine, spending a lot of money for fuel as well as for maintenance. He wants reliability and the lower-cost operation of a diesel.

*Question:* So it's not the hot-rodder who converts to diesel?

*Capanna:* Hardly. Sure, some younger drivers have got the diesel bug. Generally, though, the younger generation is looking for a lot of power and a lot of performance, which you don't normally get with a diesel. Again, typically, most conversions run to pickups.

*Question:* Pickup trucks?

*Capanna:* For the most part, yes . . . three-quarter-ton pickups, sometimes a half-ton and once in a while a ton.

*Question:* What about automobiles?

*Capanna:* Automobiles are really the toughest of all to do. And the hardest, dollars-and-sense, to justify "going diesel." With automobiles, you run into space problems you don't often confront in a pickup truck or motor home. There's simply less room in a car's engine compartment. It's harder fitting a diesel engine in there. Frankly, the few of us in the conversion business are so busy dieselizing vehicles that are easy to work on, as pickups, that we shy away from the cars.

*Question:* But you've done a lot of car conversions, some of them record-holders for mileage economy?

*Capanna:* Sure, and of course we can fit a diesel virtually into anything. But not necessarily the diesel a person would like to have or the engine his car needs to perform, dieselized, as well as it did with its gasoline engine. Sometimes the "right" diesel engine for a particular car won't fit under the hood. It's simply too

**Fig. 7.4** The Isuzu 4-cylinder model QD 90 fits nicely in the GMC model Sierra 15 engine compartment. Standard GM air conditioning is used.

big. For one example, there was this fellow who came in with his Lincoln Continental, a Mark IV as I recall, and said, "I'd like to get a diesel put in here." I asked him, "How much power do you want it to have?" And he replied, "I'd like it to be just as powerful as it is." "OK," I said, "then hold the end of this tape." He held the one end against the Continental's firewall and I ran the tape out to those windows over there . . . about 6 feet. "That," I told him, "is the size of diesel you'll need. Where would you like me to put it?"

*Question:* He laughed?

*Capanna:* No, he was disappointed. But the right diesel for the right conversion situation won't disappoint. It'll outperform the gasoline engine it replaces.

*Question:* But for that diesel-minded Continental owner, a diesel wouldn't?

*Capanna:* His wasn't a "right situation" for gasoline-to-diesel engine conversion.

*Question:* Let's illustrate the difference with an example.

*Capanna:* All right. Let's say someone comes in with a vehicle, let's say a three-quarter-ton pickup, powered by a 300- to 350-cubic-inch displacement (CID) gasoline engine. We can replace it with a 331 CID diesel that will give him every bit as much performance and greater pulling torque than his gas engine ever did. And far better economy all the way around.

*Question:* So the diesel you install is very nearly the exact match in size, cubic inch displacement, as the gas engine it replaces?

*Capanna:* Right. And that's one of a successful conversion's secrets. It's where, incidentally, diesel car makers for years went wrong. And it's why diesel cars got a reputation, deservedly, for being sluggish on the getaway. Engineering thinking went something like this: "Let's take out this big expensive-to-operate gasoline engine and put in a little economical diesel." Those little-engine cars got good fuel economy, but they didn't have anywhere near their previous performance. Or the performance of similar models, gasoline powered. The first produc-

**Fig. 7.5** Key to successful conversion is a diesel with same cubic inch displacement as the gas engine it replaces. Note high-pressure fuel-injection lines a little right of center.

tion diesel cars to come out with the right-sized engine on the first shot were the Oldsmobile and Volkswagen Rabbit. Their performance is every bit the match of their gasoline engine equivalents. And I say that not simply from the viewpoint of a converter, but as an owner. I own a 1978 diesel Olds 98.

*Question:* Conversion's first rule, then, is to match the size of what you put in to what you took out?

*Capanna:* Exactly. If you substitute a diesel with equal cubic inch displacement for the gasoline engine the vehicle formerly had, you aren't going to be disappointed.


### Fuel Economy Justifies Conversion

*Question:* Granted the diesel's better fuel economy and longer life, how can someone wanting to convert to diesel justify the cost, considering that today, and probably into the foreseeable future, diesel fuel and gasoline are virtually priced the same?

*Capanna:* That's a question a lot of people considering conversion ask, and it's got an easy answer: As the price of both fuels escalate, the savings per mile become greater if you drive a diesel. The reason you save more is because of the diesel's far better mileage.

*Question:* Better, on the average, by how much?

*Capanna:* By anywhere from sixty percent to over 100 percent—and 100 percent more miles per gallon with diesel isn't at all unusual. That's twice the mileage you got before, when it ran gasoline engined.

*Question:* The higher miles-per-gallon assumes, I suppose, a manual transmission, which fuel economy-wise is the more efficient transmission, rather than use of an automatic transmission?

*Capanna:* A manual transmission, yes, and one that's also equipped with overdrive gears. The comparative transmission figures look like this: With a standard transmission you'll get about 15 percent better diesel mileage than with an automatic. And if your manual transmission has an overdrive as well, you can expect something like 25 percent better fuel mileage than with an automatic. So right there—with a manual/overdrive transmission—you get, say, 25 percent more miles per gallon than you did running your gasoline engine with an automatic transmission. Add to this a diesel's inherent fuel efficiency over a same or nearly same size gasoline engine, and you're talking 70 percent to 80 percent more miles per gallon, anyway, with diesel. And often, 100 percent more.

*Question:* Can we spell out some parameters to help answer the "Should I convert to diesel?" question.

*Capanna:* Let's begin with mileage. The likeliest car conversion candidate is the 100-mile driver.

*Question:* The "100-mile driver"?

*Capanna:* Yes, a person who normally drives his car at least 100 miles a day— and there are plenty of people who do, as I singled out earlier. But if you don't, I'd be hard put to justify conversion on the basis of economics. Because, swapping diesel for gasoline, and making the system work, you're going to have to figure spending $4,000–$5,500 at the low end of the scale, and as much as $9,000 for some larger-engine swaps. Even at the lower end of the scale, $4,000–$5,500 for a conversion, you're talking approximately half the price of a pretty good new car—more than half the price, in fact, of a diesel Volkswagen Rabbit. And at the higher end, you're again talking more than half the price of a diesel Toronado Oldsmobile. Both of them are excellent, high-performance diesel packages. So, you've got to weigh the figures to see if you want to spend the kind of money we're talking about for a conversion; or should you buy one of the new diesel packages—a diesel Rabbit, Olds, or whatever. Coming onto the market are a lot of others, including diesel Fords and Chevrolets.

*Question:* Only a few years back, of course, the average driver didn't have that kind of choice—reasonably priced diesel production automobiles?

*Capanna:* There was virtually no choice. You either converted your car—new, old or inbetween—to diesel, or you didn't drive a diesel automobile.

*Question:* But there are even some who don't drive 100 miles a day who can logically, even economically, swap their present car's gasoline engine for a diesel?

*Capanna:* Yes, a very considerable number of people who like the gasoline engine car they drive, although not its insatiable appetite for gasoline, and plan to "drive it out" keep the car and drive it another four to five, maybe even more years. For them, the $4,000–$5,500 they may spend for a conversion becomes economical in terms of years rather than miles. Depending on the price of fuel, even an average 15,000–20,000-miles-a-year driver will save somewhere between $1,000–$1,500 annually above his prorated conversion costs—if he drives his car out, let's say, an additional five years.

*Question:* Even considering the $1,000 a year that a $5,000 diesel conversion would cost him, prorated over five years, he can save yet another $1,000–$1,500 each year in fuel simply because of the 60 percent, even 100 percent better mileage he gets from his diesel?

*Capanna:* That's right. Still, the people who need conversion most are those hurting most: vehicle owners quite literally being forced off the road by their vehicles' low-low fuel mileage and by the escalating cost of fuel. They have no choice but to convert to diesel. They simply can no longer afford to drive gasolined—or with the economics of gasoline engines.

*Question:* You're talking about the owners of pickup trucks, recreational vehicles—motor homes and the like?

*Capanna:* Precisely. Let me give you some examples and, doing so, very specifically spell out what's involved in their gas-to-diesel conversion in the way of parts, major components, shopwork, and costs—the same ingredients which go into any conversion, be it a pickup or the family car.

*Question:* The specifics of any good diesel conversion?

*Capanna:* The specifics, yes. The "what's involved in diesel conversion?" question answered in hardware and hard economics.

*Question:* A typical diesel conversion candidate who literally must convert to diesel else be forced, economically, off the road?

*Capanna:* Yes. Let's start with a pickup truck that's getting—and believe it or not, we've had some this bad—just five miles to the gallon. An extreme example, but not all that unusual. Let's say it's a three-quarter-ton pickup seldom getting better than five miles per gallon, with automatic transmission and a large, gas guzzling gasoline engine.

*Question:* He can still, once dieselized, get "stay on the road mileage" despite his automatic transmission—assuming this three-quarter-ton pickup owner wants to retain his automatic transmission?

*Capanna:* He can. If he wants automatic transmission, despite its cost in fuel, OK, but we don't generally recommend that he keep the transmission he has unless it happens to be a Chrysler automatic. We recommend the Chrysler for conversions over either Chevy or Ford because the Chrysler automatic transmission doesn't require vacuum to shift it, as do the others. You can make other types of automatic transmissions work without vacuum, by adding available accessories, but they never do quite function as well as they should.

*Question:* So if he wants automatic transmission, you'd recommend as part of the conversion a switch to an automatic, as the Chrysler, requiring no vacuum, something the diesel engine doesn't produce?

*Capanna:* Correct. But we'd prefer, to achieve maximum diesel fuel economy, that he stick with a manual transmission.

*Question:* So it is likely that the driver converting to diesel will need a new transmission in addition to the diesel?

*Capanna:* Not necessarily. Most pickup trucks have four-speed manual transmissions in them anyway. What they don't generally have is the overdrive. And overdrive, as part of the manual transmission gives you, with diesel, at least 10 percent better fuel mileage than a manual transmission without overdrive, as we mentioned before. And the entire combination: manual transmission with overdrive, 25 percent better fuel mileage, anyway, than the standard automatic transmission.

*Question:* You're drawing some fairly tight parameters as to the kind of gas engine vehicles and their major components most likely, with conversion, to give highest fuel mileage?

*Capanna:* Not all that tight, no. I am merely saying that certain components, as an overdrive-equipped manual transmission, when mated with the right-size diesel, all but guarantee a conversion package with the highest attainable fuel economy. And that, of course, is what conversion to diesel is all about.

*Question:* Is there, then, some "ideal" vehicle which, logically, would profit most from conversion?

*Capanna:* If there is any single "ideal" conversion prospect, insofar as we are concerned, it'd be a Chevrolet three-quarter-ton pickup with a standard manual transmission to which a fuel-economizing overdrive can be added quite easily in front of the transmission, giving eight speeds forward rather than the four of the standard manual transmission. With a doubling of available forward gear speeds— a gear "split" it is called—diesel performance is better, smoother, and more fuel economical because the step between each shift position of the gears is smaller. So when you shift, you don't drop as many rpms as with the normal four-speed transmission. And because you drop fewer rpms between a gear shift, you don't lose as much power in shifting.

### Advantage of "Gear Splitting"

*Question:* This "gear-splitting" thing probably deserves a bit more explaining. Many drivers aren't familiar with the term, or with overdrive gears, which are particularly advantageous, fuel economy-wise, in a diesel conversion.

*Capanna:* Well, gearing, of course, is the method used to transmit engine power to the wheels. When you start out, just to get a vehicle rolling, you need a lot of heft: muscle power. The engineers call it "torque," which literally means the rotational, twisting force needed to get the wheels moving and the car rolling. The diesel is renowned for its muscle power, for its torque, even when the engine, as when you start up, isn't nearly up to its full revolutions-per-minute. A diesel develops nearly its full torque at very low engine speeds. So it has far greater pulling power than the gasoline engine, whose muscular torque isn't developed until the engine is turning much faster and whose torque is confined to a relatively narrow range of total engine speeds. It's because of its quite fantastic torque or muscle power at low engine speeds that the diesel is so universally used in heavy equipment—in bulldozers, heavy haul trucks and, increasingly, in farm tractors—in applications where you need a great deal of muscle. Diesel has the muscle.

*Question:* And it's the gears that translate that muscle to motion—to getting the car rolling, in first gear, then moving faster the higher up the gears you go.

*Capanna:* Right. And it explains, in part, why overdrive gears appreciably add to fuel economy in a diesel conversion. Consider for a moment a diesel car with a four-speed manual transmission—with first, second, third, and fourth, or high, gears. To keep it simple, let's suppose the Owner's Manual lists the transmission gear ratios something like this:

| | |
|---|---|
| first gear | 4 : 1 |
| second gear | 3 : 1 |
| third gear | 2 : 1 |
| fourth gear | 1 : 1 |

You won't find gear ratios as even-numbered as these. You're more likely, as for example in the four-speed manual gearing of the Volkswagen diesel Rabbit, to see the ratio for first gear given as a fractional ratio: 3.45 : 1.

But we're keeping it simple. What 4 : 1 means is simply this: whatever the engine's speed, it is *reduced* through the gearing to one-fourth what it was at the engine.

*Question:* The ratio 4 : 1 is a *reduction* ratio? If, for instance, engine speed were only four revolutions per minute, then through gearing, as in first gear, with a reduction ratio of 4 : 1, the speed transmitted to the drive shaft by the gearing would be only one revolution per minute?

*Capanna:* Literally, yes. But, of course, the speed of the engine is much higher. Still, the ratio holds in our first gear 4 : 1 ratio example, so long as you're in that gear. Thus, with a 4 : 1 gear ratio, if the diesel's speed is 1,600 rpms, it is reduced to 400 rpms through the gearing, and these are the rpms transmitted to the drive shaft.

When engine speed, in a diesel particularly, is reduced like that it adds up to

**Fig. 7.6** In a conversion, you need power under the hood equal to that of a gas engine, and the proper gearing to make it work. Note the oversized radiator. (Photograph by James Joseph)

pulling power. And, to get a car rolling, that's what you need: muscular "torque." That's what you get with a 4 : 1 first-gear ratio. But once the car is rolling, you don't need start-up muscle, but rather rotational speed at the wheels. You've got the car rolling. Now you want to go. So, in second gear, once you're rolling, you'll note in our simplified example that the gear ratio is reduced to 3 : 1 which, by obvious arithmetic, increases rpms out of the gearing and to the wheels.

*Question:* Let's go over the simple math.

*Capanna:* Sure. What these reduction gear ratios mean is that whatever the engine's speed, it's divided by the ratio's first number. So, in a 4 : 1 ratio first gear, with the engine turning 1,600 rpm, you divide engine speed by 4 and get 400 rpms through the gearing. Now, in second, with a 3 : 1 gear ratio, you divide engine speed by only 3. So with the engine turning 1,600 rpm, divided by 3, you get roughly 533 rpms through the gearing—an *increase* in speed at the drive shaft and wheels. That, of course, is what you want, because you want to get going, get up speed.

*Question:* The same, of course, applies the higher up the gearing you go. In third, with yet a smaller 2 : 1 ratio, you get 800 rpms through the gearing (1,600 rpms divided by 2). And in fourth, the "high" drive gear—cruising gear on the highway—you get the engine's full rpms through the gearing. The fourth gear's 1 : 1 ratio delivers the engine's full 1,600 rpms (1,600 divided by 1) through the gearing.

*Capanna:* Right. And you're rolling down the highway. But there's one problem here, and it's where overdrive comes in.

*Question:* A problem that explains that term "gear splitting" and why overdrive gives better mileage, especially in a diesel?

*Capanna:* Yes. If you'll look back over our figures, you'll see that there is relatively little rpms difference between first and second. Once in first gear, with 400 rpms through the gearing, you shift to second, and now the gearing delivers 533 rpms—an increase, certainly, but only a matter of 133 rpms in our simplified example. Moving higher in the gearing, the rpm *difference* between gearing grows, proportionally, much greater. And that difference becomes even greater as, accelerating, you increase engine speed. Between third gear's 800 rpms, in our example, and fourth gear's 1,600 rpms, there's a big 800 rpm difference—just in the process of shifting gears. If, at the same time, you accelerated, as you would, and if the diesel were now turning 3,000–4,000 rpms, the difference in rpms between third gear and fourth might be a thousand rpms.

*Question:* It's right there, between third and fourth gear, especially, where there's a critical rpms difference and, by inference, a fuel-wasting power loss?

*Capanna:* Exactly. Shifting between third and fourth, particularly, and whether manually or with an automatic transmission, momentarily drops a big bundle of rpms. That's lost power. To prevent this, we prefer the addition of overdrive gearing—in effect, another set of gears between the higher ones the vehicle already has. That way, the rpm drop during shifting is far less, and the power loss far less.

*Question:* So, by adding additional gearing—overdrive gearing—you in effect "split" the difference in rpms between the vehicle's usual gearing?

*Capanna:* Precisely. Usually, we add an extra four gears, giving the driver eight gears if he really wants to use them. Generally, a driver will use six of the available eight gears he gets, with overdrive's "split gears" added to the transmission he now has. The important overdrive gears are, as we noted, in the higher gear-shift range, especially between third gear and fourth. Between those the overdrive "split" adds another gear which is called "third overdrive." And after the fourth gear, we add another, called "fourth overdrive."

*Question:* So now, with overdrive, the diesel conversion isn't shifted from first to second to third to fourth but, using the most often used six of the now eight available gears, with overdrive, from first to second to third to *third overdrive* to fourth and finally to *fourth overdrive*.

*Capanna:* And doing so, you drop far fewer rpms, lose far less power—which is one reason with overdrive "gear splits" you can get another 10-percent better fuel mileage—and, overall, with the right conversion package, 100-percent better mileage than what the same vehicle got with its gasoline engine.

*Question:* OK. In our conversion "package" thus far, we've substituted for the gas engine a diesel of about equal CID. And we've added overdrive gearing to the 4- or 5-speed manual transmission. What else goes into a conversion?

### Conversion Usually Calls for Larger Radiator

*Capanna:* Almost always a larger radiator.

*Question:* The old radiator hasn't cooling capacity enough for the diesel?

*Capanna:* Actually, it usually has—for *most* occasions. Underline that word "most." But on occasion, say on long, steep, hot climbs, when the original radiator isn't big enough, you can ruin the diesel. To ensure yourself, you put in a larger radiator—in most cases, a radiator with twice the cooling capacity of the gas-engined radiator it replaces.

*Question:* To get that double capacity, the conversion's new radiator has to be wider and higher than the one it replaces?

*Capanna:* That's usually the way it works. There is usually space enough where the old one went to fit in the new.

*Question:* What about the gas engine vehicle's fuel tank?

*Capanna:* The fuel tank or tanks are left as they are. We just drain out the gasoline, that's all. But there's one other thing you've got to do: remove the tank's fuel line and take off the gasoline filter that's on the end of it. And throw that filter away.

*Question:* The gasoline fuel-tank filter is discarded?

*Capanna:* Yes. The material that the gasoline fuel filter on the end of the fuel line in the tank is made of isn't compatible with diesel fuel. Leave the filter in there, and the little holes in it will swell shut. So the diesel won't get fuel.

*Question:* So the fuel line in the tank is put back without a filter?

*Capanna:* It is. But you install a substitute for it, actually a far more efficient filter, where the filter is easier to reach—between the diesel fuel tank and the diesel's fuel pump. Actually, of course, the diesel engine comes with one fuel filter already installed. It's called the "secondary fuel filter," which anticipates that you'll install another, the "primary fuel filter" (the one replacing the tank's filter you discarded) upstream of it—that is, between the fuel tank and the "secondary" filter that comes installed on the engine.

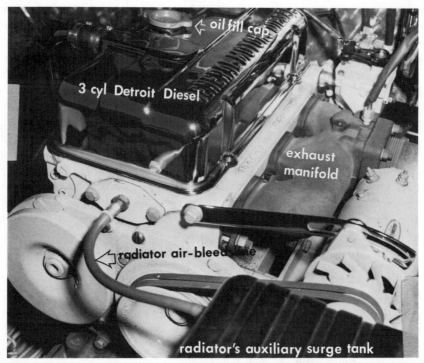

**Fig. 7.7**   Chromed and glittering conversion uses trusty 3-cylinder Detroit (GM) industrial/automotive diesel, rated 101 hp at 2,890 rpm. Note radiator surge tank. (Photograph by James Joseph)

*Question:* So the diesel conversion package includes a replacement fuel filter for the one removed from the tank's fuel line?

*Capanna:* Yes. And the replacement, as I indicated, is located somewhere—usually in the engine compartment—where it's easy to reach and to service, something you couldn't do with the gas tank's old gasoline filter.

*Question:* So there's quite a difference in filtering ability between the gasoline filter you discard and the diesel fuel filter you add?

*Capanna:* A big difference. One reason there is is that diesel fuel must be kept extremely clean. The filter we add to replace the tank's old gasoline one gets rid of contaminants down to one micron size—contaminants so small you can't see them without a microscope.

*Question:* What else must we add to this conversion?

*Capanna:* Well, a lot of piping, brackets, and, of course, engine mounts. The engine mounts are custom-made. And you've got to make brackets for the air conditioning components and for the power steering pumps—the reason being that these components, although retained from the original engine compartment hardware, will likely have to be mounted in other than their original places. That's because the diesel may be larger than the gas engine it replaces—or, more probably, of a bit different shape. So parts that snugged around the gas engine may have to be relocated to snug around the diesel. And you've got to plumb—put in lines—for the turbocharger.

*Question:* Assuming the conversion is turbocharged?

*Capanna:* Well, almost always we put in a turbocharger.

*Question:* Instrumentation?

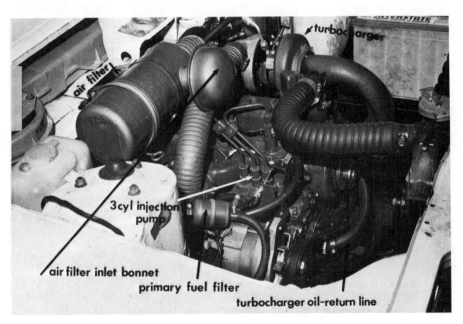

**Fig. 7.8** Turbocharger kit can add up to 30–50 percent more horsepower and can increase fuel economy significantly. Virtually all conversions are turbocharged. (Photograph by James Joseph)

*Capanna:* We don't have much in the way of instrumentation. We put in a pyrometer to keep track of turbo temperature. And we put in a water-level warning light to let the driver know if the water's low in the radiator. That just about does it, insofar as instruments are concerned, in most diesel conversions.

*Question:* What about a new fuel gauge? There's something, I think, about switching from gasoline to diesel fuel that makes the old gas gauge read inaccurately?

*Capanna:* Not exactly inaccurately, just differently. But we generally don't switch gauges. What happens is this: Because diesel fuel is thicker, has greater viscosity than gasoline, the fuel gauge float, the same one used when there was gasoline in there, floats a little higher. So, on the fuel gauge, you get a different proportionate level reading than when you ran gasoline fueled.

*Question:* With the fuel float floating higher, the gauge is likely to show "full" when the tank level is actually some gallons below that mark?

*Capanna:* Right. When you completely fill up with diesel, you'll experience being able to go over 100 miles before the gauge comes off the full line. But from then on, it usually moves pretty fast—toward half-full, quarter-full, etc. That's because now the tank level is going down and the float is following it down. But the diesel conversion driver gets accustomed to a lingering gauge reading of full, then a faster-than-normal drop after 100 miles or so.

*Question:* What about an extra battery? Most production diesels have two, or at the least, an oversized single.

*Capanna:* If you're going to drive—or if you live—in a cold climate, then you'll need two batteries in your conversion. They help turn the engine over when it's cold. But the fact that production cars usually have two doesn't necessarily mean someone living in warm climates—Florida, the South, Texas, Southern California—needs two. The manufacturer puts two batteries in there because he doesn't know where the car is going to be driven. So he plays safe with the two rather than just one. But the one we put in usually has a 100-amp rating.

*Question:* All this sounds pretty expensive. Are we still talking in the $4,000-to-$5,500 range for the conversion? Whatever the case, we'd better put some price tags on the various components we've talked about.

### Conversion Not Cheap

*Capanna:* Diesel conversions don't come cheap. Let's start with the engine. The "cheapest" diesel engine runs about $3,000—for a 4-cylinder diesel. Put in a Caterpillar V-8, and you're talking $8,000 for the diesel. So the range is from $3,000 to $8,000 for an automotive diesel at today's prices.

*Question:* And what, roughly, are some price tags for the other components?

*Capanna:* A turbocharger: anywhere from $300 for just the turbocharger, the barebones unit, to $900 for a complete kit—we call them "bolt-on" turbo-kits because they come complete with all the hardware you need, and you simply bolt things into place.

*Question:* Assuming an owner keeps his manual transmission, what about the parts to adapt it to the diesel?

*Capanna:* A manual transmission may not need them. But the automatic transmissions do. We make the adapters here in the shop. They cost anywhere from $175 to $400.

*Question:* What about the labor involved in a conversion, in hours?

*Capanna:* They add up to about 200 hours.

*Question:* A lot of hours, hauling out the gasoline engine and putting in the diesel. What's the total labor bill for all those hours?

*Capanna:* I can't really quote hourly labor rates. We've got a package price for conversions, and that includes the labor.

*Question:* So, to get it all down in figures again, what kind of package prices are we talking about?

*Capanna:* Normally, from about $4,500 to $9,000, depending how big the vehicle is, what engine you want, what combinations you want in the transmission.

*Question:* You're talking a lot of money.

*Capanna:* Right. And a lot of time.

*Question:* All right, let's say somebody wants to convert his pickup truck, motor home, even his car, assuming he's a high-mileage driver and can expect, in reasonable time, to recoup most of his diesel conversion costs by spending less per mile for fuel. Around the country are only, really, a relatively few "conversion specialists" like yourself. Can a vehicle owner have the gasoline-to-diesel conversion done locally, by someone not a specialist in gasoline-for-diesel swapping?

*Capanna:* Yes. But you've got to find somebody locally who is pretty good at fabricating and machining. That, or buy such things as transmission adapters special-ordered and ready-made. And then there's some welding. But there are a lot of guys around who can do that. Machine tools help. But you really don't have to have them. Basically, all it takes is a hacksaw, a welder, and some moxie.

*Question:* Still, some of the doing takes very considerable skill?

*Capanna:* Not more skill than a *real* mechanic has. You've got, of course, to make sure when putting in the transmission, if you're doing that, that it's dead center of the crankshaft. Otherwise, the transmission is going to be forever jumping out of gear. That, or breaking the end off the jackshaft. Probably adapting the transmission, and getting it very precisely fitted in, is the most precision part of the conversion. As for the rest of it, it doesn't matter that much if something is one sixteenth of an inch off-kilter.

*Question:* So a conversion can be done locally, if a vehicle owner buys the basic components and the special parts from a conversion specialist as yourself?

*Capanna:* Yes.

*Question:* You sell diesel engines, I know, as well as turbo kits for some engines, transmission adapters, and the like. Do you send an instruction book to help someone and his local mechanic get the conversion right?

*Capanna:* No, we don't. But I'm as close as the phone if someone buys components, including the engine, and needs help.

### Conversion Demands Knowledge

*Question:* Do manuals come with a diesel engine—maybe step-by-step instructions telling how to install it?

*Capanna:* No, when you buy an engine you get just the Owner's Manual, much as would a new vehicle owner. But it doesn't tell you anything about how to do an installation. The manual just tells you about the engine. That's all. To do an installation locally, you'll need two additional books—a Parts Book and an Overhaul Book. The first lists engine parts and tells you how to order them. The second—more familiarly known as a Shop Manual—tells you how to overhaul an engine, and, sometimes, how to install it.

*Question:* I assume these two pretty essential books aren't for free.

*Capanna:* Costs vary. But together they can run as high as $40 or so. Costs vary with the engine maker, who generally sells both manuals. You can order them by mail.

*Question:* But, of course, if a vehicle owner finds a good local mechanic, and he does the job, he'll order all the parts needed, along with the various manuals, if he feels he needs those, too?

*Capanna:* Right. Diesel conversion isn't generally something you find many drivers doing themselves. It takes a lot of time and a lot of doing.

*Question:* How might one spot "a good local mechanic" able to do the job?

*Capanna:* I'm not sure I can tell you how to spot one, but I can tell you what an "honest-to-goodness" mechanic is: someone who has a mechanical mind; who understands when, to make something fit, it has to go up or down or sideways. If a mechanic understands how to fit things in, and if he's able to picture what has to be done in his mind, and can make it work, he can install a diesel engine.

*Question:* Then in diesel conversions things just don't fit normally into place? The engine, for example, just doesn't "drop in"?

*Capanna:* Never. A lot of people come in and see one of our engines sitting in a vehicle, and they say, "Heh, it fits right in." Well, it didn't. That's not the case, ever. It fits because we made it fit.

*Question:* The payoff, obviously, is a diesel conversion that delivers its promise: long, minimum-maintenance engine life, good road performance and 60 percent, maybe as much as 100 percent, more miles per gallon than with the old gasoline engine.

*Capanna:* It all goes back to the "right situation" we spoke of at the outset. Convert with a lot of miles and years ahead of you—and especially a pickup truck, motor home, or the like, that's driving you to the fueling poor farm—and a diesel conversion will deliver its promise. And for some drivers who expected less, far more than they had even hoped for.

*Question:* Still, a diesel conversion isn't for everybody or every vehicle?

*Capanna:* Certainly not.

# Chapter 8

# Troubleshooting

Troubleshooting is nothing more than a systematic, clearheaded analysis of what's wrong. In simplest, most practical terms, it is a form of elimination. If, typically, the needle of the dashboard's temperature gauge suddenly edges toward the boiling mark, there's an obvious coolant system problem. In a diesel's coolant system, as in a gasoline engine's, there are only a few things that can go wrong to cause the system to overheat, and you don't have to be an automotive, much less a diesel, whiz to sleuth them out. You simply *eliminate* with a quick, visual inspection those parts of the system that are obviously *right;* that done, what's *wrong* often becomes almost immediately apparent.

Even before the radiator has cooled enough for you to remove its pressure cap safely, you can eliminate half a dozen probable causes while the system is still under pressure. Leaks—or the absence of leaks—in hoses, connections, the water pump itself, or in the radiator core structure are easily spotted. With the radiator cooled and its cap removed, a quick glance tells you whether the coolant level is at the proper full mark.

As shown in one of the troubleshooting ''symptom/cause/what to do'' charts on the following pages, you have already eliminated the majority of ''probable causes'' for an overheating coolant system. Only a few more remain. Of these, one possible cause is a loose radiator fan-drive belt. On many diesel engines, although certainly not all, the radiator fan is belt driven by the crankshaft while the water pump is driven by the engine's timing gear. Assuming for the engine you're troubleshooting that the fan is belt driven, you can test the belt by hand, to feel whether it has tension or is too loose. If still in doubt, you can check visually with engine running whether the belt, being loose, is slipping on the pulley through which it drives the fan. Your verdict: The fan is operating normally.

For many coolant systems, only three or four possible causes for overheating remain. You've already eliminated, in less than five minutes' time, all of the

177

others. The water pump itself may be internally defective, the thermostat may be stuck closed and preventing coolant from circulating through the radiator, the radiator may be clogged, or the temperature gauge itself may be faulty. Of these four possible causes of coolant system overheating, the last two are the least likely. If the system was indeed hot when you opened the hood, then the gauge that gave you first warning was correct and working; so that eliminates the gauge. What eliminates the possibility of radiator clogging was the suddenness of the overheating. Clogging builds gradually in a radiator, gradually causing the system to run hotter and hotter—and this happens over time, not suddenly; so clogging is eliminated.

Troubleshooting, you're now down to just two probable causes: the water pump or the thermostat. If the water pump isn't leaking (and it isn't, as your preliminary visual leak check showed), then it's probably the thermostat. In any engine, a defective thermostat leads the list as the most frequent cause of overheating. Change-out and replacement of the thermostat and water pump are simple jobs, well within the skill of many diesel owners.

But even if you never intend to take a wrench in hand, troubleshooting has its rewards. One of them is better insight into your diesel vehicle and its engine. Sleuthing a problem to its probable causes also puts you on more nearly equal (and more knowledgeable) terms with the mechanic when you take the vehicle in to have the trouble corrected. And troubleshooting builds confidence, in yourself as a diesel owner and in the vehicle you own and drive.

The troubleshooting charts in this chapter have been carefully excerpted and abbreviated from service and Owner's Manuals of major engine and engine component makers. Shown, generally, are common diesel and diesel system problems that, at one time or another, may confront the diesel owner. Almost all are within the grasp—and solution—of anyone who has read this book.

Even should your diesel *never* develop *any* of the listed symptoms, you'll be forewarned, and forearmed. And if a symptom should develop, you won't panic. With considerable self-assurance, you'll be prepared, through the often quick process of elimination, to analyze whether an apparent problem is a problem at all—and, if it is, whether it is serious enough for a mechanic's attention.

Troubleshooting can save you time, and money you may not need to spend on a mechanic's correction. The troubleshooting charts that follow are like the first aid kit under your seat (or, as in the Mercedes-Benz, tucked away in its own compartment). You never really expect to need or use it. But should the need arise, it's there.

## QUICK-CHECK TROUBLESHOOTING GUIDE

Elsewhere in this chapter are specific trouble-diagnosis guides for several popular diesel engines. By contrast, the following *quick-check guide,* devised by the Ford Motor Company, is designed to pinpoint, quickly, the probable cause of an apparent problem in virtually any make or model of diesel engine. Unlike the chapter's more specific ones, this quick-check guide doesn't suggest remedies.

Rather, it narrows to a few probable causes and sources the most common of diesel engine symptoms. To make diagnosis even easier, it pinpoints problems that are probably purely mechanical (a clogged air cleaner, for example) and those most likely to be involved with an engine's fuel system (for example, the presence of air in fuel-system lines). As a universal quick-diagnostic guide, it is one of the most valuable of its kind for any owner of a diesel vehicle.

## DIESEL ENGINE WILL NOT START
### Starter does not crank the engine
1. Battery discharged
2. Electrical lead(s) disconnected
3. Faulty starter switch
4. Faulty key-starter switch
5. Faulty starter switch
6. Hydraulic lock, water, or oil in combustion chamber

### Starter cranks engine slowly
1. Battery not fully charged
2. Battery cable(s) loose
3. Electrical connections corroded or dirty
4. Engine oil too heavy
5. Faulty starter motor

### Starter cranks engine
*Mechanical*
1. Blocked air cleaner
2. Improper engine timing
3. Poor cylinder compression

*Fuel System*
### Fuel NOT reaching injection pump
1. Insufficient fuel in tank
2. Blocked fuel line
3. Restricted fuel filter
4. Air leaks in fuel line
5. Faulty fuel lift pump

### Fuel reaching injection pump
1. Air in fuel system
2. Control rod sticking
3. Excess-fuel device inoperative
4. Faulty injectors

## ENGINE OVERHEATS
*Mechanical*
1. Insufficient water in cooling system
2. Insufficient oil in crankcase
3. Fan belt loose or broken
4. Plugged radiator
5. Thermostat stuck
6. Timing incorrect (diesel injection pump)
7. Faulty water pump
8. Radiator leaking
9. Air in cooling system
10. Radiator cap not sealing or defective
11. Internal engine leakage
12. Exhaust gas leakage into cooling system
13. Cylinder head gasket improperly installed

14. Hot spots in engine due to poor coolant circulation
15. Extended engine idling
*Fuel System*
1. Faulty injector(s)

ENGINE KNOCKS
*Mechanical*
1. Diluted or thin oil
2. Insufficient oil supply
3. Low oil pressure
4. Excessive crankshaft end play
5. Flywheel runout excessive
6. Excessive connecting rod or main bearing clearance
7. Bent or twisted connecting rod
8. Crankshaft journals out-of-round
9. Excessive piston ring side clearance
10. Excessive piston-to-cylinder bore clearance
11. Broken rings
12. Excessive piston pin clearance
13. Piston pin retainer loose or missing
14. Excessive camshaft end play
15. Worn timing gear teeth
16. Excessive timing gear backlash
17. Valve rocker(s) sticking
18. Valve spring(s) broken
19. Improper injection timing
*Fuel System*
1. Faulty injector
2. Air in system

## ENGINE KNOCKING

Diesels may "knock"—a rough, rattling sound like the knock in a gasoline engine, but from different causes—for a number of reasons. The main reason for diesel knock is delayed combustion. In a diesel, ignition (combustion) should begin *before* the entire fuel charge has been injected into the cylinder or precombustion chamber. If combustion is delayed—that is, if ignition does not take place before the entire charge is delivered—the engine may smoke or knock. There are two distinct types of diesel knock:

*Diesel or "Delayed" Knock:* When the delay period before ignition is long, a large quantity of atomized fuel (sometimes, in fact, the entire charge) accumulates in the combustion chamber. Then when ignition *does* take place, it is more violent—as you might suspect—and the sudden high pressure from igniting so large a fuel charge causes the knock (called "diesel knock") heard in some engines. Unlike the knock in a gasoline engine, which is caused by burning the last portion of fuel, in a diesel the knock occurs with the burning of the first portion of the large quantity of injected fuel which, due to delayed ignition, has accumulated at the top of the cylinder. Diesel knock may be due to improper fuel (too low a cetane number, for example) or to injector or injector pump problems.

*Preignition Knock:* This is a quite different kind of knock: ignition *before* the piston has reached top dead center and *before* the injector has injected a charge of fuel. One cause is a dripping or leaking injector, which leaks some fuel into the combustion chamber, where it is ignited before the normal fuel charge is injected. Crankcase oil, slipping past faulty cylinder rings and into the combustion chamber, may be ignited also, causing preignition knock. Often preignition knock, far less violent than diesel knock simply because there is less fuel or oil to ignite, is barely audible, and sometimes it is not audible at all. Nonetheless, it can cause a diesel to run rough.

Both types of knock are the result of uncontrolled ignition. For that reason alone, although there are plenty of others, the problem should be corrected.

**Knocking Declines**

| *In a Gasoline Engine With:* | *In a Diesel Engine With:* |
| --- | --- |
| Higher engine speed | Lower engine speed |
| Lower engine loading | Higher engine loading |
| Lower compression | Higher compression |
| Carburetor adjustment to *either* richer or leaner mixture | Better mixing of fuel and air (more turbulence or stratification) |
| | More suitable jet spray pattern and injection pressure |
| Later timing of ignition | More favorable timing of start of fuel injection |
| Increased cooling (colder intake air, lower coolant temperature, cooler oil, sodium-cooled exhaust valves, aluminum alloy pistons and cylinder head) | Decreased cooling (warmer intake air, higher coolant temperature, warmer oil, glow plugs, etc.) |
| Smaller cylinders | Larger cylinders |
| Higher air humidity | |
| Lower air density (higher altitude) | |
| Addition to the fuel of such octane improvers as tetraethyl lead and methyl-tertiary-butyl-ether. | Addition to the fuel of such cetane improvers as amyl nitrate and hexyl nitrate. |

*ENGINE DOES NOT GIVE FULL POWER*
  *Mechanical*
    1. Clogged air cleaner
    2. Low cylinder compression
    3. Improper valve lash adjustment
    4. Faulty valves
    5. Blown head gasket
    6. Engine overheating
    7. Sticking piston rings
    8. Worn piston rings
    9. Worn cylinder walls
  *Fuel System*
    1. Restricted fuel line
    2. Faulty injectors
    3. Incorrect fuel delivery
    4. Insufficient fuel in tank
    5. Incorrect injection timing
    6. Air in fuel system

    7. Restricted fuel filters
    8. Control rod sticking
    9. Faulty fuel pump

## ENGINE IDLES ROUGHLY
### Mechanical
    1. Sticking valve(s)
    2. Broken valve spring(s)
    3. Governor idle setting incorrect
    4. Air leak in governor system
    5. Incorrect valve timing
### Fuel System
    1. Insufficient fuel in tank
    2. Air in fuel system
    3. Restricted fuel filter
    4. Improper idle adjustment
    5. Faulty fuel pump
    6. Faulty injector(s)
    7. Faulty fuel injection pump

## EXCESSIVE EXHAUST SMOKE
### Mechanical
    1. Poor cylinder compression
### Fuel System
    1. Excess fuel device locked in activated position
    2. Maximum stop screw out of adjustment
    3. Incorrect injection pump timing
    4. Faulty injector(s)
    5. Faulty fuel injection pump

## DIESEL EXHAUST SMOKE ANALYSIS
### Black or gray smoke
    1. Engine lugging
    2. Improper grade of fuel
    3. Air cleaner clogged or damaged
    4. High exhaust back pressure
    5. Improper injection pump timing
    6. Faulty injectors
    7. Improper fuel delivery
    8. Incorrect engine valve timing
    9. Engine overheating
    10. Poor cylinder compression
### Blue smoke
    1. Air cleaner oil (in oil-bath type air cleaners) too light in viscosity, or oil level in air cleaner too high
    2. Engine oil getting into combustion chamber probably past rings or valve seals
    3. Engine crankcase oil level too high
    4. Wrong grade or type of fuel
    5. Poor cylinder compression
### White smoke
    1. Wrong grade or type of fuel
    2. Cooling system temperature below normal operating temperature
    3. Faulty injector(s)
    4. Low cylinder compression

*Black smoke* consists of a large number of particles of carbon; this carbon forms when the fuel is heated in oxygen-lean regions in the combustion chamber.

*Blue smoke* consists of a large number of particles of fuel oil of about 0.5 micron diameter or less; these particles are recondensed droplets of unburned fuel or incompletely burned fuel. These small particles cause blue light to be scattered. When an engine is running fast but under light load, regions of the combustion chamber may be at too low a temperature to permit igniton, and blue smoke appears. When viewed in transmitted light, the blue smoke appears brown.

*White smoke* consists of a large number of particles of fuel oil larger than about 1.0 micron diameter. To produce white smoke, the fuel must have time to condense into larger droplets than for blue smoke. A cold engine running at light load and low speed could produce white smoke.

### Excessive Exhaust Smoke Emission

| White Smoke | Black Smoke | Blue Smoke |
|---|---|---|
| Fuel not burning; check for: | Incomplete burning; check for: | Lubricating oil being burned; check for: |
| Water in fuel | Incomplete burning | Piston rings or cylinders worn |
| Incorrect timing | Type of fuel used | Valve guides worn |
| Poor cylinder compression | Cold engine | Oil-bath air cleaner overfull |
| | Engine overload | Wrong fuel |
| | Clogged air intake system | |
| | Faulty fuel injectors | |
| | Restricted exhaust | |
| | Faulty injection pump | |

### Troubleshooting Guide:  Injector Fault Diagnosis

| Symptom/Condition | Probable Cause(s) | What To Do |
|---|---|---|
| Engine runs unevenly, misfires or has cylinder knock | **1.** Injector(s) not properly sealed in cylinder head | **1.** Check injector sealing washers and for cleanliness of seal |
| | **2.** Wrong number of sealing washers under injector(s) | **2.** Check for proper number |
| | **3.** High pressure leaks or restriction in injector(s) lines or at line unions | **3.** Visually check for leaks; remove line to knocking cylinder's injector or see dealer |
| | **4.** Injector(s) sticking | **4.** Incorrect sealing washers or inaccurate torquing; see dealer |
| | **5.** Faulty or wrong injector(s) | **5.** Change to correct/ new injectors or see dealer |
| Poor starting | **1.** All of the above probable causes *except* high pressure restriction in injector fuel line(s) | |

**Troubleshooting Guide:   Injector Fault Diagnosis (cont.)**

| Symptom/Condition | Probable Cause(s) | What To Do |
|---|---|---|
| Excessive exhaust black smoke; engine overheats | **1.** Wrong number of sealing washers under injector(s) | **1.** Check for proper number |
| | **2.** Injector(s) sticking | **2.** See #4 action above |
| | **3.** Faulty or wrong injector(s) | **3.** See #5 action above |
| Engine has lost power or consumes fuel excessively | **1.** All probable causes and actions listed under "Engine runs unevenly," above, *except* restriction in injector(s) high pressure fuel line(s) *plus* fuel line leak | |

*Note:*   Removal and reseating of engine's injector(s) is only a little more difficult than removing/replacing a gasoline engine's spark plugs. As with spark plugs, a special, simple injector extractor tool is available from many diesel specialty dealers. Extreme care must be used not to drop or impact an injector during removal; nozzle tips are particularly vulnerable to impact damage. In reseating an injector, cleanliness in the area of cylinder head bore and seat is extremely important. Final firming of an injector in place requires tightening (torquing) to specified "pound-feet" of torque. Torque wrenches are available in automotive retail stores. The correct torque to be used can be obtained from your dealer or from local injection specialists. If the injector's nozzle or nozzle valve is worn or damaged, the injector must either be replaced or sent to an injector specialist for repair.

**Troubleshooting Guide:   Oldsmobile V-8 Diesel**

(used in most General Motors cars and pickup trucks, including Oldsmobile, Cadillac, GMC and Chevrolet pickup trucks, and others). This *abbreviated* guide includes some routine tests and corrective steps within the capability of many diesel vehicle owners.

**Diesel engine: 8-cylinder V-8, 350 CID, 120 hp (net) at 3,600 rpm.**
  **Compression ratio: 22:1**

| Symptom/Condition | Probable Cause(s) | What To Do |
|---|---|---|
| Engine will not crank | **1.** Loose or corroded battery cables | **1.** Check connections at batteries, engine block, and starter solenoid |
| | **2.** Discharged batteries | **2.** Check generator belt adjustment and generator output; recharge/ replace batteries |
| | **3.** Starter defective | **3.** See your dealer or serviceman |
| Engine cranks slowly but will not start | **1.** Battery cable connections loose or corroded; batteries undercharged | **1.** Check connections as above; have batteries and charging system checked |
| | **2.** Wrong engine oil | **2.** Drain and refill with oil of recommended weight (viscosity) |

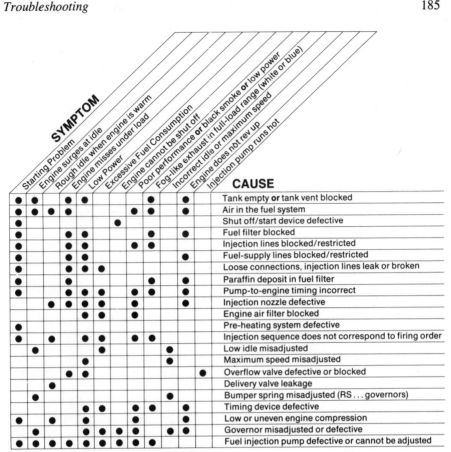

**Fig. 8.1** Troubleshooting guide assumes that the engine is in good working order and properly adjusted and that the electrical system has been checked and, if necessary, repaired. (Courtesy of Robert Bosch Corporation)

### Troubleshooting Guide: Oldsmobile V-8 Diesel (cont.)

| Symptom/Condition | Probable Cause(s) | What To Do |
|---|---|---|
| Engine cranks normally, but will not start | 1. Incorrect starting procedure | 1. See your Owner's Manual; The Olds manual carries this notice: "Do not try to start the engine with the WAIT light on. In most cases, the engine will not start, and cold air and fuel entering the engine will further delay starting." |
| | 2. No voltage to fuel solenoid; glow plugs or glow plug control system inoperative | 2. See your dealer |

**Troubleshooting Guide:   Oldsmobile V-8 Diesel (cont.)**

| *Symptom/Condition* | *Probable Cause(s)* | *What To Do* |
|---|---|---|
| | **3.** No fuel to injection pump or to injection nozzles | **3.** See dealer |
| | **4.** Incorrect or contaminated fuel | **4.** Drain and flush fuel system; refill with clean fuel |
| Engine starts, but will not continue to run at idle | **1.** Slow idle incorrectly adjusted | **1.** Adjust idle screw |
| | **2.** Restricted fuel system; contaminated fuel | **2.** See dealer; drain and refill with clean fuel |
| Engine starts, idles rough, WITHOUT abnormal noise and/or smoke | **1.** Slow idle incorrectly adjusted | **1.** Adjust idle screw |
| | **2.** Injection line leaks | **2.** Wipe clean injection lines and their connections; run engine and check visually for leaks; correct/have corrected |
| | **3.** Injection system problem: air in injection lines to nozzles; internal nozzle leaks; nozzle malfunction | **3.** See your dealer |
| Engine starts, idles rough, WITH excessive noise and/or smoke | **1.** Injection pump timing incorrect | **1.** Make sure timing mark on injection pump is aligned with mark on adapter |
| | **2.** High pressure lines incorrectly installed | **2.** Check routing of lines to injectors (firing order is 1-8-4-3-6-5-7-2) |
| | **3.** Nozzle(s) malfunction | **3.** See your dealer |
| Engine misfires above engine idle speed, but idles OK | **1.** Plugged fuel filter | **1.** Replace filter |
| | **2.** Incorrect or contaminated fuel | **2.** Check and correct |
| | **3.** Incorrect injection pump timing | **3.** See check listed above |
| Fuel leaks on ground, but no engine malfunction | **1.** Loose or broken fuel line or connections | **1.** Examine complete fuel system, including fuel tank, lines, fuel return lines, and injection lines; find source of leak; repair/have repaired |

**Troubleshooting Guide: Oldsmobile V-8 Diesel (cont.)**

| Symptom/Condition | Probable Cause(s) | What To Do |
|---|---|---|
| Noticeable loss of power | 1. Restricted air intake | 1. Check/replace air cleaner element |
| | 2. Plugged fuel filter | 2. Replace filter |
| | 3. Plugged vent in fuel tank cap | 3. Remove fuel cap; if loud "hissing" noise is heard, vent in fuel cap is plugged; replace cap (Slight hissing sound is normal) |
| | 4. Pinched or otherwise restricted fuel-return system | 4. Examine fuel lines for restrictions and correct |
| | 5. Contaminated or incorrect fuel | 5. Drain/flush fuel system; refill with proper, uncontaminated fuel |
| Noise: A "rap" from one or more cylinders (sounds like a rod bearing knock) | 1. Air in fuel system | 1. Check for air leaks in fuel line and correct |
| | 2. Air in high pressure (injection) line(s) | 2. Loosen injection line at nozzle(s) of each cylinder suspected of causing noise, and bleed air from line; if you are not familiar with this simple procedure, see your dealer |
| Noise: Objectionable overall combustion noise above normal noise level with excessive black smoke | 1. Timing not set to specifications | 1. Make certain that timing mark on injection pump is aligned with mark on adapter |
| | 2. Injection pump internal problem | 2. See your dealer |
| | 3. Possible serious internal engine problem | 3. See your dealer |
| Engine overheats | 1. Leak in coolant system, in oil cooler system, or coolant recovery system not operating | 1. Check for leaks and correct; in coolant recovery system, check coolant recovery jar, hose and radiator cap, and correct |
| | 2. Fan belt slipping or damaged | 2. Replace or adjust |
| | 3. Thermostat stuck closed | 3. Replace |
| | 4. Head gasket leaking | 4. See your dealer |

**Troubleshooting Guide:   Oldsmobile V-8 Diesel (cont.)**

| Symptom/Condition | Probable Cause(s) | What To Do |
|---|---|---|
| Instrument panel's oil warning light remains ON at idle | 1. Oil cooler or oil cooler line and oil restricted | 1. Remove restriction in cooler or cooler line |
| | 2. Oil pump pressure is low | 2. See dealer for oil pump repair |
| Engine will not shut off with key | 1. Injection pump's fuel solenoid does not return fuel valve to the OFF position | 1. (To shut off engine, pinch the fuel return line at the injection pump; use a pliers if necessary; engine will shut down. (Fuel return line returns unburnt fuel from the injection pump to the fuel tank). |

*Note:*   Some diesel engines, such as the Mercedes-Benz, have an emergency engine-STOP lever, plainly marked as such, located under the hood near the fuel pump. Pushing it shuts off the engine.

**Troubleshooting Guide:   Volkswagen Rabbit Diesel**

**Diesel engine: 4-cylinder, 90 CID, 48 HP (net maximum output) at 5,000 rpm. Compression ratio: 23:1**

| Symptom/Condition | Probable Cause(s) | What To Do |
|---|---|---|
| Car will not start. Engine will not turn over or turns over too slowly | 1. Safety belts (both driver and passenger belts for Rabbits equipped with automatic seat belt system) may not be connected | 1. Check safety belt connections and reconnect |
| | 2. Battery is run-down or dead | 2. Charge or replace battery; check cause for high current consumption causing battery's condition |
| | 3. Loose connections: | 3. Check to be sure connections are tight: |
| | a. at battery | a. check connections at battery and ground strap; retighten if necessary |
| | b. at starter | b. check solenoid connections on starter |
| | 4. Starter failure | 4. See your dealer |

**Troubleshooting Guide:   Volkswagen Rabbit Diesel (cont.)**

| *Symptom/Condition* | *Probable Cause(s)* | *What To Do* |
| --- | --- | --- |
| Engine turns over, but won't start | **1.** Improper starting procedure | **1.** See ''Starting'' section in your Owner's Manual |
| | **2.** No fuel in tank | **2.** Fill the tank |
| | **3.** Glow plugs aren't working (glow plugs are not getting voltage because of trouble in plug relay, car's ignition switch or relay switch on fuse box); or glow plugs themselves are malfunctioning | **3.** Check all electrical and fuel connections, including glow plug wires, in engine compartment for tightness; if no quick correction is obvious, see your dealer |
| Warm engine, but hard to start | **1.** Improper starting procedure | **1.** See ''Starting'' section in your Owner's Manual *Note:* Owner's Manual says this when starting an *already warm* VW diesel: ''DO NOT DEPRESS ACCEL-ERATOR WHILE STARTING. No matter what the outside temperature is, turn the key all the way to the right to start engine. DO NOT PRE-GLOW.'' |
| Car hard to start in winter | **1.** Battery low or run down | **1.** Check, then charge or replace battery |
| | **2.** Improper starting procedure for starting in cold weather when engine is cold | **2.** See ''Starting Cold Engine'' section in your Owner's Manual. In part, this section reads: (When starting a cold engine at outside temperatures *below* 32°F): ''Depress accelerator *fully* while starting. No matter what the outside temperature is, pull out knob for cold start device (on left of steer-ing column). Turn key to PRE-GLOW (Pos. 2). Glow plug light should be on. As soon as glow plug light goes out, turn key to start engine. Approximately 2 minutes after starting, *fully* push in knob for cold device.'' |

**Troubleshooting Guide:   Volkswagen Rabbit Diesel (cont.)**

| Symptom/Condition | Probable Cause(s) | What To Do |
|---|---|---|
| | **3.** Wrong weight of fuel and/or lube oil | **3.** *Fuel:* Switch from regular #2 diesel fuel to "winterized" #2; or, if none is available locally, you can "winterize" regular #2 by adding as little *regular* gasoline as possible to regular #2 diesel (20% to 30% gasoline, by volume, but no more, says Volkswagen). Even more fluid in cold weather is #1 diesel fuel used in most other car diesels in sub-zero weather, but it should *not,* specifically warns VW, be used in the VW Rabbit diesel. Here is Volkswagen's warning against fueling with #1 diesel: "The use of any other fuel (other than #2 or winterized #2 diesel) may cause you additional expense and may also affect your warranty." *Lube oil:* Switch to a winter grade. In single-grade *diesel* lube oil, VW's Owner's Manual recommends use of SAE 10W diesel lube oil if current or anticipated outside temperatures are below, or predicted to fall below, about 22° F |
| Engine heats up excessively while driving; temperature gauge's needle enters red danger zone, or temperature warning light comes on | **1.** Insufficient coolant | **1.** Add if necessary |
| | **2.** Failure of radiator fan or thermo switch | **2.** See your dealer |
| | **3.** Insufficient cooling due to fog lights or insect screens (when mounted, for example, in front of radiator) blocking radiator's cooling area | **3.** Remove accessories that block air flow through radiator |

**Troubleshooting Guide:**    **Volkswagen Rabbit Diesel (cont.)**

| Symptom/Condition | Probable Cause(s) | What To Do |
|---|---|---|
| | **4.** Mountain driving in hot weather, especially with air conditioner on while towing a trailer | **4.** Slow down and turn off air conditioning, which should return engine temperature to normal; if not, check for other probable causes above |
| Oil pressure warning light comes on while driving (brake warning light may also come on, but in case of brake-system-only problem, only brake warning light will come on) | **1.** Oil pressure dangerously low | **1.** STOP IMMEDIATELY (this *does not* mean you can drive to nearest service station); check lube oil level; if level is OK, check connections of oil pressure switch and warning light; if oil level low, do not restart engine until you have filled to proper oil level |
| Alternator warning light comes on while driving | **1.** Belt that drives alternator and water pump may be broken or slipping | **1.** *Stop at once;* turn off engine and replace or adjust drive belt. *Note:* Broken or slipping belt means your water pump probably is no longer working. Coolant is not circulating through engine. If engine is not now over-heated, it shortly will be. Overheating can *quickly* ruin a diesel engine. |
| | **2.** Alternator is not charging battery | **2.** If problem is not a slipping or broken drive belt, turn off all unnecessary electrical loads (turn off radio, air conditioning, heater, etc.) and drive to nearest service station or VW dealer; if alternator is no longer charging battery or not charging it enough, battery will soon run down |
| Brake warning light comes on when brakes are applied | **1.** Failure in one circuit of dual brake system | **1.** First make sure you haven't forgotten to release the parking brake fully; if the parking brake is released, but |

## Troubleshooting Guide: Volkswagen Rabbit Diesel (cont.)

| Symptom/Condition | Probable Cause(s) | What To Do |
|---|---|---|
| | | brake warning light comes on when applying brakes, pull off road and stop; with careful road-shoulder starts and stops, test remaining effectiveness of braking system; you may be able to drive slowly to nearest service station; if not, you may have to have car towed to service station or to nearest dealer |
| Strong odor of diesel fuel while parked or driving | 1. Leak in fuel lines or fuel cap | 1. Check fuel lines and their connections, and tighten connections if necessary; check fuel cap—it might be missing; if trouble isn't obvious, see your dealer |
| Strong odor of hot oil and increased engine noise | 1. Crankcase ventilation system is disconnected or broken | 1. Turn off engine; reconnect or replace crankcase ventilation hose |

## Troubleshooting Guide: Nissan 6-33 and 6-33T (turbocharged) Diesel

(a popular engine in diesel conversions and available—since 1980 models, in turbocharged version—in International Harvester's four-wheel drive sports/utility Scouts, including the Scout II and SS-II, Scout Traveler, and Scout Terra)

**Diesel engine: 6-cylinder, 198 CID, 81-brake horsepower at 1,800 rpm (101 hp in turbocharged version, designated 6-33T, the "T" for turbocharged) Compression ratio: 22:1**

| Symptom/Condition | Probable Cause(s) | What To Do |
|---|---|---|
| Noise in engine's air intake system (high-pitched sound changing with engine speed, especially when accelerating) | 1. Loose filter case cover | 1. Tighten cover |
| Exhaust emits large amount of black smoke; high fuel consumption | 1. Clogged air intake filter | 1. Replace filter |

Note: This *abbreviated* guide includes some routine tests and corrective measures within the capability of many diesel vehicle owners.

**Troubleshooting Guide:   Nissan 6-33 and 6-33T (turbocharged) Diesel (cont.)**

| Symptom/Condition | Probable Cause(s) | What To Do |
|---|---|---|
| Engine knocks and exhaust also emits black smoke | 1. Injection pump timing or injection fault, as too high injection pressure or faulty injection nozzle | 1. See your dealer for adjustment of timing and pump; cleaning of injection nozzle |
| Engine speed does not reach its rated maximum rpms | 1. One or more faulty injection nozzles, causing drop in injection performance; sticking nozzle needle is most probable cause | 1. Replace nozzle(s) or see your dealer |
|  | 2. Governor fault; weak or broken governor spring | 2. See your dealer to repair or replace spring or governor parts |
| Engine speed exceeds rated maximum rpms | 1. Governor adjustment (mechanical governor); ruptured governor diaphragm (pneumatic governor) | 1. See your dealer for adjustment/diaphragm replacement |
|  | 2. Fuel pump dirty or poor rack and pinion action | 1. See your dealer |
| Engine tends to overheat; coolant temperature rises to 212°F and tends to stay there. | 1. Faulty water pump, causing drop in its performance; pump water leak | 1. Replace defective parts or the pump |
|  | 2. Clogged radiator or dirty radiator water | 2. Clean/flush radiator |
|  | 3. Loose V-belt(s) | 3. Tighten, restoring V-belt(s) tension |
|  | 4. Defective thermostat (thermostat won't open) | 4. Replace thermostat |
|  | 5. Water leakage; low water level caused by damaged gasket, defective coolant system hose(s) | 5. Repair defects/ replace defective parts |
| Engine stops immediately after starting | 1. Clogged fuel filter element, creating high element pressure, caus- ing fuel to escape through filter's overflow valve | 1. Replace fuel filter element |
|  | 2. Water in fuel | 2. Drain/clean fuel tank |

**Troubleshooting Guide:   Nissan 6-33 and 6-33T (turbocharged) Diesel (cont.)**

| Symptom/Condition | Probable Cause(s) | What To Do |
|---|---|---|
| | **3.** Air in fuel (damaged fuel line, loose line connection, damaged fuel system gasket) | **3.** Repair/replace faulty fuel line; replace gasket |
| | **4.** Clogged fuel tank vent hole | **4.** Clear the vent hole |
| | **5.** Damaged fuel feed pump | **5.** See your dealer for pump repair/replacement |

# Glossary

*additives:* Any of a number of chemicals and compounds that may be added to diesel fuel or lube oil to modify, improve, or prevent changes in the oil's natural characteristics. Thus a widely used additive improves an oil's antirusting characteristics while it is in storage.

*bore:* Diameter of the cylinder, given in inches or centimeters.

*bottom dead center (B.D.C.):* See stroke.

*brake horsepower* (abbreviated ''bhp''): The horsepower actually delivered by the engine at the output end of its crankshaft (flywheel). So named because a braking device is used to measure this usable engine output power.

*cetane* or *cetane number* (pronounced **''see**-tane''): A number indicating the ignition quality of diesel fuel. Specifically an arbitrary number given to the lapse between the time instant fuel is injected into the combustion chamber and the instant ignition starts. The higher the cetane number, the faster, and thus better, a fuel's ignition quality. Most diesel fuels have cetane numbers between 35 and 55. Cetane defines the characteristics of diesel fuel much as octane defines the characteristics of gasoline.

*CID:* Abbreviation for ''cubic inch displacement,'' used to describe the volume of the cylinders swept by the pistons.

*cloud point:* The temperature at which diesel fuel becomes cloudy due to the formation of wax crystals. A fuel's ''pour point'' occurs at a somewhat lower temperature.

*combustion chamber:* In the cylinder of a diesel, the area remaining between the top of the cylinder and the top of the piston when the piston, on its compression stroke, has reached its farthest upward travel (top dead center). This so-called ''chamber'' is where the main combustion takes place.

*compression ratio:* The ratio of a cylinder's maximum volume to its minimum volume, indicating to what degree air is compressed within the cylinder. Typically high diesel compression ratios—such as 20:1, the maximum volume figure shown first—indicate high compression, thus heat of compression sufficient to self-ignite the diesel's fuel charge.

*cranking:* The starting cycle of a diesel engine. Powered by the vehicle's battery, the starter motor rotates the crankshaft, moving the pistons in their cylinders to create heat of compression sufficient to combust the injected fuel, thus starting the diesel.

*cubic inch displacement* or *piston displacement* (abbreviated CID or ''cu. in. displ.''): The

195

volume of air displaced in the cylinders by the action (stroke) of the pistons. Given in cubic inches. *To calculate displacement,* multiply the area of a piston (in square inches) × its travel (stroke, in inches) × the number of pistons.

*cylinder:* The cylindrical chambers, machined into a diesel engine's block, through which the pistons move.

*direct injection:* The injection of fuel, under high pressure, directly into the top of a diesel's cylinders, thus directly into the "combustion chamber."

*downstream/upstream:* The relative position of various fuel system components in the fuel's *direction* of flow, from the fuel tank to the injectors. Thus, every fuel system component is "downstream" from the fuel tank, but may be either "downstream" or "upstream" in relation to another component.

*flash point:* The temperature at which a diesel fuel vaporizes sufficiently to be ignited by a flame in open air. Used only as an index of fire hazard (far less for diesel fuel than for gasoline) and has no relationship to the fuel's combustion within an engine. Most states set either 100°F or 150°F as the minimum flash point for diesel fuel.

*fuel additives:* Additives used almost exclusively in fuel to modify, inhibit, or improve its characteristics. Thus, a "pour point depressant," a chemical fuel additive, lowers the temperature below which diesel fuel will no longer flow.

*fuel bacteria:* Any of numerous microorganisms that can live in and thrive on kerosene-based fuels, including diesel.

*horsepower* (abbreviated "hp"): A standard measure of engine power. One horsepower equals the force needed to raise 33,000 pounds a distance of one foot in one minute.

*indirect injection:* The injection of fuel into a small chamber (called the "precombustion chamber"), connected to the main cylinder, rather than directly into the top of the cylinder.

*in-line engine:* A diesel all of whose cylinders are in a straight line.

*lean fuel mixture:* An air/fuel mixture containing a high proportion of air. If the air fuel mix is too lean, present is more air (oxygen) than can be burnt by the fuel during combustion. One indication of too lean a fuel mixture is white exhaust smoke.

*litres:* Another way, growing popular, of expressing an engine's cubic-inch displacement. For example, the Mercedes-Benz 300SD diesel, with a 183-cubic-inch displacement, is also a "3-litre" engine (1 litre equals 61 cubic inches, thus: $\frac{183}{61} = 3$ litres).

*naturally aspirated diesel:* One that "breathes naturally"—takes in air without aid from such devices as turbochargers.

*piston:* The moving member within a diesel's cylinders. On its upward compression stroke, the piston compresses the air to fuel-ignition temperature, the power of whose ignition forces the piston downward, driving the crankshaft.

*pour point:* The temperature at which diesel fuel ceases to flow. Fuel with a pour point of + 10°F will no longer flow below that temperature.

*revolutions per minute* (abbreviated "rpm"): The rotational speed produced by a diesel, measured in terms of the revolutions per minute of its output crankshaft. In diesel vehicles, a *tachometer* is the instrument used to gauge and show the engine's rpms (speed) at any given moment.

*rich fuel mixture:* An air/fuel mixture containing a high proportion of fuel, usually more fuel than can be completely burnt during combustion. One indication of too rich a fuel mixture is black exhaust smoke.

*stoichiometric* (pronounced "stoy-key-o-**met**-ric): The ideally correct air/fuel mixture, which is neither too lean nor too rich, and in which all the fuel and all the oxygen are completely consumed during combustion.

*stroke:* The distance traveled by a piston within its cylinder from its bottom-most position (called *b*ottom *d*ead *c*enter, or B.D.C.) to its top-most position (called *t*op *d*ead center, T.D.C.), measured in inches or centimeters.

*sulphur content:* A measure of the amount of sulphur found to some degree in virtually all diesel fuels. Since sulphur produces an engine-corrosive acid, preferred is a fuel with a low sulphur content.

*supercharger:* Like a turbocharger, a device that forces more air into a diesel's cylinders than the engine, naturally aspirated, would normally take in. But unlike the turbocharger, which is powered by the engine's exhaust gases, the supercharger is mechanically driven by the engine.

*tachometer:* An instrument used to gauge and show the engine's revolutions (speed) at any given moment.

*thermal efficiency:* How efficiently a diesel converts its fuel to output power. Expressed as a ratio of energy output (at the pistons) divided by energy input (the fuel's energy), at any given time. A diesel is far more thermally efficient than a gasoline engine.

*top dead center* (T.D.C.): See *stroke.*

*torque:* The rotational *force* delivered to the crankshaft by the pistons. Expressed in foot-pounds (ft/lbs) of force. The diesel is renowned for developing high torque at relatively low engine speeds.

*turbocharger:* A device designed to force more air into a diesel's cylinders during the pistons' suction stroke than the engine, naturally aspirated, would normally take in. Turbochargers, powered by the diesel's own exhaust gases, increase combustion, effectively boosting engine horsepower. They also help compensate, when a diesel is operated at high altitude, for air's oxygen deficiency.

*upstream:* See *downstream/upstream.*

*Vee-engine* (also called V-engine, as a V-8): A diesel whose cylinders are arranged in two banks, forming a Vee, the angle between the banks seldom exceeding 90-degrees. The Vee configuration permits a diesel to be smaller and more compact than an in-line engine with the same number of cylinders.

*viscosity:* The fluidity of a liquid, such as diesel fuel or lube oil. The *higher* its viscosity, the thicker and *less fluid* an oil; the lower its viscosity, the thinner and *more fluid* an oil. Viscosity changes with temperature, as an oil becomes more fluid as temperature rises and less fluid as temperature falls. Under the widely used SAE (Society of Automotive Engineers) viscosity number classification system, an oil may be single-grade (as SAE 30) or multigrade (as SAE 5W-30, also written as 5 W-30). SAE viscosity numbers without a W are based on an oil's tested viscosity at 210°F. So-called "winter grades" of lube oil, with a W (most are multigrades), are based on the oil's viscosity at 0°F.

*volatility:* For a diesel fuel, the temperature range over which it vaporizes during refining. Because the refining process involves distilling (vaporizing and then condensing the oil), diesel fuel is often called a "distillate fuel."

# Appendices

## CONVERSION SPECIALISTS

Despite the rush to dieselize, relatively few firms or individuals specialize in custom-converting the average owner's car, pickup truck, motor home, or other utility vehicle to diesel. Those who *do* are mostly in the West, especially in California, where diesel conversions (notably of recreational vehicles and light trucks) have been popular for more than a decade and long before current escalating fuel prices forced almost anyone with a gas-guzzler to consider conversion to diesel.

The list of conversion specialists which follows is not all-inclusive, although it may be the best currently available. Many local shops and garages that occasionally do diesel conversions do not think of themselves as "conversion specialists." Yet some of these nonspecialists (almost none of them listed below) are among the most specialized of diesel converters; often they specialize in the conversion of only one make and type of vehicle (for example, Ford pickup trucks) and may elect to install only one make of diesel engine. Within their limited specialty, they may turn out excellent conversions.

Even conversion specialists tend to be modest-size operations, shops handling one to half a dozen jobs at a time. And if there is any typical conversion specialist, it is probably either a veteran diesel mechanic who learned his trade working on diesel trucks or a "speed mechanic," one of the highly skilled competition car specialists now turned to far slower-going diesel vehicles.

One way to find a good diesel conversion specialist locally is to inquire at the new car dealer who sells the make of car you'd like dieselized. Dealers ordinarily know who, locally, are in the business of reshaping to diesel the brands of automobiles and light trucks they handle. Another way is to consult your local Yellow Pages. Diesel conversion specialists generally list themselves in the phone book under "Engines—Diesel" (because, besides installing diesels, they also sell diesel engines) or under "Engines—Rebuilding & Exchanging."

Usually, the so-called "factory branches" of major truck and machinery makers—formidable local operations dealing in Caterpillar, Cummins, International Harvester, and Detroit diesel engines and equipment—aren't interested in handling your car or light truck conversion. They will, however, sell the conversion specialist or diesel mechanic the engine he needs to do your job. But many factory branch people, though expert in heavy-

198

duty diesel engines for transport and industry, concede they have but limited expertise in "light-duty applications," meaning cars and pickup trucks. Moreover, their shop equipment is usually sized for heavy diesel testing and repair, not for the light-duty engines that go into owner-vehicle conversions. With a few notable exceptions, factory branches queried during research for this book replied with a resounding "no," when asked if they did car or light truck diesel repair or conversion.

Here, however, are some specialists who do—specialists in gasoline-to-diesel conversions. The list is by no means complete and we extend apologies to anyone who may have been inadvertently omitted.

### California

C & F. Engineering
contact: Emmett Core
222 W. Arvin Street
Oildale, CA 93308
(805)399-3603

Cal's Engine & Machine Shop
contact: Larry Bunch
2146 Main Street
Escalon, CA 95320
(209)838-3780

Ed Fell Diesel Conversions
contact: Ed Fell
5225 Flagstone Street
Long Beach, CA 90808
(213)425-7090

Lynn Diesel Enterprises
contact: R. S. Lynn
1100 Watt Avenue
Sacramento, CA 95825
(916)487-9805

Sacramento Clean Air Terminal
contact: Read B. Chilcoat
8646 Everglade Drive
Sacramento, CA 95826
(916)383-1801

DLR/Energy Saving Systems
& Mfg. Co.
contact: Richard Weggesser
Star Rt. Box 100-H/Brown Road
Inyokern, CA 93527
(714)377-5539

Wilcap Company
contact: Tony Capanna
2930 Sepulveda Blvd.
Torrance, CA 90510
(213)326-9200

Don Winton Diesel Engineering
contact: Don Winton, Sr.
P.O. Box 3846
Downey, CA 90242
(213)920-1140

Woodland Diesel Service
117 East Street
P.O. Box 162
Woodland, CA 95695
(916)662-8192

### Illinois

Diesel Conversion of Illinois
Rt. #1, Powers Road
Huntley, IL 60142
(312)669-5040

### Michigan

Ron Rogers
9230 Belding Road
Rockford, MI 49341
(616)874-8325

### Missouri

Jim Cheek Enterprises
contact: Jim Cheek, Mike Walk
4109 W. Sunshine
Springfield, MO 65807
(417)862-7481

### Nevada

Mentzer Detroit Diesel, Inc.
contact: Dik Buxton
1550 Kleppe Lane
Sparks, NV 89431
(702)359-1713

Northern Nevada Diesel
contact: Robert Boyer
1409 Industrial Way
Gardnerville, NV 89410
(702)782-5740

### New Mexico

The Turbo Shop, Inc.
contact: T. J. Carr
110-B Utah NE
Albuquerque, NM 87108
(505)265-8494

### South Carolina

AAA Diesel Service
contact: Russ Topping
Black River Road
Camden, SC 29020
(803)432-8611

*Texas*

Diesel Conversion Services, Inc.
   contact: David Knowlton
   539 Delgado Street
   San Antonio, TX 78207
   (512)733-9733
Dallas Diesel
   contact: Howard Bond
   628 W. Ridgewood
   Garland, TX 75044
   (214)278-8572

Diesel America
   contact: George Barre
   5623 E. Paisano Drive
   El Paso, TX 79925
   (915)772-1451

## DIESEL CAR CLUBS AND MAGAZINES

If you drive a diesel car, you may be interested in joining one of the several clubs serving diesel drivers. Here is brief information on three of them:

*Diesel Automobile Association* (DAA)
   Membership/subscriptions:
      P.O. Box 1501
      Concord, NH 03301
      (617)658-3330 (Wilmington, MA/New England office)
   Executive office:
      801 West 181st Street
      New York, NY 10033
      (212)781-2947

National organization for diesel car owners and businesses that serve them, with membership throughout the United States, Canada, and Mexico. DAA is deeply involved in advancing diesel car technology (at both the production and congressional levels), in breaking down diesel permit requirements in the few states that still have them, and in advancing its members' appreciation and enjoyment of their diesel cars. Members receive DAA's semiannual magazine, *Diesel Motorist,* periodic newsletters, transcripts of DAA conferences and seminars with diesel experts, and can participate in DAA-sponsored tours to diesel manufacturers here and abroad, including DAA-arranged European delivery of diesel cars. DAA activities of a more technical nature include the club's growing involvement in the development of new, hopefully lower-cost diesel fuels, such as hydrogen (through DAA's "Diesel-Hydrogen Research Institute"). Working with a major diesel converter, DAA expects shortly to introduce a limited-production, high-performance diesel automobile, specifically, the Chrysler LeBaron, custom redesigned, and powered by a 6-cylinder turbocharged Nissan-Turbo diesel engine. Declares club president, Robert A. Gibbons, "DAA aims to be much more than merely a 'club' of diesel car enthusiasts."

Membership is $25 annually for individuals, $100 a year for corporate members.

*Mercedes-Benz Club of America, Inc.*
   P.O. Box 9985
   Colorado Springs, CO 80932
   (303)633-6427

Long established (founded 1955), with a big membership (12,000-plus) this is the enthusiasts' club for owners of Mercedes-Benz cars, many of them Mercedes "Ds" for diesel. Currently, about 30 percent of the membership own Mercedes diesels, with "diesel members" projected to rise to 50 percent of membership in the next few years. The club's business manager, Donn Wald, directs a United States/Canada network of some fifty local sections (among the largest: Los Angeles, New York City, San Francisco/Oakland, and Washington, D.C.) that generally meet monthly, usually for dinner, to hear technical speakers, compare M-B car notes, and socialize. Also big among club members are rallies, including the annual (May) European Rally, which includes a tour of Mercedes-Benz's Stuttgart, West Germany, main factory and the Mercedes-Benz Museum, one of cardom's best. Club chapters are coordinated by six directors-at-large and nine regional vice-presidents.

Annual dues are $25; for two years, $48.

*Diesel Car Club of Oregon*
     6610 N.E. Davis Street
     Portland, OR 97213
     (503)234-4179

This seven-year-old club of diesel enthusiasts from all over Oregon meets three or four times a year, usually in the Salem area, bringing local diesel authorities from Peugeot, Perkins, GM, and Mercedes-Benz before car-owning diesel buffs. Before meetings it issues an excellent and informative newsletter of three or four pages. Membership, says club secretary James W. Cox, now nudges the 120 mark.

Annual dues are $5.

### Magazines for Diesel Buffs

*Diesel Car Digest*
     P.O. Box 160253
     Sacramento, CA 95816
     Quarterly. Annual subscription: $7.50 (United States), second-class mail; first class, $10 (United States, Canada, and Mexico); foreign, air mail, $13 (except Canada and Mexico)

Diesel car buffs' own slick-paper and highly informative quarterly magazine, launched in 1976 by editor/publisher (and automotive engineer) Robert E. Flock. Subtitled "The quarterly journal of the light-duty diesel," *Diesel Car Digest* focuses on new diesel cars, vans, and pickup trucks and is especially strong on diesel conversions and on answering its now some 7,000 readers' operational and maintenance questions. Great gift for diesel car owners and fans.

*Diesel & Gas Turbine Progress* (North American edition)
     P.O. Box 26308
     Milwaukee, WI 53226
     Monthly. Controlled circulation (free to those in the diesel engine business). Others: $20 annually (United States and Canada); $25 (all other countries).

Along with its parallel monthly, the *International Engine Drive Systems Magazine* in the worldwide edition, *Diesel & Gas Turbine Progress* is the dominant voice of technical developments, especially in the heavy-duty engine segments (truck, bus, machinery, on-site power, marine) of the diesel and gas turbine industry. Now it also focuses on car and light vehicle developments. Worldwide, it is dieseldom's most widely read technical journal.

### THE DIESEL OWNER AND STATE LAWS

First, the good news: Two states, Maine and Michigan, which until recently required their diesel-driving citizens to purchase fuel-use permits, have rescinded the requirement. Michigan did so on August 1, 1979 and Maine on September 14, 1979. Now the bad news: Six states, Arizona, Idaho, Massachusetts, New Hampshire, Utah, and Wyoming, still require that resident owners of diesel vehicles obtain, in some instances at no cost, a fuel-use permit. In all but one state, Massachusetts, nonresident diesel fuel users (motorists merely passing through) are exempt from fuel permit laws affecting residents. But at least one state, Arizona, suggests that drivers through the state, "for their own peace of mind," says a state official, obtain at any Arizona port of entry a "Visitor Permit" authorizing diesel purchase. New Hampshire's fuel-use tax (called a "road toll") for resident diesel car owners is the nation's steepest—up to $72 a year. Most other states—with the exception of Idaho, New Hampshire, and Wyoming—levy only a nominal (usually $1) permit fee, or no fee at all. Where fees run higher it is usually because diesel fuel is not state-taxed at the pumps, as is gasoline.

"The problem," one state spokesman explains, "is that diesel fuel has heretofore been used mainly by farmers, contractors, and truckers—all of whom pay the usual state highway fuel tax not at the pump, but by special levies. Since we don't tax diesel at the pumps, we've got to collect our normal road tax some way. That's why diesel owners are licensed and must pay in a lump sum the state fuel taxes they'd normally pay at the pump by the gallon." In nearly all states, of course, if you store diesel fuel (or any other type of fuel subject to state road taxes), you need a special permit. Again, because fuel in home storage tanks isn't taxed at the pumps, you must pay your state's usual pump tax (and federal highway taxes, too) on every gallon.

Back in the good news column: Even the few states requiring any kind of diesel fuel-use permit seem on the brink of second thoughts. Insiders predict that virtually all such discriminatory laws will shortly be erased from state law books. Even where they exist, use laws—with some notable exceptions—are hard to enforce. Many state officials themselves seem confused about their own statutes. Enforcement is spotty, a conclusion reached both in this book's state-to-state research and by the American Automobile Association.

Here is a brief rundown of state fuel-use laws:

### Arizona

Resident diesel owners must apply for a "Use Fuel" permit (a "Use Fuel" being diesel, butane, or propane), the no-cost permit exempting you from filing diesel purchase reports with the state, as required of commercial diesel users. The permit should be carried in your vehicle, available should any questions arise when you fuel. Nonresidents, while exempt, may obtain free at any Arizona port of entry a "Visitor Permit" to buy fuel.

For the resident use-fuel exemption permit, write:

Tax Revenue Section
Motor Vehicle Division
Arizona Department of Transportation
P.O. Box 2100, 234M
Phoenix, AR 85001

### Idaho

Complicated laws on fuel taxes have Idaho in a state of considerable confusion. Resident owners of diesel vehicles whose gross weight is under 8,000 pounds (which would include automobiles and pickup trucks) must buy a Special Fuels license and sticker. Its annual cost of up to $63 is based on the owner's estimate of his vehicle's fuel economy, on its average miles per gallon. Resident owners of diesel vehicles with a gross weight over 8,000 pounds (large motor homes, typically) simply pay their state fuel tax—9½ cents per gallon, same as for gasoline—at the pump and need not apply for the fuels license. Nonresidents, who pay Idaho's tax at the diesel pump, are exempt.

This two-tiered tax situation by vehicle weight finds some diesel owners who buy their annual Special Fuels license paying their road taxes twice—once when they buy the fuels license and again at the pumps, because diesel is taxed there, too. Of course, the double-taxed diesel owner can submit the pump tax bill to the state for reimbursement or, better yet, can ask the service station operator to deduct the tax from the pump's total reading. But some Idaho residents say it's easier to pay twice than to haggle with the state over a fuels tax refund. Says a state official, "If a diesel owner drives into a station and has the Special Fuels sticker, the station is not supposed to charge the fuels tax. The tax has already been paid. Some stations have refused to deduct the state tax from the total meter reading. Instead, they tell the double-taxed diesel owner to go fight with the state.''

Almost as confusing is Idaho's fuels tax schedule. Here's how it works: You apply at your County Assessor's Office, where you are asked, "How many miles per gallon does your diesel vehicle average?" Based on *your* mpg estimate, here's what you pay:

| Owner's Estimate of Vehicle's MPG | Monthly Tax | Total Annual Tax |
|---|---|---|
| under 14 mpg | $5.25 | $63.00 |
| 15 to 19 mpg | 3.70 | 44.00 |
| 20 to 24 mpg | 2.85 | 34.20 |
| 25 to 29 mpg | 2.35 | 28.20 |
| 30 to 34 mpg | 2.00 | 24.00 |
| 35 to 39 mpg | 1.70 | 20.40 |
| 40 to 44 mpg | 1.50 | 18.00 |
| 45 to 49 mpg | 1.35 | 16.20 |
| 50 to 54 mpg | 1.20 | 14.40 |
| over 55 mpg | 1.10 | 13.20 |

## Massachusetts

Massachusetts is the only state requiring *both* resident and nonresident diesel owners (automobiles, recreational vehicles, and motor homes included) to obtain a Special Fuels User License at $1 to operate on the state's roads. With your application made and fee paid, the state will send you a Special Fuels User License card and decal, the license card to be carried in the vehicle and the decal to be placed on the outside of the driver's door. ''But,'' says a Massachusetts official, ''so many Mercedes-Benz owners complained about our decal decorating their car doors that we've relented.'' The Special Fuels User License decal may now be displayed on the car's rear window (and, vouches one state tax spokesman, even in your glove compartment, if you insist).

However you choose to display it, resident and nonresident diesel owners in Massachusetts cannot legally drive the state's highways without a fuels user's license. The license is applied for on Form MF-VA, Department of Revenue License Application. To obtain the license form write:

Massachusetts Department of Revenue
P.O. Box 7012
Boston, MA 02204

## New Hampshire

Residents who own diesel pleasure vehicles must obtain a permit and pay a $24–$72 annual road toll, because no fuel tax is collected at diesel pumps in New Hampshire. Nonresidents are exempt.

The road toll fee is based on the weight of your diesel vehicle, according to the following schedule:

| Vehicle's Weight | Annual Fee |
|---|---|
| 0 to 3,000 lbs | $24 |
| 3,001 to 5,000 lbs | $48 |
| 5,001 to 8,000 lbs | $72 |

The road toll may be paid annually or quarterly, or prorated monthly. You're issued a license card, to be carried in your car, as proof of fee payment. To obtain your state's "Application for User's Fuel Licenses" (Form RT129) write:

State of New Hampshire
Department of Safety
Division of Motor Vehicles
Road Toll Administration
James H. Hayes Safety Building
Hazen Drive
Concord, NH 03301

*Utah*

Resident diesel owners must apply for a free "filing exemption," so they don't have to report or keep records of diesel fuel purchases, as must commercial diesel-fuel users. Nonresidents are exempt. To apply for Utah's "Special Fuel Permit," which in effect exempts you from your state's diesel fuel-use law, write:

Utah State Tax Commission
1095 Motor Avenue
Salt Lake City, UT 84116

*Wyoming*

Resident diesel owners pay a special $50 annual road-use tax, in addition to the usual vehicle registration fee, when registering or relicensing their vehicles. The fee is paid at the County Treasurer's Office at the county seat where the vehicle is registered. Nonresidents are exempt.


### DIESEL FUEL DIRECTORIES

Although more and more service stations are installing diesel pumps, fuel can sometimes be hard to find, especially if you're driving in unfamiliar territory. To make diesel fueling and diesel "stops" less elusive, a number of diesel fuel station directories are available. Some are offered free of charge by oil companies and generally list only the issuing company's own diesel stops. Others, such as Mercedes-Benz's modestly priced ($2) station guide, list diesel stops across the United States and Canada. In choosing fuel stop guides, consider your own driving habits. If you drive mostly within an area served by one or two oil companies that issue fuel directories, their no-cost guides should be local guide enough. If you expect to travel widely, you'll need a nationwide guide to fueling stops. Some fuel stop guides, even the nationwide ones, are merely compilations of diesel stops listed in various oil company guides—and why pay for a compilation, when you can get the companies' guides at no cost, although not as conveniently packaged as the compilations? Other nationwide guides, however, list many additional stops in areas where oil companies have not, as yet, issued guides of their own.

Unfortunately, fuel stop guides go out of date rather quickly, and not all guide publishers, oil companies among them, update their listings annually, even though new diesel fuel stops are continually being added. And some stations that may have dispensed diesel are closing; the post-OPEC attrition among stations has been significant. Today's 185,000 service stations of all types contrast with some 220,000 in 1974. Of the remaining total, perhaps 20,000—about 11 percent—dispense diesel, says a leading industry source. Some of these, however, are far off the interstate routes traveled by most diesel users. Still, the diesel boom is in many areas triggering a veritable rush to "dieselize," as former no-diesel stations put in diesel pumps.

The best fuel directories not only tell you a listed station's usual hours, but the type of diesel fuel—#2, winterized #2, or #1—it dispenses. Chevron's 42-page "Diesel Fuel

Locations for Autos and Trucks'' does even more: It lists Chevron truck stops and diesel stations catering to automobile drivers separately in some 26 states, including Alaska, served by Chevron and also notes listed stations' weekend hours when they differ from the weekday usual. Some diesel outlets are merely notated "Sundays—closed" in the directories.

Although truck stops will almost always fuel your car, pickup or motor home, they are decidedly truck oriented. For some diesel drivers, merely getting into and out of a busy truck stop's service area, what with big rigs all around, can be a bit harrowing. Besides, some truck stop attendants are less than solicitous of the diesel driver, whose vehicle's tank may hold a mere twenty gallons or so of diesel, while the behemoth trucks that constitute the stop's VIP patrons regularly fuel up with 100 to 200 gallons. Many diesel drivers feel decidedly uncomfortable in the busiest of truck stops. Knowing how to read a fuel guide that does not plainly label "truck stops" can steer you to stations better set up to serve the diesel car driver rather than the diesel truck driver. Although not invariably, fuel stops within a town or city are probably service stations with a pump or two dispensing diesel, and stations listed along interstate or major U.S. highway routes are more likely to be truck stops. One indication of which kind, of course, is a station's name; many truck stops call themselves just that—as, for example, Bosselman Truck Stop, an Amoco station on the outskirts of Big Springs, Nebraska.

Along interstate routes, you can nowadays often find diesel even if you don't have a fuel directory, or if the ones you have list only one company's stations. More and more, the interstate system is being posted with signs—typically, "GAS, DIESEL"—directing you to the next off ramp and its diesel-dispensing station. For most diesel vehicle owners, a fuel guide is a glove-compartment comfort. Here is a list of a number of available fuel directories, and how to obtain them. Where a charge is mentioned for a guide, the price is only approximate.

### Oil Company Directories (no charge)

*Amoco Oil Company*

    *Diesel Fuel Directory*. Lists stations by city and state. Does not show type of diesel fuel dispensed. Includes brief discussion of diesel fuel. Notes states that require diesel-user permits. Sixty pages. Shows diesel stops in 43 states and District of Columbia where Amoco operates. Write to Customer Service Department, AMOCO, 200 East Randolph Drive, Chicago, IL 60601.

*Exxon Oil Company*

    *Exxon Truck Stop and Diesel Fuel Directory*. Twenty-page, trucker-oriented guide for 34 states and Washington, D.C. Classifies stops by services, shows hours open and types of diesel fuel dispensed. Available from Exxon diesel fuel stations, or write Exxon Company, USA Consumer Affairs Department, P.O. Box 2180, Houston, TX 77001.

*Gulf Oil Company*

    *Diesel Fuel Outlets, U.S.A.* Barebones listing of its diesel outlets in 29 states and District of Columbia. Twenty-five pages. Write to Public Affairs Department, Gulf Oil Corporation, P.O. Box 1563, Houston, TX 77001.

*Mobil Oil Corporation*

    *Mobile Retail Diesel Service Stations Directory*. Comprehensive list of its diesel stops by states. Available from Mobile diesel fuel stations or write to Mobile Travel Services, 150 East 42nd Street, New York, New York 10017.

*Phillips Petroleum Company*

*Diesel Directory*. Lists stations by city and state and specifies services available. Write to Customer Service Department, Phillips Petroleum Company, Bartlesville, OK 74004.

*Standard Oil Company of California* (Chevron)

*Chevron Diesel Fuel Locations for Autos and Trucks*. Extensive, detailed listing of diesel stops in the United States and British Columbia, Canada. Separately lists auto and truck stops (truck stop services, including type of diesel fuel dispensed, more detailed than auto stop listings), also mileage chart, energy tips, and description of Chevron diesel fuels and engine oils. Forty-two pages. Available from some Chevron diesel fuel stations or write to Retail Sales, Standard Oil of California, 575 Market Street, San Francisco, CA 94105.

*Standard Oil of Ohio (Sohio)*

*Directory of Retail Outlets Dispensing Diesel Fuel*. One-page, super barebones listing of diesel stops in Ohio, Pennsylvania, Michigan, Indiana, and Kentucky. Write to Marketing Department, The Standard Oil Company, Midland Building, Cleveland, OH 44115.

*Sun Oil Company* (Sunoco and DX)

*A Guide to Sunoco DX Service Stations Selling Diesel Fuel*. State-to-state listing of its diesel fuel outlets. Available from some Sunoco DX diesel stations or by writing Sunmark Industries, P.O. Box 7368, Philadelphia, PA 19101.

*Texaco*

*Directory for Purchasing Texaco Diesel Fuel*. State-to-state, United States-only listing of Texaco diesel outlets. Available at truck stops, Texaco zone offices, or by writing Texaco Travel Service, 2100 Hunters Point Avenue, Long Island City, NY 11101.

*Union Oil Company*

*Union 76 Diesel Fuel Locations*. Fold-out single sheet listing diesel stops in twelve western states, including Texas, Hawaii, and Alaska. Noted are truck stops and 24-hour stations. Available from some Union 76 diesel outlets or write Customer Service Department, Union Oil Company of California, Box 7600, Los Angeles, CA 90051.

### Diesel Car Manufacturers' Directories

*Mercedes-Benz*

*Directory of Fuel Stations (and Authorized Mercedes-Benz Dealers)*. Mercedes-Benz's version of the Hammond guide (see below). Excellent, comprehensive listing of some 15,000 diesel stops in the United States and Canada.
No cost to Mercedes-Benz buyers, $2 to others. Available from Mercedes-Benz dealers (but price may be higher than when ordering direct from Mercedes-Benz of North America, One Mercedes Drive, Montvale, NJ 07645.

*Oldsmobile*

*Where to Buy Diesel Fuel: A Directory of Diesel Fuel Stations, USA and Canada*. An excellent no-cost, 141-page compilation (plus others) of major brand stations, including 7,000 retail diesel fuel outlets, with 24-hour outlets noted. Available from local Oldsmobile zone offices or write Diesel Fuel Guide Headquarters, General Motors Corp., Room 317-B, 465 W. Milwaukee, Detroit, MI 48202.

*Peugeot*

> *Peugeot Diesel Directory*. Good state-by-state free guide to diesel stations in the United States write to Peugeot Incorporated, One Peugeot Plaza, Lyndhurst, New Jersey 07071.

### Independently Published Directories

*Diesel Fuel Guide*. State-by-state, comprehensive listing of some 11,300 fuel stops in all fifty states and Canada. Annually revised. $6.95. Write to Diesel Fuel Services, Inc., P.O. Box 256, South Salem, NY 10590.

*Edna Connelly's Diesel Fuel and Truck Stop Guide*. Excellent fuel stop guide by city and state, showing services, hours, etc., all keyed to state maps. A trucker's fuel stop location favorite. Annually revised. $6.95 plus 75 cents for shipping. Available from many truck stops or by writing Edna Connelly, P.O. Box 6268, Reno, NV 89513.

*Hammond Diesel Stop Directory and Road Atlas*. Among the most detailed and comprehensive guides of diesel stops in United States and Canada, which locates stations by maps and cross index. Includes diesel fuel tax, permit information. $4.95. Available from many bookstores or by writing Hammond Incorporated, Maplewood, NJ 07040.

### Association-Published Directory

*National Truck Stop Guide*. Comprehensive listing of the largest and leading truck stops along the nation's interstate and primary highways. Coded to show such truck services as acceptance of credit cards, whether food, lodging, and repair services available, and kinds of diesel fuels usually available. $1. National Association of Truck Stop Operators, P.O. Box 1285, Alexandria, VA 22313.

## ASSOCIATION OF DIESEL SPECIALISTS DIRECTORY

The A.D.S. directory of specialized diesel experts across the United States and Canada is available to nonmembers at $15. For names of new members not listed or for A.D.S. members in Mexico or abroad, contact the association's international headquarters: Association of Diesel Specialists, 1719 West 91st Place, Kansas City, MO. 64114, Phone: (816) 444-3500, Executive Director: Betty Puckett.

*Alabama*

Alabama Diesel Co.
  3328 6th Avenue South
  Birmingham, AL 35222
  (205)324-4406
Alabama Diesel Co.
  3341 Old Selma Road
  Montgomery, AL 36108
  (205)262-6624
Birmingham Electric Battery Co.
  2230 2nd Avenue South
  Birmingham, AL 35233
  (205)251-3211
Huntsville Diesel Service
  914 Bob Wallace
  Huntsville, AL 53801
  (205)534-3034
Industrial Hydraulics, Inc.
  209 South 20th Street
  Birmingham, AL 35233
  (205)251-1095

Saunders Engine & Equipment Co. Inc.
  840 Dumaine Road
  Mobile, AL 36601
  (205)456-4507
Test-Calibration Company
  3408-B Beltline Park Drive North
  Mobile, AL 36617
  (205)457-1333

*Alaska*

Alaska Diesel Service Inc.
  403 East Fireweed
  Anchorage, AK 99503
  (907)272-9589

*Arizona*

"Charlie" C. Jones Battery & Electric Co.
  2440 W. McDowell Road
  Phoenix, AZ 85009
  (602)272-5621

Perkins Diesel Service
    747 South Country Club Drive
    Mesa, AZ 85202
    (602)964-5273
Southwest Diesel & Electric Corp.
    1830 North 27th Avenue
    Phoenix, AZ 85009
    (602)269-2471

*Arkansas*

Northeast Diesel Service
    1309 Falls Street
    Jonesboro, AR 72401
    (501)932-7425
Taylor Diesel Service of Arkansas, Inc.
    2120 East Broadway
    Little Rock, AR 72119
    (501)945-2326

*California*

Advanced Diesel Injection, Inc.
    2035 Main Street
    San Diego, CA 92113
    (714)232-6452
Allen Fuel Injection, Inc.
    2035 Butte House Road
    Yuba City, CA 95991
    (916)673-4180
Automotive Diesel & Electric Co., Inc.
    2374 East Date Street
    Fresno, CA 93712
    (209)266-6334
Berge's Diesel Fuel Systems, Inc.
    110 S. Irwindale Avenue
    Azusa, CA 91702
    (213)334-5017
Coast Fuel Injection, Inc.
    1590 Industrial Avenue
    San Jose, CA 95112
    (408)287-7600
Collins Diesel Injection, Inc.
    1420 E. Miner Avenue
    Stockton, CA 95205
    (209)948-4410
Diamond Diesel Service, Inc.
    2550 East 12th Street
    Oakland, CA 94601
    (415)532-8500
Diamond Diesel of Santa Rosa
    300 West Robles No. K
    Santa Rosa, CA 95401
    (707)528-1232
Diesel Control Corp.
    226 North Marine Avenue
    Wilmington, CA 90744
    (213)835-5651
Diesel Electric Sales & Service, Inc.
    329 12th Avenue
    San Diego, CA 92101
    (714)232-3073

Diesel Fuel Systems
    18016 South Vermont Avenue
    Gardena, CA 90248
    (213)327-3921
Diesel Injection Sales & Service
    1552 Cypress Street
    Oxnard, CA 93030
    (805)483-9339
Diesel Injection Service
    932 West Mill Street
    San Bernardino, CA 92410
    (714)885-0590
Diesel Motive
    13523 Norwalk Boulevard
    Norwalk, CA 90650
    (213)868-3738
Dumas Diesel Injection
    2521 East Carson Street
    Long Beach, CA 90810
    (213)518-1260
Fuel Injection Sales & Service, Inc.
    10612 Pioneer Boulevard
    Santa Fe Springs, CA 90670
    (213)944-3261
H. G. Makelim Co.
    219 Shaw Road
    South San Francisco, CA 94080
    (415)873-4753
National Pump & Injector Sales & Service, Inc.
    2307 East Belt Street
    San Diego, CA 92113
    (714)232-0831
Pimentel & Son
    6450 Bay Street
    Emeryville, CA 94602
    (415)655-7442
Sacramento Diesel Pump & Injector Service
    414 16th Street
    Sacramento, CA 95814
    (916)448-8297
Turbocharger, Inc.
    12215 Woodruff Avenue
    Downey, CA 90241
    (213)869-0983
United Diesel Service
    1903 Penn Mar Avenue
    South El Monte, CA 91733
    (213)448-0521
Valley Automotive & Diesel Service, Inc.
    1870 Dogwood Road
    El Centro, CA 92243
    (714)352-0984

*Colorado*

Central Motive Power, Inc.
    6301 North Broadway
    Denver, CO 80217
    (303)428-3611
Colorado Diesel & Purifiers, Inc.
    2061 West Hamilton Place
    Englewood, CA 80110
    (303)761-5135

Diesel Services, Inc.
    450 South 9th Street
    Grand Junction, CO 81501
    (303)243-7218
Diesels Inc.
    727 6th Street
    Greeley, CO 80631
    (303)356-2672
Mitchcon Corporation
    8109 E. 39th Avenue
    Denver, CO 80207
    (303)333-2317
Specialized Diesel Service
    302 North 2nd
    Lamar, CO 81052
    (303)336-2828

*Connecticut*

Acme Auto Supply, Inc.
    544 New Park Avenue
    West Hartford, CT 06110
    (203)232-4444
The Clark-Son Co., Inc.
    354 Davenport Avenue
    New Haven, CT 06519
    (203)787-6746
H & L Diesel
    47-1 Essex Street
    Deep River, CT 06417
    (203)526-5941

*Florida*

Atlantic Diesel Service
    State Road 621 East
    Lake Placid, FL 33852
    (813)465-3756
Dade Diesel Co., Inc.
    2747 N.W. 34th Street
    Miami, FL 33142
    (305)633-8491
Everglades Diesel Injection Service, Inc.
    243 S.W. 33rd Court
    Fort Lauderdale, FL 33315
    (305)522-1780
George's Diesel Service
    1015 Loxahatchee Drive
    West Palm Beach, FL 33409
    (305)686-7251
Inland Diesel Fuel Injection Service, Inc.
    2877 W. Tharpe Street
    Tallahassee, FL 32303
    (904)576-0139
Interstate Diselect, Inc.
    4220 North Orange Blossom Trail
    Orlando, FL 32804
    (305)293-7971
L & J Diesel Injection Service, Inc.
    122 West 29th Street
    Hialeah, FL 33012
    (305)885-3175

Stuart Diesel Service Inc.
    6515 Adamo Drive
    Tampa, FL 33619
    (813)626-7105
Taylor Diesel Service, Inc.
    228 North Myrtle Avenue
    Jacksonville, FL 32204
    (904)356-2641

*Georgia*

Auto Electric & Diesel Company
    810 Lambert Drive, N.E.
    Atlanta, GA 30324
    (404)876-3622
Diesel Injection and Electric Co.
    4767 Clark Howell Highway
    College Park, GA 30349
    (404)768-8754
Testmaster Inc.
    309 Main Street
    Garden City, GA 31408
    (615)965-6642

*Idaho*

Eastern Idaho Diesel
    405-406 College
    Idaho Falls, ID 83401
    (208)523-5766
Goold Auto Electric
    217 2nd Avenue N
    Twin Falls, ID 83301
    (208)733-2679

*Illinois*

Area Diesel Service
    North University
    Carlinville, IL 62626
    (217)854-2641
Diesel Injection & Turbo Service Inc.
    725 Princeton Avenue
    Villa Park, IL 60181
    (312)833-6262
Diesel Pump & Injector Service
    High 121
    Mt. Pulaski, IL 62548
    (217)792-3796
Illinois Auto Electric Company
    656 County Line Road
    Elmhurst, IL 60126
    (312)833-4300
Precision Industrial Corp.
    Precision Fuel Systems
    60 Gordon Street
    Elk Grove Village, IL 60007
    (312)439-9122
Triangle Diesel Injection Sales and Service, Inc.
    R.R.#1
    Kankakee, IL 60901
    (815)933-4172

*Indiana*

Craigville Diesel & Auto
   P.O. Box 44
   Craigville, IN 46731
   (219)565-3184
Eagle Machine Co., Inc.
   635 East Market Street
   Indianapolis, IN 46206
   (317)637-2521
Evansville Auto Parts, Inc.
   5 East Riverside Drive
   Evansville, IN 47713
   (812)424-8264
Jasper Engine and Transmission Exchange
   U.S. 231 South
   Jasper, IN 47546
   (812)482-1041
Kolb Diesel Sales & Service
   703 S. Barker Avenue
   Evansville, IN 47712
   (812)464-9141
Smith Bros. Diesel Inj. Service Inc.
   117 South Morgan Street
   Mentone, IN 46539
   (219)353-3961
Turbo & Diesel Injection Co.
   450 W. Troy Avenue
   Indianapolis, IN 46225
   (317)783-5451
Wabash Diesel Service
   4860 N. 13th Street
   Terre Haute, IN 47805
   (812)466-5751

*Iowa*

Diesel Specialties, Inc.
   3211 Delaware
   Des Moines, IA 50313
   (515)265-7318
Diesel Specialties, Inc.
   4505 Harbor Drive
   Sioux City, IN 51102
   (712)255-1601
Iowa Diesel Injection Service
   515 Packwaukee Street
   New Hartford, IA 50660
   (319)983-2361
M.M. Supply Co., Inc.
   206 12th Street
   Des Moines, IA 50306
   (515)288-0192
Midwest Diesel Injection Service, Inc.
   Highway 20 East
   Fort Dodge, IA 50501
   (515)576-5501
Red Oak Diesel Clinic, Inc.
   2500 North 4th Street
   Red Oak, IA 51566
   (712)623-2221

*Kansas*

Bell Engine Service, Inc.
   3810 West 10th
   Great Bend, KS 67530
   (316)792-4333
Hutchinson Diesel Service
   401 North Poplar
   Hutchinson, KS 67505
   (316)662-3111
Power Products Fuel Injection Service
   923 Zerr Road
   Garden City, KS 67846
   (316)275-4347

*Kentucky*

Diesel Injection Service Co., Inc.
   4710 Allmond Avenue
   Louisville, KY 40221
   (502)361-1181

*Louisiana*

Bergeron's Diesel Fuel Injection Service
   P.O. Box 512
   Eunice, LA 70535
   (318)546-6630
Arthur A. Castille Company, Inc.
   106 West St. Peter Street
   New Iberia, LA 70560
   (318)364-2321
Diesel Injection Equipment Co., Inc.
   1101 Enterprise Boulevard
   Lake Charles, LA 70601
   (318)433-3506
Gerhardt's Inc.
   819 Central Avenue
   Jefferson (New Orleans), LA 70181
   (504)733-2500
J. L. Hebert's Engine Sales & Service, Inc.
   166 North Liberty Street
   Opelousas, LA 70570
   (318)942-7939
Johnnie's Diesel Injector Service, Inc.
   613 Papworth Avenue
   Metairie, LA 70005
   (504)834-3212
Landry & Simoneaux Diesel Service, Inc.
   1657 Highway 90 East
   Morgan City, LA 70380
   (504)384-3631
McQueen's Injection Service
   1201 Cypress Street
   West Monroe, LA 71291
   (318)325-9641
Vaughan & Bush, Inc.
   1050 Grimmett Drive
   Shreveport, LA 71107
   (318)222-8432
Waldron Diesel Specialists
   327 New Orleans Avenue
   Houma, LA 70360
   (504)876-0403

John M. Walton, Inc.
  1050 Carondelet Street
  New Orleans, LA 70190
  (504)525-0556
Womack Brothers, Inc.
  6983 Airline Highway
  Baton Rouge, LA 70805
  (504)356-0136


### Maine

Atlantic Fuel Injection, Inc.
  Route 302
  North Windham, ME 04062
  (207)892-8545
Central Equipment Co.
  101 Bennoch Road
  Stillwater, ME 04489
  (207)827-4435
Connell Diesel & Electrical Inc.
  305 Warren Avenue
  Portland, ME 04103
  (207)797-6800


### Maryland

Arundel Fuel Injection Corp.
  1111 Wilso Drive, Desoto Industrial Park
  Baltimore, MD 21223
  (301)525-3700
B & D Fuel Injection Service, Inc.
  4800 Stamp Road
  Temple Hills, MD 20031
  (301)899-1626
Baltimore Diesel Service, Inc.
  6110 Holabird Avenue
  Baltimore, MD 21224
  (301)633-6777


### Massachusetts

Boston Fuel Injection & Engine Service Co., Inc.
  261-263 Northern Avenue
  Boston, MA 02210
  (617)542-6646
Connell Diesel & Electrical Inc.
  395 University Avenue
  Westwood, MA 02090
  (617)329-5810
Dario Diesel Service, Inc.
  182 Southwest Cutoff
  Worcester, MA 01604
  (617)753-8177
G & K Diesel Service
  178 Tosca Drive
  Stoughton, MA 02072
  (617)344-2593
C. A. Krohne & Sons, Inc.
  500 West Columbus Avenue
  Springfield, MA 01105
  (413)781-5824


### Michigan

Diesel Equipment Sales & Service Inc.
  578 E. Main Street
  Potterville, MI 48876
  (517)645-7684
Diesel Injection Service, Inc.
  430 54th Street, S.W.
  Grand Rapids, MI 49508
  (616)531-1030
D. A. MacPherson, Inc.
  County Road 653
  Iron River, MI 49935
  (906)265-5197
Metro Diesel Fuel Injection, Inc.
  24526 Capitol Avenue
  Redford Township, MI 48239
  (313)531-2230
Northern Diesel Controls Service
  3755 Utica Road
  Sterling Heights, MI 48078
  (313)739-7222


### Minnesota

Diesel Components, Inc.
  12050 Riverwood Circle
  Burnsville, MN 55337
  (612)890-2885
Diesel Service & Supply
  111 East 19th Street
  Hibbing, MN 55746
  (218)263-5725
Diesel Service Company
  1253 Eagan Industrial Road
  St. Paul, MN 55121
  (612)454-5530
Rochester Fuel Injection Service
  6360 Highway 63 South
  Rochester, MN 55901
  (507)288-8038
Zip's Diesel Injection Service
  Highway 152, South
  St. Cloud, MN 56301
  (612)251-6816


### Mississippi

Haygood of Mississippi, Inc.
  Highway 49 South
  Jackson, MS 39308
  (601)939-5471
J & H Diesel Service, Inc.
  P.O. Box 5261
  Greenville, MS 38701
  (601)378-8711
Precision Fuel Injection Service
  113 E. South Street
  Jackson, MS 39202
  (601)948-2894
Tupelo Diesel Service
  782 Westmoreland Drive
  Tupelo, MS 38801
  (601)844-1361

Wansley's Fuel Injection Service
1247 Meridian Avenue
Laurel, MS 39440
(601)425-1426

### Missouri

Diesel & Electric Sales & Service, Inc.
2810 Nicholson
Kansas City, MO 64120
(816)241-3400
Diesel Fuel Injection Service, Inc.
9331 South Broadway
St. Louis, MO 63125
(314)631-2500
Electrical & Magneto Service Company, Inc.
1600 Campbell
Kansas City, MO 64108
(816)421-3711

### Montana

Gomer's Diesel & Electric, Inc.
308 2nd Avenue South
Great Falls, MT 59405
(406)761-5530
Gomer's Diesel & Electric, Inc.
2400 Palmer
Missoula, MT 59801
(406)728-7620
Midwest Diesel Injection Service
10 Second Street West
Havre, MT 59501
(406)265-6841
Original Equipment, Inc.
905 Second Avenue North
Billings, MT 59102
(406)245-3081

### Nebraska

Automotive Diesel Inc.
1100 J Street
Auburn, NB 68305
(402)274-3632
Automotive Sales & Service
414 West B Street
McCook, NB 69001
(308)345-4365
Diesel Service, Inc.
215 East 2nd Street
Kimball, NB 69145
(308)235-4797
Midwest Diesel Injection Service
Highway 275 West
Beemer 68716
(402)528-3303
R.P.W. Inc.
7402 L Street
Omaha, NB 68103
(402)339-7872

### Nevada

Nevada Diesel Service, Inc.
301 West Miller Avenue
North Las Vegas, NV 89030
(702)642-5717
Sierra Diesel Injection Inc.
2525 Mill Street
Reno, NV 89502
(702)329-4232

### New Hampshire

New England Diesel Fuel Inj. Inc.
10 Spencer Street
Lebanon, NH 03766
(603)448-2828

### New Jersey

Battery & Electric Service Company
100 East Main Street
Somerville, NJ 08876
(201)725-5344
Diesel Powered Products
226 Chapel Heights Road
Sewell 08080
(609)589-6866
Dover Diesel Service
Green Pond Road
Rockaway, NJ 07866
(201)627-7733
Jersey Diesel Sales
566 Smith Street
Perth Amboy, NJ 08861
Trenton Diesel Service & Supply Co.
50 Cunningham Avenue
Trenton, NJ 08610
(609)587-0448

### New Mexico

Central Motive Power, Inc.
808 Second Street, N.W.
Albuquerque, NM 87103
(505)247-0184

### New York

A & D Diesel Service, Inc.
143-147 21st Street
Brooklyn, NY 11232
(212) 788-4222
Donnelly Diesel Service, Inc.
25 Dingens Street
Buffalo, NY 14206
(716)823-2525
East Coast Diesel Service, Inc.
22 North Prospect Avenue
Lynbrook, NY 11563
(516)887-9220
Kozaczek Bros.
Route 9W
Newburgh, NY 12550
(914)562-2625

Dick Laing Diesel Service
Arterial Highway
Binghamton, NY 13901
(607)722-1430
McGlynn Diesel Service Inc.
627 West Merrick Road
Valley Stream, NY 11580
(516)561-2203
Specialized Diesel Services, Inc.
5972 Court Street Road
Syracuse, NY 13206
(315)463-8575
Union Carburetor Diesel & Electric Inc.
378 Mt. Hope Avenue
Rochester 14620
(716)232-2700.

### North Carolina

Coastal Diesel Service Inc.
1700 Highway 70 East
Newbern, NC 28560
(919)633-2025
Diesel Equipment Company
212 Atwell Avenue
Greensboro, NC 27406
(919)373-8331
Diesel Fuel & Electric Service, Inc.
Route 1, Box 97
Midland, NC 28107
(704)888-5898
Diesel Injection Sales & Service, Inc.
4209 North Graham Street
Charlotte, NC 28213
(704)596-6010
Diesel Injection Sales & Service, Inc.
Highway 54 West
Raleigh, NC 27606
(919)851-1220

### North Dakota

Knopik Diesel & Electric
Route 2, Box 204
Dickinson, ND 58601
(701)227-0301
Midland Diesel Service & Engine Company
25-27-1/2 Street South
Fargo, ND 58102
(701)237-6937
Midway Diesel & Electric Inc.
1724 40 Avenue South East
Mandan, ND 58554
(701)663-9215

### Ohio

Columbus Diesel Supply Company
201 North Fourth Street
Columbus, OH 43215
(614)228-6663

Diesel Injection Service Co., Inc.
3032 Reading Road
Cincinnati, OH 45206
(513)281-5315
Findlay Diesel Injector Service, Inc.
407 Walnut Street
Findlay, OH 45840
(419)423-1447
Fluid Mechanics, Inc.
2221 Brookpark Road
Cleveland, OH 44134
(216)351-6967
Northwest Fuel Injection Service, Inc.
330 North High Street
Columbus Grove, OH 45830
(416)659-2124
Ohio Diesel Injection Sales & Service
1230 Market Street
Youngstown, OH 44502
(216)744-8903
Standard Motor Parts, Inc.
200 Carroll Street
Akron, OH 44304
(216)535-7161

### Oklahoma

American Electric Ignition Co., Inc.
124 N.W. 8th Street
Oklahoma City, OK 73101
(405)236-3551
Industrial Ignition Co.
1808 N.W. 2nd
Oklahoma City, OK 73106
(405)235-3788
Moore & Son's Diesel Service
P.O. Box 117
Drummond, OK 73735
(405)493-2261
Schoenhals Engine Service
R.R. #2, Box 200
Shattuck, OK 73858
(405)938-2569
Thompson's Diesel Fuel Injection Specialists,
Inc.
5700 S.W. Kenworth Avenue
Oklahoma City, OK 73148
(405)943-8536

### Oregon

Automotive Products, Inc.
1700 S.E. Grand Avenue
Portland, OR 97214
(503)235-1947
Oregon Fuel Injection, Inc.
865 Conger Street, #12
Eugene, OR 97402
(503)485-1434
Smitty's Diesel Service, Inc.
P.O. Box 1730
Roseburg, OR 97470
(503)672-8231

*Pennsylvania*

Advanced Diesel Specialists, Inc.
  Rte 93, RD 1, Box 312
  Hazleton, PA 18201
  (717)454-2426
Automotive Ignition Company, Inc.
  301 Meade Street at Trenton Avenue
  Pittsburgh, PA 15221
  (412)243-3080
Automotive Supply Company
  1917 Margaret Avenue
  Altoona, PA 16601
  (814)944-9447
A. R. Beatty Diesel Sales & Services
  5251 Kuhl Road
  Erie, PA 16510
  (814)899-0427
C. V. Diesel Service, Inc.
  RR 3, Box 81B
  Greencastle, PA 17225
  (717)597-3184
Fuel Injection Sales & Service, Inc.
  RD 3
  Allentown, PA 18104
  (215)395-3718
Miller Diesel Inc.
  6030 Jonestown Road
  Harrisburg, PA 17112
  (717)545-5931
Penn Diesel Service Co.
  RD 3, Box 624, Fairville Avenue
  Harrisburg, PA 17112
  (717)545-4207
Philadelphia Diesel, Inc.
  Rte 940, Box 272
  Mt. Pocono, PA 18344
  (215)922-2007
Sardello, Inc.
  2700 Neville Road
  Pittsburgh, PA 15225
  (412)771-2766
Sorington Fuel Injection
  Box 246, RD 2
  Somerset, PA 15501
  (814)445-7457
Sullivan Bros., Inc.
  Creek Road and Langoma Avenue
  Elverson, PA 19520
  (215)942-3686
United Diesel, Inc.
  3625 Butler Street
  Pittsburgh, PA 15201
  (412)621-9815

*Rhode Island*

E. F. English & Sons, Inc.
  RD 8
  Esmond, RI 02917
  (401)231-0210

*South Carolina*

Diesel Injection Sales & Service, Inc.
  1413 Bluff Road
  Columbia, SC 29202
  (803)799-8720
Superior Diesel, Inc.
  6819 Rivers Avenue
  Charleston, SC 29411
  (803)553-8331

*South Dakota*

D. K. Diesel Injection Service
  109 3rd Street, S.W.
  Watertown, SD 57201
  (605)886-2750
Dakota Diesel Service, Inc.
  North Highway 77
  Sioux Falls 57101
  (605)336-6531
Mattern's Diesel Injection Service
  East Highway 12
  Aberdeen, SD 57401
  (605)886-2750

*Tennessee*

Acme Diesel Inc.
  4724 Rutledge Park
  Knoxville, TN 37914
  (615)524-3005
Automotive Electric Corporation
  3250 Millbranch Road
  Memphis, TN 38116
  (901)345-0300
Diesel Sales & Service Co.
  103 Jubilee Drive
  Chattanooga, TN 37421
  (615)894-4050
Diesel Sales & Service Co.
  423 West Main Street
  Johnson City, TN 37601
  (615)928-1661
Diesel Sales & Service Co.
  2236 McCalla Avenue
  Knoxville, TN 37915
  (615)546-7751
Diesel Sales & Service Co.
  928 Main Street
  Nashville, TN 37206
  (615)227-2242
Mid South Diesel Injection Service
  3166 Connahbrook Drive
  Memphis, TN 38116
  (901)396-0750
Taylor Diesel Service, Inc.
  1075 South Third Street
  Memphis, TN 38101
  (901)948-4467

## Texas

Abilene Diesel Injection Service, Inc.
725 Walnut
Abilene, TX 79604
(915)673-7031

Central Fuel Injection
16 North 10th
Temple, TX 76501
(817)778-5851

Central Texas Diesel Injection Service, Inc.
5018 E. 1st Street
Austin, TX 78702
(512)385-4890

Diesel Fuel Injection Service, Inc.
P.O. Box 4320
Brownsville, TX 78520
(512)831-4744

Diesel Injection Sales and Service, Inc.
5558 Leopard Street
Corpus Christi, TX 78408
(512)882-7668

Diesel Injection Service, Inc.
1001 Slaton Road
Lubbock, TX 79408
(806)745-4122

Diesel Injection Service of Texas, Inc.
2850 Stevens Road
Odessa, TX 79762
(915)367-8638

Doug's Fuel Injection Service
2 Miles West 83
Weslaco, TX 78596
(512)968-3722

Gerhardt's Inc.
5601 Braxton Drive
Houston, TX 77036
(713)789-8860

Gibbs Diesel Injection Sales and Service
912 N. Timberland Drive
Lufkin, TX 75901
(713)634-7793

Houston Fuel Injection Service
2219 McAllister Street
Houston, TX 77092
(713)682-0010

Magneto & Diesel Injector Service
6931 Navigation Boulevard
Houston, TX 77011
(713)928-5686

Schwing Diesel Co.
4848 Leopard Street
Corpus Christi, TX 78408
(512)883-7223

Spitzer A & I
1055 Hawkins
El Paso, TX 79926
(915)778-6326

Texas Fuel Injection Service
4828 Calvert Street
Dallas, TX 75247
(214)631-0127

Weber Diesel Service
123 West Carolina
San Antonio, TX 78210
(512)534-5445

Wichita Diesel Injection Service
210 Jalonic
Wichita Falls, TX 76307
(817)767-0502

Wilson Battery & Electric Service
618 Jackson
Amarillo, TX 79105
(806)373-1727

Womack Diesel Service
1626 N. Austin
Seguin, TX 78155
(512)379-0030

## Utah

Diesel Electric Service & Supply Co., Inc.
652 West 1700 South
Salt Lake City, UT 84115
(801)972-1836

Diesel Injection & Turbo Sales
2295 South 300 West
Salt Lake City, UT 84115
(801)486-3151

Fuel Injection Service Company, Inc.
1197 South 300 West
Salt Lake City, UT 84101
(801)487-0881

## Virginia

Blue Ridge Diesel Injection, Inc.
1016 Delaware Street
Salem, VA 24153
(703)389-7296

Central Diesel, Inc.
1603 Jefferson Davis Highway
Richmond, VA 23224
(804)233-9814

Diesel Injection Sales & Service, Inc.
1120 East Brambleton Avenue
Norfolk, VA 23516
(804)622-5691

Industrial Diesel, Inc.
2514 Alabama Avenue
Norfolk, VA 23513
(804)857-6171

Virginia Diesel Service Inc.
1120 Bruce Street
Richmond, VA 23224
(804)232-8988

## Washington

Advanced Diesel & Supply Co., Inc.
2929 East Sprague Avenue
Spokane, WA 99202
(509)535-0336

Hatch And Kirk, Inc.
  5111 Leary Avenue, N.W.
  Seattle, WA 98107
  (206)783-2766
Huston's Auto Parts
  423 West Main Street
  Chehalis, WA 98532
  (206)748-4407
Northwest Fuel Injection Service
  East 1112 Nob Hill Boulevard
  Yakima, WA 98901
  (509)452-8564
Seattle Injector Company, Inc.
  1410 Airport Way South
  Seattle, WA 98134
  (206)623-1135
Spokane Diesel Pump Repair, Inc.
  E. 628 Pacific Avenue
  Spokane, WA 99202
  (509)838-3556
Tri Cities Diesel Injection Service, Inc.
  707 South Oregon
  Pasco, WA 99301
  (509)547-2591

*West Virginia*

Craig Motor Service Company, Inc.
  131 West Pike Street
  Clarksburg, WV 26301
  (304)623-3421

*Wisconsin*

Diesel Injection Service, Inc.
  1571 Ivory Drive
  Sun Prairie, WI 53590
  (608)256-1003
Diesel Specialists, Inc.
  620 Clark Hinkle Street
  Green Bay, WI 54303
  (414)499-1475
Eau Claire Diesel Service
  1337 Western Avenue
  Eau Claire, WI 54701
  (715)835-1498
Fuel Injection & Electric, Inc.
  1625 North Barker Road
  Brookfield, WI 53005
  (414)784-4500
Fuel Systems, Inc.
  12730 Robin Lane
  Brookfield, WI 53005
  (414)781-4353
La Crosse Diesel Service, Inc.
  Highway 35 South
  La Crosse, WI 54601
  (608)788-2300

*Wyoming*

Turbo/Injection Service
  6917 West Yellowstone
  Casper, WY 82601
  (307)266-6760

*A.D.S. Members: CANADA*

*Alberta*

Camrose Diesel Injection Ltd.
  44 Grand Drive
  Camrose
  (403)672-5309
G. C. L. Diesel Injection Service Ltd.
  16722 110th Avenue
  Edmonton T5P 1G9
  (403)453-6786
Hutton's Limited
  131 11th Avenue
  Calgary T2R OC1
  (403)269-3725
Loveseth Industrial Division
  15906 114th Avenue
  Edmonton T5M 2Z4
  (403)452-7321
United Diesel Injection
  4210 103rd Street
  Edmonton T6H 4S4
  (403)434-8517

*British Columbia*

Dynamic Engineering Co. Ltd.
  1270 Frances Street
  Vancouver V6A 1Z5
  (604)253-4427
Fred Holmes Fuel Injection Sales & Service, Ltd.
  25 Victoria Drive
  Vancouver V5L 2C1
  (604)253-7585
Interior Fuel Injection Service, Ltd.
  4600 29th Street
  Vernon V1T 5B9
  (604)545-0774
Kamloops Fuel Injection Ltd.
  1330 Dalhousie Drive
  Kamloops V2C 5P7
  (604)374-5393
N. W. Fuel Injection Service
  835 Agnes Street
  New Westminster V3M 1H4
  (604)524-2828
Northern Diesel Services Ltd.
  9716 17th Street
  Dawson Creek V1G 4B3
  (604)782-8910
Valley Fuel Injection Ltd.
  A10-33733 King Road, R.R. #2
  Abbotsford V2S 4N2
  (604)853-6096

Vulcan Diesel Service
  940 100th Avenue
  Dawson Creek V1G 1L6
  (604)782-2190
Wilson And Proctor Limited
  808 Devonshire Road
  Victoria
  (604)385-3481

### Manitoba

Auto Electric Service (Western) Ltd.
  170 Fort Street
  Winnipeg R3C 1E1
  (204)943-5637
Brown & Murray Ltd.
  237 Front Street
  Winnipeg R3C 1E2
  (204)943-8401
Hendypower Diesel Injection Service
  1090 Kenaston Boulevard
  Winnipeg R3P OR7
  (204)475-9100
Pritchard Engineering Co., Ltd.
  111 Bannister Road
  Winnipeg R3C 3A1
  (204)633-9213
Western Diesel Fuel Injection Service Ltd.
  401 Braecrest Drive
  Brandon R7A 5Y6
  (204)725-1435

### New Brunswick

Stairs Brothers Ltd.
  P.O. Box 203, R.R. #6
  Salisbury
  (506)372-5007
Stairs Brothers Ltd.
  P.O. Box 1251
  Fredericton E3B 5C8
  (506)472-7851

### Newfoundland

Diesel Injection Sales & Service Limited
  122 George Street
  St. John's A1C 5M3
  (709)726-6774
Newfoundland Armature Works Ltd.
  73 Kenmount Road
  St. John's A1B 3T2
  (709)722-3471

### Nova Scotia

Stairs Brothers Ltd.
  12 Waddell Avenue
  Dartmouth B3B 1K3
  (902)469-0098

### Ontario

Auto Jobbers Warehouse Ltd.
  1301 Matheson Boulevard
  Mississauga L4W 1R1
  (406)625-8641
Bardo Diesel Ltd.
  1370 Hammond Street
  North Bay P1B 3C1
  (705)472-8641
Chatham Fuel Injection Service
  R.R. #2
  Chatham N7M 5J2
  (519)351-1033
Del Equipment, Ltd.
  139 Laird Drive
  Toronto 17
  (416)421-5851
Derek's Diesel Service Ltd.
  61 Carson Street
  Toronto M8W 3S1
  (416)255-8670
The Diesel Shop of Diesel Injection Service Ltd.
  Highway 14 North, RR #5
  Belleville K8N 4Z5
  (613)966-1017
Diesel Injection Service
  24 Bentley Avenue
  Ottawa K2E 6T8
  (613)225-9520
Diesel Technic Company
  84 Six Point Road
  Toronto M8Z 2K3
  (416)231-6920
Henninger's Diesel Ltd.
  1106 Webbwood Drive
  Sudbury P3C 3B7
  (705)675-1241
Huron Fuel Injection Equipment
  P.O. Box 788
  Clinton N0M 1L0
  (519)482-7971
Industry Diesel Service Ltd.
  1015 Industry Street
  Oakville L6J 2X3
  (416)845-3444
J & M Diesel Service
  Hyde Park Road
  Hyde Park N0M 1Z0
  (519)471-9613
Lakehead Diesel & Hydraulics Ltd.
  1095 Russell Street
  Thunder Bay P7B 5M6
  (807)622-0643
Niagara Diesel Injection Service
  Box 2460, Station B
  St. Catharines L2M 7M8
  (416)682-7982
Sharma Diesel Injection Service Ltd.
  1630 Sismet Road
  Mississauga L4W 1R4
  (416)625-3640

Simola Diesel Ltd.
   2001 Riverside Drive
   Timmins P4N 7C3
   (705)264-9518
W. Diesel Injection Service
   133 Bay Street North
   Hamilton L8R 2P5
   (416)523-7665
West Lincoln Diesel Ltd.
   R.R. #3
   Caistor Centre L0R 1E0
   (416)957-3604

### *Quebec*

International Electric Co., Ltd.
   1037 Bleury Street
   Montreal H2Z 1M8
   (514)861-1451
Laurentian Diesel Inc.
   10422 Balzac Street
   Montreal North H1H 3L4
   (514)325-8207
Montreal Diesel Fuel Pumps Inc.
   333 St. Hubert Street
   Laval H7G 2Y5
   (514)669-2679
Provincial Diesel Inc.
   730 Rose de Lima
   Montreal H4C 2L8
   (514)937-9371

Vente & Service Diesel, Inc.
   1059 St. Vallier West
   Quebec G1N 1G6
   (418)681-0631

### *Saskatchewan*

Diesel Injection Service Regina Ltd.
   2139 8th Avenue
   Regina
   (306)522-4100
Electric Motor Service Ltd.
   1234 Scarth Street
   Regina S4R 2E5
   (306)525-5464
Stan Olson Diesel Ltd.
   115 Broadway West
   Yorkton S3N 0M3
   (306)783-5501
Reg's Diesel Injection Service Ltd.
   738 5th Street
   Estevan S4A 0Y6
   (306)634-5010
Robinson Diesel Injection Ltd.
   813 46th Street East
   Saskatoon
   (306)652-5374

## SOME LEADING LUBE OIL ANALYSTS

### *East*

Analysts, Inc.
820 E. Elizabeth Avenue
Linden, NJ 07036
(201)925-9393

Ana Laboratories
111 Harding Avenue
Bellmawr, N.J 08030
(609)931-0011

### *West*

Analysts, Inc.
2910 Ford Street
Oakland, CA 94601
(415)536-5914

Watchdog, Inc.
P.O. Box 11438
Spokane, WA 99211
(509)535-9791

### *Central*

D-A Lubricant Company, Inc.
1340 W. 29th Street
Indianapolis, IN 46208
(317)923-5321

Analysts, Inc.
Box 4002
Schaumburg, IL 60194
(312)884-7877

### *South*

Optimal Systems, Inc.
P.O. Box 1182
Atlanta, GA 30301
(404)448-5235

Analysts, Inc.
12715 Royal Drive
Stafford, TX 77477
(713)494-3042

# Index